THE INDEBTEDNESS OF CHAUCER'S WORKS TO THE ITALIAN WORKS OF BOCCACCIO

(A REVIEW AND SUMMARY)

HUBERTIS M. CUMMINGS, Ph.D.

INSTRUCTOR IN THE UNIVERSITY OF CINCINNATI

A DISSERTATION

PRESENTED TO THE FACULTY OF PRINCETON UNIVERSITY IN CANDIDACY
FOR THE DEGREE OF DOCTOR OF PHILOSOPHY

"Amor, che al cor gentil ratto s'apprende."
Dante, *Inferno.* V. 100.

PHAETON PRESS
NEW YORK
1967

Originally printed 1916
Reprinted 1967

Library of Congress Catalog Card Number 67-30901

Printed in U.S.A. by
Edwards Brothers, Inc.
Ann Arbor, Michigan

PREFACE

The present work has developed from a dissertation on *Chaucer's Indebtedness to Boccaccio in Troilus and Criseyde and the Knight's Tale,* which was submitted in April, 1914, to the English Department of Princeton University as the fulfilment of a partial requirement for the degree of Doctor of Philosophy. The dissertation, never separately published, is now fully incorporated in the present, rather longer, study of the influence of Boccaccio's works over Chaucer's, and herewith makes its first appearance in print, with its earlier crudities, the writer fears, at times all too imperfectly removed.

Very early in my investigation of the Chaucer-Boccaccio problem I perceived to my regret that I should have more to do than to review and summarize. I saw that it would be my duty, also, to challenge several of the results of earlier, and very earnest investigation; but, to weigh very critically the results of other's labours, I soon realized was an inevitable function of scholarship, and so reconciled myself to the *rôle* of quasi-iconoclast. It was, accordingly, very much in the belief that an absolute truth can no more readily be obtained in the field of scholarship than in the field of philosophy, that the present investigation was undertaken.

And the work was pursued only in the hope that an approximate form of truth might be obtained, which might prove of value to students of Chaucer problems. Were the riddle in the relations existing between Chaucer and Boccaccio capable of one unquestioned solution, that solution would have been determined long ago, for scholars have long employed their wits upon it; and certainly, if the riddle had been only once and for always propounded and then answered immediately and dogmatically, the solution, however interesting it might have been, would have thrown little light upon the genius of Chaucer.

In a word, an immediate solution would have precluded, and still would preclude, its own value. It would aver one of two facts, either that the relations,—whatever they might have been, personal, literary, of friendship or of discipleship,—existing between the two poets were of no real value to Chaucer, or that Chaucer's work, having become too dependent upon those relations, would have no value for us to-day, five centuries after the poet's death. Neither of these facts is admissible. The relations existing between the two poets were of great, although not necessarily of supreme, value to Chaucer; and Chaucer, even the most arrant of Philistines would admit, is of very considerable value to us!

It has been my effort then in this review to account more definitely than before has been done for the amount of Chaucer's debt to the Italian poet's works; to investigate concretely the differing methods employed by the English poet in his treatment of the *Filostrato* in *Troilus and Criseyde*, and of the *Teseide* in the *Knight's Tale*; and to explain, so far as is possible, Chaucer's attitude to "Lollius," or, as we know him, Giovanni Boccaccio. I can only hope that future students of Chaucer and his sources may derive some little help from my labours.

It is my cordial desire to thank the many writers, named in the body of my text, for the very great assistance afforded by them to me in my investigation. And my hardly less debt to my friends, Dr. Ernest Francis Amy and Dr. Bernard Levi Jefferson, who, working over their own Chaucerian problems in Princeton, were ever at my side with kindly and helpful suggestions, I would gratefully acknowledge. It is a pleasure, too, to thank Professor Thomas Marc Parrott and Professor Charles Grosvenor Osgood of Princeton University for the ever ready sympathy and excellent counsel they accorded me as a graduate student, and as a student of Chaucer. But greatest thanks are due to Professor Robert Kilburn Root of Princeton, who led my first steps in Chaucerian studies, while I was still an undergraduate at Princeton, and guided me no less solicitously in the writing of the present work, in every act proving himself the best of counselors and friends.

HUBERTIS M. CUMMINGS.

Cincinnati, Ohio, 1916.

CONTENTS

FOREWORD

Frequent references will be made in the following pages to the Italian writings of Giovanni Boccaccio, as found in complete form in the *Moutier* edition, the volumes and contents of which are cited below together with the approximate dates of composition.

Boccaccio, Giovanni: *Opere Volgari*, 17 vols., Florence, 1827-1834.

I-IV.	*Il Decamerone* (1348-1354).
V.	*Il Decamerone* (concluded); *Il Corbaccio* (1354-5).
VI.	*Fiammetta* (about 1338).
VII-VIII.	*Il Filocolo* (after 1338).
IX.	*La Teseide* (before 1341).
X-XII.	*Commento Sopra Dante* (1373).
XIII.	*Il Filostrato* (before 1341).
XIV.	*Amorosa Visione* (about 1338).; *Caccia di Diana* (about 1338).
XV.	*Vita di Dante*; *L'Ameto* (1338-1342).
XVI	*Rime; L'Urbano* (1354 or earlier).
XVII.	*Ninfale Fiesolano* (before 1341).

Summaries of the whole or of partial contents of a number of these works will be made from time to time in this dissertation, but without regard to chronological order.

Besides the above Italian works, the following Latin works are ascribed to Boccaccio:

De Montibus, Sylvis, Lacubus, Fluminibus, Stagnis seu Paludibus.
De Casibus Virorum Illustrium.
De Mulieribus Claris.
De Genealogiis Deorum Gentilium (1359).

Editions of these works will be cited at such times when references are made to them, but Chaucer's possible use of any one of them will not be made at any time the study of my dissertation.

CHAPTER I

CHAUCER AND THE *Filocolo*

The *Filocolo* (*Opere Volgari*, Vols. VII-VIII) is one of Boccaccio's early works, a long prose romance, at times very richly coloured, crowded with classical allusions, and fairly redolent of the worship of Venus. The narrative follows:

Felice, King of Spain, and his Queen, eager to break up the infatuation of their son Florio, who later assumes the name of Filocolo, for Biancofiore, a young lady of supposedly humble origin, who has been brought up in the court as a foster daughter, contrive to separate the two lovers by sending Florio to the ducal court of his uncle Feramonte at Montorio on the pretext that the youth's education can more properly be cared for there. During his absence various machinations are attempted by the queen against Biancofiore. Among others is a ruse so managed by her that Biancofiore, supposing a great service to have been rendered to her by a youth of the name of Fileno, is induced to present the latter with her veil. Fileno follows Florio to Montorio and there, declaring that the veil, which he shows to the prince, is a pledge of Biancofiore's love for him, throws Florio into an unhappy fit of jealousy, which is dispelled only after a vision of Biancofiore, protesting her true love to Florio, has appeared to him in a dream. After this, various other attempts are made by his parents to break the passion of Florio. At last, while he is still absent, they determine to rid themselves of Biancofiore by selling her as a slave to some Alexandrian merchants. The bargain is struck, and the damsel is carried off to many wanderings. Returning presently to the Spanish court, Florio penetrates the deception of his parents, who maintain that Biancofiore is dead, and sets out determined to scour the world in search of her.

While he is on his travels, he is one day walking on the shore at Naples with several friends, when they come upon a party of young men and women in a garden, and being pleasantly welcomed remain with them for a time. Later all withdraw to a shady spot, where at the suggestion of Fiammetta, one of the ladies, they agree that one of their number shall be appointed "king" and that each member of the group shall submit to him some love problem. The suggestion results in an episode of story-telling, and the proposing of a number of *questioni d'amore*. Ere long Florio and his friends have resumed their travels in search of Biancofiore.

Meantime the girl, after many vicissitudes, has fallen into the hands of the Ammiraglio of the King of Babylonia at Alexandria, who, charmed with her beauty, confines her together with her faithful maid Glorizia, with suitable attendants, in a wonderful tower, in the hope that he may one day make her the favorite wife in the harem of his master.

While Biancofiore is still in the hands of the Ammiraglio, Florio arrives at Alexandria, and learns by a lucky chance of her presence in the marvelous tower (VIII, 138-42). A conspiracy is formed by which Florio succeeds in gaining the acquaintance of Sadoc, the castellan of the tower, an acquaintanceship that ripens into a friendship over several games of chess sagaciously played by the young lover (VIII, 142-55). Charmed by the courteous behaviour of Florio, Sadoc demands of him one day the story and purpose of his wanderings; and Florio, throwing caution to the winds, in the realization that "la fortuna aiuta gli audaci," divulges the whole tale of his love for Biancofiore (VIII, 156-61).

The castellan is moved to pity and promises, since the Ammiraglio retains in his own keeping all the keys of the tower, to smuggle Florio into Biancofiore's apartments in a basket of flowers on the day when roses are sent by the Ammiraglio to all the maidens confined in the tower (161-64).

The promise is kept, and Florio is carried by Sadoc, under the very nose of the Ammiraglio (166), in to the foot of the tower. Sadoc summons Glorizia to deliver the basket to her mistress; and Florio, hearing him call, imagines Biancofiore is approaching and impulsively protrudes his head from the basket. The maid is frightened and cries out in amazement, but recognizes Florio just in time to hide him again in the basket, before busybodies come rushing up in alarm at her cry, and carries the basket into a beautiful room in the tower (166-67). Here Glorizia explains Biancofiore's temporary absence and advises caution (168). It is then agreed between the maid and Florio that he shall be concealed behind the curtains of Biancofiore's bed ("quivi tacitamente dimorerai tanto che coricata a dormir la vedrai, e poichè addormentata sarà, siati lecito di fare il tuo disio," 168-69). When Florio is hidden, Glorizia goes to seek Biancofiore, and finds her, prostrated in melancholy over her long separation from her lover, lying on the bed of one of her companions. To comfort the damsel, Glorizia improvises a dream in which she pretends to have seen Florio entering the room of Biancofiore, and the lovers joyously united

(170-71). Encouraged by Glorizia's persistently avowed belief that Florio is seeking her in that very land ("in questo paese"), Biancofiore begins to make merry with her maids.

Florio in his place of concealment witnesses their festivities "per piccolo pertugio," masters his impatience to rush out and embrace Biancofiore, and awaits nightfall (172-74).

Glorizia and Biancofiore come into the latter's bedroom, and, while preparations are made for retiring, converse of Florio and their vicissitudes (174-76). Finally the damsel creeps into her bed, and, unable to sleep for a time, sighs for Florio and prays to Venus, "Or ecco io m'acconcio a dormire, e attendo nelle mie braccia il disiato bene, o santa Dea "(176-77).

Florio controls his ardour until Biancofiore finally falls asleep, then boldly enters her bed and draws her into his arms. She wakens in fright to find herself in a young man's embraces, but her fears are allayed when she learns he is Florio (179). Before, however, she finally surrenders to him, she requires Florio to show her a ring, with which she had long before presented him. Florio shows it to her on his finger and volunteers to espouse her with it (180-81). They rise and, clothed in rich apparel, pledge their marriage vows before Hymen, Juno, and Venus (181-82). Then they call Glorizia to rejoice with them for a time, before they at last retire together (182-83). For a few nights they continue their amorous delights (183-85), until they are discovered by the Ammiraglio asleep in one another's arms (184-85).

The latter is infuriated and condemns them to be burned alive; but they are rescued by Florio's friends. In the end it appears that Biancofiore is the niece of the Ammiraglio, and the two are permitted by him to marry.

They wander about in other adventures, and are finally restored to Spain, where the discovery that Biancofiore is of noble birth secures to them full pardon, and where after the death of King Felice they enjoy a prosperous reign (185-378).

The general dissimilarity of this summary of the *Filocolo* to the story of Chaucer's *Troilus and Criseyde* will, of course, at once strike the reader. Boccaccio's is a story of constant lovers happily united in the end; and Chaucer's is a story of a love ruined by a faithless woman. Nevertheless it has been an accepted belief among Chaucerians for a number of years that an immediate influence was exercised by the

Filocolo over *Troil.* This attitude of belief, accepted among others by Professor J. S. P. Tatlock (*Boccaccio and the Plan of the Canterbury Tales, Anglia*, 1913, 69-117) and the French scholar Èmile Hyacinthe Legouis (*Geoffroy Chaucer*, Paris, 1910, 121-22), is due entirely to sections of Professor Karl Young's admirable piece of Chaucerian scholarship, *The Origin and Development of the Story of Troilus and Criseyde*, Chaucer Society, 1908, pp. 139-68. That the belief is quite erroneous the present writer has concluded after a minute study of Professor Young's work on *Filocolo-Troilus* relations.

It was Professor Young's belief that the intrigue leading up to Troilus's and Criseyde's first night and certain similar details were influenced by the intrigue and certain minor details leading up to the first night of Florio and Biancofiore.

In his enthusiasm for the influence of Italian literature upon the works of the English poet, Professor Young premised that it "is *à priori* not in the least surprising" that Chaucer, an assiduous reader of the *Filostrato* and the *Teseide*, "should have known and used another of Boccaccio's early works" (*Origin and Development of the Story of Troilus and Criseyde*, 140). Proceeding then to summarize the episodes in the *Filocolo* and *Troil.* which lead to the first night of the lovers in each work, he found in them much the same general situation. The characters of the Italian romance, Biancofiore and Florio, meet on this occasion, he believed, in much the same way as Criseyde and Troilus do. His next step was to examine the details in the general situations of *Filocolo* and *Troil.*, and as the result of his study of the two works he decided that there exist seven minor circumstances in Chaucer's account which offer *definite* parallels to seven minor circumstances in the account of Boccaccio. Upon these seven resemblances he built his thesis.

To discuss Professor Young's contentions competently it is necessary, first to present his seven parallels;

I. In each case the *innamorata* is led to believe that her lover is far away.

II. According to both accounts the lover, concealed in an adjoining chamber, observes through a small orifice the merry-making in which his lady takes part.

III. In each case the go-between, while keeping the lover concealed, prepares the mind of the *innamorata* for his coming by vague suggestions of such a possibility.

IV. The jealousy of the lovers figures prominently in both stories.

V. In both accounts the lady takes oaths from her lover before finally admitting him to her bed.

VI. In both stories the lovers make use of rings.

VII. Although there is in Chaucer's poem no formal ceremony of marriage like that in *Filocolo* before the image of Cupid, the English poem does show a parallel in the interchanging of rings just mentioned, in the hymn of Troilus to Love and to "Citherea the swete," and in Criseyde's acceptance of his vows.

Separate study must be made of each of these parallels.

"Pandarus," asserts Professor Young à *propos* of the first of them, "is explicit upon this point" of Troilus's being far away,

"He swor hir, 'nay, for he was out of towne,'" (III, 570), while Glorizia, the nurse of Biancofiore, is also "unequivocal,"

"Or ecco, disse Glorizia, tu nol puoi avere, egli non c'è, ne cio può venire" (*Filocolo*, Vol. II, p. 175), and Biancofiore (four pages later!) says to Florio, "Come può essere che tu qui sii ora ch'io ti credeva in Ispagna?" (II, 179). The parallel seems, at first appearance, rather striking, but when we discover in the *Filostrato*, the great source, it will be remembered, of Chaucer's poem, another equally striking one, its value becomes less impressive. This parallel has escaped Professor Young's attention. When, in the Italian poem, the favourable moment comes for an assignation of Griseida and Troilo, Pandaro finds himself constrained to inform her that Troilo was *alquanto di lontano*, only later to evince his ability to insure a speedy return of the absent lover.

> *Pandaro dolessi*
> *Di Troilo, che 'l dì davanti andato*
> *Era con certi, per bisogni espressi*
> *Della lor guerra, alquanto di lontano,*
> *Bench' el dovea tornare a mano a mano.* (III, 21.)

To the above passage rather than to the *Filocolo* must be attributed the reference in *Troil.* to the absence of the young knight from town. In itself it obviates all necessity for further research into the origin of *Troil.* III, 570.

In his second parallel Professor Young makes much of the similarity between the concealment of Troilus and that of Florio. Troilus views the merriment of Pandarus and Criseyde through a little window "in a stewe" (III, 595-614), while Florio in "una camera" contiguous to the room in which Biancofiore and her companions begin "a far festa" witnesses the pastimes of his love "per piccolo pertugio" (II, 168, 172), i. e., a tiny opening, not necessarily a window at all. But had Professor Young fully exercised his caution, he would have perceived that, once it is posited that Troilus should be hidden in the house of Pandarus, a lover of his propensities would be bound to spy upon the merry-making of his lady and her uncle. It takes no great literary invention, such as Florio gazing through a tiny opening, to influence the creation of a scene of a man hiding in a neighboring room and from his place of concealment watching the activities of his friends. Figures in hiding have ever been, in all literatures, a commonplace. Eaves-droppers, malicious or well disposed, are by no means unusual conventions in mediaeval romances. Husbands regularly set spies upon their wives in that and in other varieties of literature. By chance or by purposed hiding chevaliers frequently discover things to their own advantage. No device could have been more simple or more likely to be uninspired by a literary influence than Chaucer's permitting the lovelorn Troilus, secretly bestowed in an adjoining room, within hearing distance of Criseyde's voice, to indulge his longing to peep at the lady every second that he remained in concealment.

Moreover the figure of Troilus concealed in the house of Pandarus is not a diametrically different one from that of Troilus, abed in the house of Deiphebus feigning illness, and awaiting the approach of Criseyde (*Troil.* II, 1753-57). On this occasion also Troilus is an eaves-dropper.

> But now to yow, ye lovers that ben here,
> Was Troilus nought in a cankredort,
> That lay, and mighte whispringe of hem here?
>   (II, 1751-53)

It should be remembered, too, that the reason for Troilus's concealment is that Criseyde is accompanied by her women, who must not be permitted to know of her clandestine amour with the knight. It is only after they are safe abed that the intrigue of the three Trojans can mature (III, 687-768). Similarly in Boccaccio's *Filostrato*, the chief source of *Troil.*, Troilo is obliged to remain in hiding until Griseida's household "sen fu ito a dormire" and "la casa rimasta tutta cheta." (*Filostrato* III, 26-27, *Opera Volgari*, Vol. XIII.)

Surely Chaucer's imagination was broad enough to span the tiny cleft between the place of Troilo's hiding in the *Filostrato*, III, 25, the "certo luogo rimoto ed oscuro," and the "litel windowe in a stewe" of *Troil.* III, 601, without the assistance of a "piccolo pertugio" in the *Filocolo.*

Let us observe Professor Young's third parallel. It is not wholly evident that the preliminaries to the *innamoramento* in *Troil.* and in the *Filocolo* are similar. Glorizia's preparation of the mind of Biancofiore for the coming of Florio is not pre-eminently like Pandarus's preparation of the mind of Criseyde for the coming of Troilus. Rather in telling Biancofiore of her "nuova visione, che nel sonno di lui e di te queste notte m'apparve" (II, 171), Glorizia is decidedly unlike Pandarus, who prepares Criseyde's mind by swearing that Troilus is out of town and by adding the assurance, "I pose that he were" here,

> "Yow thurfte never have the more fere.
> For rather than men mighte him ther aspye,
> Me were lever a thousand-fold to dye." (III, 571-4)

And the more she enlarges upon her vision, the less Glorizia's looks like the *preparation* of Pandarus—if it be correct to speak of the lines just quoted from Chaucer's text, as Professor Young would term them, as *preparation* of the mind of the enamoured Chriseyde for the coming of Troilus through the vague suggestions made by Pandarus of such a possibility. Let me submit the dream of Biancofiore's nurse in fuller detail than Professor Young does. "E pareami che egli avesse indosso una gonella quasi di colore di vermiglia rosa, e sopra essa un drappo, il cui colore quasi simigliante mi pareva a' tuoi capelli; e pareami tanto lieto quanto io mai lo vedessi, e solamente rimirava te, che nel tuo letto soavemente dormivi; a cui e' mi parve dire: o Florio, come e perchè venisti tu qui?" After the response made by Florio in the dream, and repeated in her account by Glorizia, she continues: "Tu allora mi parea che ti svegliasse, e piena di maraviglia riguardandolo, appena potevi credere ch' egli desso fosse; ma poi riconosciutolo, grandissima festa faciavate." (II, 171). More of her dream there would be little use in presenting here. Enough has been quoted to illustrate the total unlikeness of the passages in the *Troil.* and the *Filocolo,* which Professor Young is fain to parallel. No real similarity can be detected in Pandarus's oath that Troilus was out of town and Glorizia's dream that Florio had been in the bedroom of Biancofiore, leaning over her sleeping figure. Yet such is the similarity Professor Young proposes.

We may now consider his fourth parallel, the jealousy of Troilus and that of Florio.

Very great is the difference in the occasions for the jealousy of these two lovers. Troilus in reality merely assumes a pretext of jealousy, after Pandarus has falsely declared to Criseyde that her lover is unhappy, because he suspects that she is favourable to the suit of one Horaste (III, 806-807). Florio is jealous of one Fileno, who shows him a "velo" which he says Biancofiore's own hand has given him as a token of her love, whereas it is only through the machinations of Florio's queen-mother, who is opposed to the infatuation of the prince for Biancofiore, that the damsel has presented him the veil in gratitude for a service he has apparently rendered her. (I, 246-251). There is no such flaunting of a favour before the eyes of Troilus. Moreover the jealousy of Troilus and the jealousy of Florio are manifested on widely different occasions. Florio is jealous when he is separated far away from Biancofiore by his designing parents; Troilus is apparently jealous when his lady is on the eve of surrendering herself to his embraces.

The paralleling of jealousy in two lovers cannot then denote a real influence of the *Filocolo* over the *Troil.* unless it is shown that they reveal the quality in somewhat parallel situations. Moreover the jealousy of Florio is never, like that of Troilus, employed as a pretext for gaining admission to his mistress. It is even possible, too, that Troilus's jealousy was suggested to Chaucer by certain passages *à propos* of Troilo's *gelosia*, in Boccaccio's *Filostrato* (I, 49; II, 75; IV, 139-145; VII, 18).

The fifth parallel, proposed by Professor Young, is hardly deserving of the name. "In both stories the lady takes oaths of her lover before finally admitting him to her bed." Criseyde merely takes "swich othes as hir list devyse" (III, 1143), from Troilus, and feels then that there is no cause for bidding him rise from her bedside; Biancofiore on the other hand passively accepts the vow of espousal, which is freely offered her by Florio, and then rises to join with him in formal marriage ceremonies before Hymen and Juno and Venus (II, 181).

The sixth parallel really ought to be combined with the fifth. "In both stories the lovers make use of rings" to be sure, but observe that in the *Filocolo* only one ring is used, and that one of a very interesting history, while in the *Troil. rings are interchanged.* In the Italian romance the ring was one which possessed a certain magical virtue. The owner of it could at any moment, by the mere examination of the stone in its setting, determine, through any temporary change in its colouring, whether his mistress was at that particular moment in any peril or oppressed with any sorrow. This ring Biancofiore had given to her lover before the days of their separation from one another. (*Filocolo* I, pp. 110, 111, 113, 116). When at last the two are united, Florio, entirely of his own initiative, proposes to espouse Biancofiore with this ring beseeching her, "nè credere che io sì lungamente aggia affannato per acquistare amica, ma per acquistare inseparabile sposa, la quale tu mi sarai," and then declaring immediately, "e fermamente, avanti che altro fra noi sia, col tuo medesimo annello ti sposerò alla qual cosa Imeneo, e la santa Giunone e Venere nostra dea siano presenti" (II, 181). In *Filocolo*, it will be perceived then, the ring is used preceding the marital vows; in Chaucer's poem however the rings are interchanged playfully after the union of Troilus and Criseyde has been consummated.

It is highly improbable that Chaucer should need a source for the old familiar picture of two lovers exchanging rings, or, if he had needed some picture from which to make so simple a copy as his proves to be, that he should take for his model the elaborate marriage ceremony of Florio and Biancofiore, which I am sorry I cannot quote at length here (II, 181-82)—and then by some canny Chaucerian magic transform their one ring into two, or even more.

Professor Young's seventh parallel also infringes upon the boundaries of the one preceding it. He maintains that the English poem shows a parallel to *Filocolo* "in the interchanging of rings just mentioned, in the hymn of Troilus to Love and to 'Citherea the swete,' and in Criseyde's acceptance of his vows." It is a hazardous parallel. The interchanging of rings, we have already seen, is altogether unlike the formal marriage of Florio and Biancofiore. And it is equally unsafe to parallel a hymn sung by Troilus, after he has Criseyde in his arms, with one which Florio sings, as he stands with his lady before the image of Cupid. The temerity of such an effort is especially apparent, when we realize that whatever credence one might have given to the validity of this single parallel, it is only supported by other parallels, the futility of which has just been demonstrated. Moreover, we remember, as Professor Young seems to forget, that Troilus's song is, after all, only Chaucer's substitution for the beautiful song which was sung by Troilo in the *Filostrato* to Love as the creator and preserver of all things (*Filostrato*, III, 74-89). Or to put it briefly, *a parallel for the hymn of Troilus is discoverable in the immediate source of the English poem.*

Criseyde's acceptance of the vows of Troilus, once she is in her lover's embrace, constitutes, too, no real parallel to Biancofiore's acceptance of the vows of her lover, only after the image of Cupid genially inclines his head in answer to the prayers of the two lovers as they stand before it.   (II, 182)[1]

The seven parallels cited above are then demonstrably inadequate. Upon them can be based no contention that Chaucer was aided by the *Filocolo* in the development of *Troil*. I cannot agree with Professor Young, therefore, that, "from the evidence before us, without pursuing details further, we are justified . . . in inferring a literary connection between this episode in the *Filocolo* and the similar episode in *Troilus and Criseyde*."   And, of course, without the support of his parallels the whole of Professor Young's contention must fall, for without them the likeness of the general situations in *Troil*. and *Filocolo* deteriorates into a mere similarity between two groups of three persons each, and each group involved in a love intrigue, where one person arranges with some subtlety for a meeting of the other two "in the bedchamber of the *innamorata*, the latter being unaware that her lover is concealed near at hand." In view of that truth, the differences in the measures taken by the two go-betweens, one a man, Pandarus, and the other a woman, Glorizia, to bring about the meeting of the lovers, become more and more divergent. Nor can they obviate, by any strain of the imagination, the dissimilarity between Biancofiore's desires and Criseyde's scruples, between Pandarus's wish "to avert scandal and overcome the lady's scruples" and Glorizia's "to avert scandal and personal disaster to the lady." Finally we cannot base a literary connection between *Troil*. and the *Filocolo* upon the mere fact that in each work one of the important characters is a go-between.

---

[1] One can find in Boccaccio's *Teseide* (*Opere Volgari*, Vol. IX) quite as relevant a parallel to the invocations accompanying the espousals of Troilus and Criseyde as the one in the *Filocolo*. Observe the marriage scenes of Teseo and Ippolita:

> Ripresi adunque i lasciati ornamenti,
> Di Citerea il tempio fero aprire,
> Serrato ne' lor primi mutamenti;
> Qui fe' Teseo Ippolita venire,
> E dati i sagrifizii riverenti
> A Venere, sposo con gran disire,
> Ippolita, l'aiuto d'Imeneo
> Chiamando, quivi il gran baron Teseo.   (*Tes*. I, 134)

Were such a step possible, it would be even easier to trace an influence of the *Filocolo* over Keats's *Eve of St. Agnes* than it has been for Professor Young to trace an influence of the Italian work over *Troil.* A number of Professor Young's parallels may be easily fitted to Keats' poem. In that latter work the lady Madeleine, though not led to believe so by any special agency, believes that her lover is far away. Porphyro, concealed in Madeleine's chamber, watches from a closet the lady's preparations to retire.

There are, too, more striking resemblances between the *Filocolo* and the *Eve of St. Agnes.* In each work the go-between is a woman, the body-servant of the lady. The old woman Angela, like Glorizia, conceals the heroine Madeleine's lover in her room. Porphyro, like Florio, bends long over his mistress ere she awakes and recognizes him. Madeleine, like Biancofiore, on being awakened, is frightened, only to be reassured by her lover a moment later.

One might too, very relevantly, parallel Biancofiore's dream, as included in the dream fabricated by Glorizia, who pretended to have dreamed that Biancofiore dreamed that she was in the arms of Florio and that she woke to find her dream was true, with Madeleine's dream that she was in the arms of Porphyro and her wakening to find herself really there. And like Florio, and entirely unlike Troilus, Porphyro is secretly introduced into his lady's chamber before the lady herself enters. To pursue resemblances further would be futile. We know that Keats was not influenced by the *Filocolo*; and yet one can see that a better case can be constructed for the influence of that work over Keat's poem than over Chaucer's *Troil.* Professor Young has based too much on two or three fortuitous parallels, and has paralleled, we have seen, two or three situations that obviously present no really close similarity.

And the dissimilarity between the *Filocolo* and *Troil.* grows as one glances at the two works *in toto.* The Italian work is filled with far wanderings and all sorts of miraculous adventure. It contains a long episode of story-telling. It covers a life-time, and it ends a comedy. On the other hand *Troil.* is a unified piece of work, describing no wanderings to make up for weakness or sluggishness in plot, and citing no miracles of any form. It contains no story within a story. It covers a brief period of time, and it ends a tragedy. Such great dissimilarities more than militate against the effectiveness of such parallels as Professor Young has offered. Indeed they argue convincingly the futility of them.

It is unfortunate that in so excellent a work as his *Origin and Devel-opment of the Story of Troilus and Criseyde* Professor Young should have introduced the theory, and more unfortunate that he should have come to believe in the actual influence of the long prose romance over *Troil.*   Chaucer, who was able to invent so many new episodes in his poem, the picture of Troilus riding beneath the window of Cris-eyde, the meeting at the house of Deiphebus, the prophecies and divination of Cassandra, and numerous others, certainly it must be con-ceded by all critics—even by those who would be unwilling to grant to the poet the high inventive power which Professor Young in full confidence acknowledges he possessed—was fully competent to invent the details of the intrigue in the house of Pandarus without the immed-iate assistance of any one of the myriad mediaeval romances of clandestine love.   And if Chaucer had known the *Filocolo* it is incon-ceivable that he, who so thoroughly culled out from Boccaccio's *Teseide* so many beauties and incorporated them into his several works, should have neglected to avail himself of any of all the rich store of them in that most tapestried of Italian prose romances.

To conclude then, we have no reasonable ground for the assumption that the *Filocolo* in any way influenced the writing of the *Troilus and Criseyde*, or even for the belief that Chaucer was at all acquainted with the Italian work when he wrote his own great poem.

CHAPTER II

CHAUCER AND THE *Amorosa Visione*

In the preceding chapter it was discovered that there is no sufficient ground for believing that Chaucer employed in *Troil.* certain details of Boccaccio's prose romance, the *Filocolo*. Such a discovery leads us to inquire whether Chaucer knew any other of Boccaccio's Italian works besides the *Filostrato* and the *Teseide*, with which, it has long been known, he was acquainted. Will it be possible to show that others too of these works, which scholars have with varying degrees of confidence suggested or asserted were known to Chaucer, can be no more categorically enumerated in the list of Chaucer's Italian readings than the long romance of Florio and Biancofiore? The question must be weighed deliberately.

In a group of *Chauceriana* compiled and published by a German scholar, E. Koeppel, (*Anglia Zeitschrift für Englische Philologie*, 1891-92, pp. 227-67), a list of parallels is prepared which is designed to reveal relations between the *Amorosa Visione* (*Opere Volgari*, Vol. XIV) and Chaucer's *Parliament of Fowls*, as well as between the Italian work and the *House of Fame* (pp. 233-38). The German scholar is so impressed with his compilation as to conclude: "Das sind die fälle, welche mir dafür zu sprechen scheinen, dass Chaucer auch die *Amorosa Visione* mit aufmerksamkeit gelesen hat. Stofflich berührt sich Boccaccio im weiteren verlauf seiner dichtung noch sehr häufig mit Chaucer, ohne dass wir jedoch, bei dem reichlichen fliessen anderer quellen, anlass haben, in seinen versen Chaucers vorbild zu suchen (pp. 237-8)." The conclusion is not categorical, but we perceive that Koeppel himself believed that Chaucer had read the *A. V.* "attentively."

Writing in the *Modern Language Notes* (Vol. X, pp. 190-92), Professor Clarence G. Child observes, "Koeppel's parallels (reference is here made only to the *House of Fame*) identify in a very interesting way, the *Lady Fame* of Chaucer with Boccaccio's *Gloria del popol mondano* and show that both poems speak of Virgil, Lucan, Ovid, and Statius, and in much the same fashion (p. 190)." From this observation Professor Child proceeds to the further remarks—obviously made, though not specifically so stated, in regard to resemblances between the *A. V.* and the *H. F.*—"One of the features of similarity is the citation of stock examples in history and mythology of loving maidens

left forlorn. These, with their stories told at various lengths, take
up a good part of the *Visione*; in Chaucer they are used to illustrate
the fact that Aeneas was not alone in his 'greet trespas,' and all but
two (Demophon and Phillis, and Theseus and Ariadne), are dismissed in a line or so."

Subsequently Professor Child investigates Chaucer's versions of
the stories of Theseus and Ariadne, Demophon and Phyllis, Aeneas
and Dido, and finds in them certain features which he believes are the
result of the English poet's indebtedness to the accounts of those
three pairs of lovers presented by Boccaccio in the *A. V.*

It will be necessary for us to scrutinize more closely the work of
Koeppel and of Professor Child.

The *A. V.* belongs, as do most of Boccaccio's erotic compositions
before the *Decamerone*, to the period of his Neapolitan pleasuring, and,
like many of them, is inscribed to his "Fiamma," Maria d'Acquino,
the "Fiammetta" of other works. It is a long poem, written in
terza rima, and composed of three introductory acrostic *sonnetti*
and of fifty *capitoli*, each, with the exception of one slightly shorter
and two slightly longer, eighty-eight lines in length. The editor of
the *Moutier* edition of it pronounces the poem "la miglior produzione
poetica del Certaldese" and "un vero gioiello di poesia italiana del
secolo decimoquarto." The three *sonnetti* are acrostics which contain in order all the initial letters of the first verse of each *terzina*
throughout the whole of the poem, and reveal it to be a jewel made
with the subtlest of mediaeval workmanship.

As its name indicates, the *A. V.* belongs to the *genre* of love and
dream-lore poetry. In a long vision the devotees of Venus are given
precedence over the followers of Glory or Fortune. The narrator
falls asleep and presently dreams that a lady, "gentil piacente e
bella," appears to him and volunteers, if he wishes it, to lead him into
a place where he shall have his every desire satisfied. Responding
agreeably to her invitation, he seems to follow her into a noble castle,
at the gateway of which he pauses to examine an inscription in letters
of gold written above. While the two stand thus, they are joined
by two youths, whom the lady leads then with the narrator into the
castle, where they find themselves in a great hall resplendent with
gold. Here first they behold a lady in purple vestments, with seven
other ladies on the right and left of her, and likewise a great crowd of
philosophers, painted upon a wall (*Capitoli* I, IV). At the left of
this lady they perceive a group of poets, including all the famous ones

of Latin and Greek antiquity and Dante, whose work their female guide stops for a while to praise (*Cap.* V). They then pass on to another painting depicting the "Gloria del popol mondano" (VI), a lady in whose train follow numerous heroes and heroines from sacred and profane history, from classical mythology, and from the mediaeval romance cycles, figures whose stories are in most instances merely touched upon (VII-XII). Of being able to count these numerous followers of Glory the narrator despairs at this moment, and, at the suggestion of his guide, turns his attention to a mountain of gold, silver, and precious stones (XII) upon which he beholds a number of famous misers, including Midas (XIII-XIV).

He next turns to a part where are painted many stories, and where first he beholds pictures of Amor and Venus (XV). After observing these he sees depicted the tales of many famous lovers from Jove and Europa to Tristram and Iseult (XVI-XXIX). Like the devotees of Glory, these, also, are too numerous to remember; and the narrator, evidently wearied, again turns to his beautiful guide (XXIX), who proceeds to show him the fates of them who follow Fortune (XXX-XXXVII). After some moralizing upon these victims, the lady invites the narrator to look with her upon glorious and eternal things, and leads him through a little door from the hall into a delightful garden (XXXVII), where he discovers a fountain and by it figures sculptured in marble, besides numerous other charms (XXXVIII-XXXIX). In the garden he sees Citherea and her son and many beautiful ladies, with one after another of whom he falls in love (XL). Presently he finds other groups of ladies dancing (XLI-XLII), and ere long still another group, seated, crowned with wreaths, and discoursing of Love (XLII). These ladies he names and describes at some length (XLIII-XLIV), until one with whom he is especially enamoured comes up to him, and, opening his breast, writes her own name in letters of gold upon his heart, and then puts a ring upon his finger (XLV). For some time he stands contemplating the charms of this lady, until she asks him how he has come thither; whereupon he tells her of his guide, and is sent by her to bring the latter (XLV-XLVII). The two ladies greet each other cordially and learn soon one another's worth. Subsequently the guide takes the second lady, with whom the dreamer is in love, salutes her as a "daughter of virtue," and in a stately speech presents her with the dreamer, giving her a moment later to him (XLVIII). The two lovers then part from the guide temporarily, and are just about to experience the ultimate delight of their love in one another's arms, when the narrator seems to wake in bitter disappointment to find all his pleasure is but a dream (XLIX). While he stands weeping in his disappointment, he is rejoined by the lady who had been his guide into the garden, and is, in a moment, overjoyed at being told by her that the pleasure he had dreamed he had been disappointed of he shall soon have in its entirety (L.). Thereupon his real awakening occurs; and the narrator ends with a plea to his lady for favour for both himself and his poem, as she reads his vision, assuring her that Love has given him to her, and religiously commending her to the Lord of All Peace (L.).

In this summary of the *A. V.* one finds no marked similarities to any of Chaucer's narratives. The castle, the gates, the processions of poets and philosophers and lovers, the groups of ladies, gardens, fountains, and the dreamer and his guide themselves are all stock properties of mediaeval poetry. They offer no valid testimony as to literary relationships unless supported by really striking verbal parallels. A careful investigation of the *A. V.* for such possible details of influence over Chaucer's work has not revealed to me any further material of that or of any other sort which is of significance; and I am brought therefore to the conclusion that any belief that Chaucer may have known and used the *A. V.* must rest on the foundation of Koeppel's and Child's several testimony, i. e., it must rest upon three parallels between the *A. V.* and the *P. F.*, upon eight parallels between the *A. V.* and the *H. F.* cited by the German scholar, and upon the similarities in Chaucer's and Boccaccio's brief narratives of the tales of three pairs of lovers in the *H. F.* and the Italian work, instanced by the American professor. An examination of this evidence becomes then imperative. It will be necessary to conduct it in considerable detail.

First, let us consider the parallels between the *P. F.* and Boccaccio's poem. Koeppel begins: "Zu dem herkömmlichen apparat der visionendichtung gehört es, dass sowohl in der *A. V.* wie auch in dem *P. F.* den im traume wandelnden dichtern führer zur seite treten, dem Italiener eine allegorische frauengestalt, dem Engländer der Africanus. Beachtenswert ist jedoch, dass beide dichter im traume, nachdem sie ihre begleitung bereits gefunden haben, dieselbe gottheit, Venus, welche sie mit demselben namen anrufen, bitten, ihnen bei dieser dichtung behilflich zu sein (p. 234)."

In consideration of the admission made by Koeppel in the first of the two sentences just quoted, to the effect that, since the *A. V.* and the

P. F. are vision poems, they both naturally contain the conventional
figure of a guide for the dreamer, it seems indeed strange that he
should argue anything "beachtenswert" in the fact that the authors of
the two poems, which belong to the *genre* of courtly love poetry,
wherein Venus and her son are perennially celebrated, should in-
voke the assistance of "this same divinity Venus." An invocation
of that deity for inspiration in a love poem is an almost inevitable
convention in mediaeval poetry.

If one examines Koeppel's first pair of parallels,

O somma e graziosa intelligenza,
Che muovi il terzo cielo, o santa Dea,
Metti nel petto la tua potenza;
Non sofferir che fugga, o *Citerea*,
A me l' ingegno all' opera presente,
Ma più sottile e più in me ne crea,
Venga il tuo valor nella mia mente.
    (*A. V.* II, 1-7)

Infiamma me tanto più ch' io non sono,
Che 'l tuo ardor, di ch' io tutto m' in-
voglio,
Faccia piacere quel di ch' io ragiono.
    (*A. V.* II. 10-12)

Citerea! thou blisful lady swete,
    That with thy fyr-brand dauntest
        whom thee lest,
And madest me this sweven for to mete,
Be thou my help in this, for thou mayst
    best;
As wisly as I saw thee north-north-west,
When I began my sweven for to wryte,
So yif me might to ryme and to endyte.
    (*P. F.* 113-119),

one finds in it verbal resemblances in the names *Citerea* and *Citherea*.
No repetition of the same attributes or achievements of the goddess
occurs in the two passages, nor is there in them further similarity of
any sort. Furthermore it is true that in the *Teseide*, which we have
long known contributed the long description of the abode of Venus in
the *P. F.* (Cf. *Tes.* Lib. VII, sts. 51-66 with *P. F.* 183-291), Boccaccio
no less than in the *A. V.* appeals to that goddess for guidance in
in his work.

> Siate presenti, o Marte rubicondo,
> Nelle tui armi rigido e feroce,
> E tu, Madre d'Amor, col tuo giocondo
> E lieto aspetto, e 'l tuo Figliuol veloce
> Co' dardi suoi possenti in ogni mondo;
> E sostenete la mano e la voce
> Di mi, che intendo i vostri effetti dire
> Con poco bene e pien d'assai martire. (*Tes.* I, 3)

This quotation I submit not as a parallel, but only as further evidence
that Chaucer could find instances of the conventional invocations of
Venus as readily in works of Boccaccio with which he was undoubtedly

familiar as in the *A. V.* And Chaucer's proclivity for making such appeals to Venus is again notably evinced in the Proem of Book III of *Troil.*, where he adroitly incorporates Troilo's hymn in praise of the goddess (*Fil.* III, 74-89) into an author's invocation (*Troil.* III, I-44).

Koeppel's second and third pairs of parallels between the *A. V.* and the *P. F.*,

> *A. V.* II, 20-24; 34-35.   *P. F.* 120-122.
> *A. V.* III, 13-21.   *P. F.* 127-133,

involve another convention of dream lore.   In both poems, he urges, the dreamer is brought to the gate or door of an enclosure above which inscriptions appear; and then he takes pains to draw his parallels closer than this, but wholly without the aid of verbal similarities.   The mind of the wary student turns instinctively at once to the myriad walled gardens of weird and antique aspect, or to other no less fascinating enclosures situate in the realms of mediaeval poetry or pictorially woven on mediaeval tapestry, only to have the student declare inwardly that parallels fully as significant can be drawn between these luminous gardens and Chaucer's garden in the *P. F.* as those drawn by the German scholar between the gardens of the *A. V.* and the *P. F.*   The *Roman de la Rose* and the *Divina Commedia*, such a student knows, will furnish abundant material for constructing parallels, and yet supply a relatively small part of the material upon which he may draw.   Compare Chaucer's translations in the *Romaunt of the Rose*: A. 135-45; 146-474; 475-482; 525-537.   We need quote for illustration only a few of these lines:

> Alle thise thinges, wel avysed,
> As I have you er this devysed,
> With gold and asure over alle
> Depeynted were upon the walle.
> Squar was the wal, and high somdel:
> Enclosed, and y-barred wel,
> In stede of hegge, was that gardin.
> (A. 475-81)

> Tho gan I go a ful gret pas
> Envyroning even in compas
> The closing of the square wal,
> Til that I fond a wiket smal
> So shet, that I ne mighte in goon,
> And other entree was ther noon. (A. 525-530)

So far then as parallels can at all be drawn between the *P. F.* and the *A. V.* they remain precarious. They embrace no similarities that are convincing. Professor Child himself evidently was unimpressed by such of them as Koeppel drew, for he does not in his article in any way build upon them as a foundation. In the parallels, however, drawn by the German scholar between the *H. F.* and the *A. V.* he discovers matter which to him seems significant and upon which he builds. Let us test the significance of his discovery and the structure which he frames upon the basis of it.

Koeppel points out features which he is inclined to consider parallel in the two poems as follows:

I.　A hall richly ornamented with gold (*A. V.*, IV, 9-10; *H. F.* 1342-6.)

II.　Interior walls adorned with paintings, on one of which,—in Boccaccio's poem but not in Chaucer's, — is pictured an exceedingly beautiful female figure (*A. V.*, VI, 43-4, 48; *H. F.*, 1364-7).

III　This lady is in each case laden with jewels and imperially enthroned (*A. V.*, VI, 49-50, 58-61; *H. F.*, 1360-1, 1364-5, 1393-94).

IV.　Information is given to both poets,—to Boccaccio by means of an inscription, to Chaucer by the announcement of heralds,—as to the identity of this beautiful woman(*A. V.*, VI, 75; *H. F.*, 1310-13).

V.　In the presentation of four great poets amid a larger series of great literary figures, by Boccaccio in the train of Philosophia, who is represented with her disciples in a painting, and by Chaucer standing on a series of pillars extending from the two sides of the throne of the Lady Fame, Vergil (*A. V.*, V, 7-9, 13-16; *H. F.*, 1483-5); Lucan (*A. V.*, V, 19-22; *H. F.*, 1499-1502); Ovid (*A. V.*, V, 25-27; *H. F.*, 1486-9); Statius (*A. V.*, V, 34-36; *H. F.*, 1460-61); and in the mention of certain of their works in association with the names of these poets.

Let us study these five very general resemblances. The passages describing the gold-ornamented halls reveal no verbal parallels; and the halls themselves are after all so commonplace in the land of faerie that we may omit them from further discussion. The paintings on the walls are too usual a convention in mediaeval description to deserve comment. The verses however in which the two beautiful female figures are presented do involve a verbal parallel, and must not be too lightly dismissed. In the *A. V.* we read of the lady,

> . . . *mai natura con sua arte*
> *Forma non diede a si bella figura,* (VI, 43-44),

and of the "feminyne creature" in the *H. F.*

> *That never formed by nature*
> Was swich another thing y-seye (1366-7).

The description of ladies, however, as celestial beings excelling nature is common in fourteenth century literature. Dante's Beatrice, Petrarch's Laura, and even Boccaccio's Fiammetta are frequently so described in the verses of their lovers. It is ever a query with an infatuated poet whether so lovely a creature as the sweet woman who has fascinated him could be fashioned by the hands of nature. Observe Chaucer's Criseyde and Boccaccio's Griseida:

> Criseyde was this lady name a-right;
> As to my dome, in al Troyes citee
> Nas noon so fair, for passing every wight
> So aungellyk was hir natyf beautee,
> That lyk a thing inmortal semed she,
> *As doth an hevenish parfit creature,*
> *That down were sent in scorning of nature.*
> > *(Troil.* I, 99-105)

> Avea Calcas lasciata in tanto male,
> . . . .
> Una sua figlia vedova, la quale
> *Si bella e si angelica a vedere*
> *Era, che non parea cosa mortale,*
> Griseida nomata, al mio parere.   (*Fil.* I, 11)

It would seem hazardous then to suggest that Chaucer in describing a lady as being unlike anything previously formed by nature must needs have depended upon some special model furnished him by some particular piece of literature. It is of interest, also, to note that Chaucer used the two verses just quoted from Koeppel's parallels merely as a preface to his long fantastic description of the creature **Fame:**

> For altherfirst, soth for to seye,
> Me thoughte that she was so lyte,
> That the lengthe of a cubyte
> Was lenger than she semed be;
> But thus sone, in a whyle, she
> Hir tho so wonderliche streighte,
> That with hir feet she therthe reighte,
> And with hir heed she touched hevene,
> Ther as shynen sterres sevene.   (*H. F.* 1368-1376)

The two prefatory verses indicate nothing more than that this creature, whose stature varies before the poet's eyes from less than the
length of a cubit to the measureless length of the distance between
heaven and earth, is without a parallel among all the objects of
nature. Boccaccio's lines on the other hand have no other design
than to assure us that nature never shaped a lovelier female than this
lady, "la Gloria del popol mondano," whose stature, it should be
observed, never varies in magnitude. And the continuation of
Boccaccio's description of "Gloria" further obviates resemblance:

> Non Citerea allor ch'ell'amò Marte,
> Nè quando Adon le piacque, con sua cura
> Si fe' sì bella, quando infra gran gente
> Donna pareva lì leggiadra e pura. (*A. V.*, VI, 45-48)

To argue that a real parallel is found in the two passages from the
Italian and the English poem, as quoted by Koeppel, would, it is
evident then, require an elastic imagination.

It would, however, not be difficult to believe that a real source
parallel was discoverable in the next two passages cited by Koeppel,—
or rather five passages, for he is at pains to assemble fragmentary
excerpts with the intervals between them omitted,—if other similarities were exhibited in the descriptions of the two ladies, richly laden
with jewels and enthroned. The German scholar introduces Boccaccio's "Gloria del popol mondano" to us as follows:

> *Tutti li soprastava* veramente
> *Di ricche pietre* coronata e d'oro (VI, 49-50)
> . . . .
> Il suo vestire a guisa imperïale
> Era, e teneva nella man sinestra
> Un pomo d'oro: e'n trono alla reale
> Vidi sedeva. . . . (VI, 58-61)

and Chaucer's "Fame" thus:

> But *al on hye*, above a dees,
> Sitte in a *see imperial*. . . . (1360-61)
> I saugh, perpetually y-stalled,
> A feminyne creature. . . . (1363-65)
> But, lord! the *perrie* and the *richesse*.
> I saugh sitting on this goddesse! (1393-94)

His italics appear indeed significant. But if we glance at the more
complete portraits of the two ladies in the *A. V.* and the *H. F.*, these

lesser items of resemblance begin to look merely accidental. "La
Gloria del popol mondano" is a figure of entrancing beauty:

> Tutti lì soprastava veramente
> > Di ricche pietre coronata e d'oro,
> > Nell' aspetto magnanima e possente:
> Ardita sopra un carro tra costoro
> > Grande e trionfal lieta sedea,
> > Ornato tutto di frondi d'alloro,
> Mirando questa gente: in man tenea
> > Una spada tagliente, con la quale
> > Che 'l mondo minacciasse mi parea.
> Il suo vestire a guisa imperïale
> > Era, e teneva nella man sinestra
> > Un pomo d'oro: e'n trono alla reale
> Vidi sedeva, e dalla sua man destra
> > Due cavalli eran che col petto forte
> > Traeano il carro tra la gente alpestra.
> E intra l'altre cose, che iscorte
> > Quivi furon da me intorno a questa
> > Sovrana donna, nemica di morte,
> Nel magnanimo aspetto fu, ch'a sesta
> > Un cerchio si movea grande e ritondo
> > Da' piè passando a lei sopra la testa
> Nè credo che sia cosa in tutto 'l mondo,
> > Villa, paese dimestico o strano,
> > Che non paresse dentro da quel tondo.
> Era sopra costei, e non invano,
> > Scritto un verso, che dicea leggendo:
> "Io son la Gloria del popol mondano" (VI, 49-75)

The lady "Fame" on the other hand is a creature of mystery rather
than of beauty. She is possessed of strange mystical eyes, of many
ears and tongues, and partridge wings upon her feet. Moreover her
stature is a variable one.

> > But al on hye, above a dees,
> > Sitte in a see imperial,
> > That maad was of a rubee al,
> > Which that a carbuncle is y-called,
> > I saugh, perpetually y-stalled,
> > A feminyne creature;
> > That never formed by nature

Nas swich another thing y-seye.
For altherfirst, soth for to seye,
Me thoughte that she was so lyte,
That the lengthe of a cubyte
Was lenger than she semed be;
But thus sone, in a whyle, she
Hir tho so wonderliche streighte,
That with hir feet she therthe reighte,
And with hir heed she touched hevene,
Ther as shynen sterres sevene.
And ther-to eek, as to my wit,
I saugh a gretter wonder yit,
Upon hir eyen to beholde;
But certeyn I hem never tolde;
For as fele eyen hadde she
As fetheres upon foules be,
Or weren on the bestes foure,
That goddes trone gunne honoure,
As Iohn writ in thapocalips.
Hir heer, that oundy was and crips,
As burned gold it shoon to see.
And sooth to tellen, also she
Had also fele up-stonding eres
And tonges, as on bestes heres;
And on hir feet wexen saugh I
Partriches winges redely.
But, lord! the perrie and the richesse
I saugh sitting on this goddesse!   (1360-94)

If Chaucer's depiction of the lady "Fame" was affected by the picture of the "Gloria" of Boccaccio, should not the surmise be warrantable that other details than the jewels and the enthronement would appear in the English poet's portrait? Might we not very well expect "Fame" also to wear a crown, made of "perrie" and "richesse," instead of having these signs of wealth "sitting" upon her (whether upon her head, her arms, or her garments Chaucer does not vouchsafe to tell us), and to be, furthermore, seated upon a throne resting upon a chariot drawn by horses "tra la gente alpestra?" Should not her brow, too, be adorned with laurel? Should she not, too, have a sceptre in her right hand, and a golden ball in her left? In fine, should we not be justified in expecting to find in the lady

"Fame" another such conventional figure as the throned monarch we find in the lady "Gloria del popol mondano?" These questions can, I believe, with reason be answered only in the affirmative. The more one tries to visualize the lady "Fame" the less one can see of Boccaccio's lady in her. The "perrie" and the "richesse" are in fact too much a property of romance to postulate an influence of the *A. V.* over the *H. F.* And finally there is too much of the lady Philosophy, as described in Book I, prose 1, of Chaucer's translation of Boethius' *Consolation*, a lady of varying stature and of rich attire, in Chaucer's "Fame," for one to see in her really anything of "la Gloria."

We pass over the third general resemblance pointed out by Koeppel, in regard to the information given us by each poet as to the identity of the beautiful lady, in order to consider the lists of famous writers cited by Chaucer and Boccaccio. Koeppel observes, "Zu beiden seiten des trones der Chaucer'schen Fama stehen auf metallenen pfeilern berühmte autoren. Man hat für dieses motiv an die ver-sammlung der grossen heiden in Dantes Limbo erinnert; Chaucer könnte auch an Petrarcas '*Trionfo della Fama*' gedacht haben, dessen drittes kapitel mit den namen berühmter schriftsteller überfüllt ist. Viel beachtenswerter jedoch scheint mir, das Boccaccio unmittelbar von dem bilde der Gloria ein anderes gemälde geschildert hat, welches die Philosophie mit den sieben wissenschaften und ihren jüngern zeigt. Unter diesen jüngern finden wir sechs der von Chaucer genannten dichter, und zwar äussert sich Boccaccio bei vier derselben, wie Chaucer nach bei allen, mit kurzen worten über ihre hauptwerke."

The six writers mentioned by the two poets are:

Vergil	(*A. V.*,	V,	7-8,	13-16;	*H. F.* 1483-85),
Lucan	("		19-22;		" 1499-1502),
Ovid	("		25-27		" 1486-89),
Statius	("		34-36;		" 1460-61),
Homer	("		17;		" 1466),
Claudian	("		50;		" 1509),

the last two being named only, with no comment made upon their works.

There is, of course, nothing unusual in the citation of two series of poets' names. Koeppel himself points out the fact that such citations occur in Petrarch's *Trionfo della Fama* and in Dante's *Inferno*. If we turn to the *Trionfo della Fama* we find mentioned in it only two of the above six poets, Homer and Virgil.

> . . . e quell' ardente
> Vecchio a cui fur le Muse tanto amiche,
> Ch'Argo e Micena e Troia se ne sente.
> Questi canto' gli errori e le fatiche
> Del figliuol di Laerte e della Diva;
> Primo pittor delle memorie antiche.
> A man a man con lui cantando giva
> Il Mantoan, che die par seco giostra;
> Ed uno al cui passar l'erba fioriva.　(*T. della F.*,
> 　　　　　　　　　　　　　　　　　　III, 10-18)

In Dante's "Limbo" we find three of the six poets, or four, if we wish to add to Homer, Ovid, and Lucan, the poet Virgil, Dante's companion on the journey through Hell, whom the other three advance to greet.

> Lo buon maestro cominciò a dire:
> 'Mira colui con quella spada in mano,
> Che vien dinanzi a'tre sì come sire:
> Quegli è Omero poeta sovrana
> L'altro e Orazio satiro, che viene,
> Ovidio è il terzo, e l'ultimo Lucano.'　(*Inf.* IV, 85-90)

Later on in Dante's *Purgatorio* we see a great deal of the poet Statius, the sixth poet cited by Koeppel as being mentioned by both Chaucer and Boccaccio; by one as "Stazio di Tolosa," and by the other as "the Tholosan that highte Stace." In the *Purgatorio* he is, it should be noted, named by himself as a native of Toulouse, a fact that certainly makes Chaucer's mention of him look more like a borrowing from Dante than one from Boccaccio's *A. V.*

> Tanto fu dolce vocale spirto,
> Che Tolosano, a se mi trasse Roma,
> Dove mertai le tempie ornar di mirto.
> Stazio la gente ancor di la mi noma;
> Cantai di Tebe, e poi del grande Achille,
> Ma caddi in via con la seconda soma.　(*Purg.* XXI, 88-93)

As we glance over these quotations from Petrarch and Dante, we begin to wonder why Koeppel should regard the list of names in the *A. V.* as so *noteworthy*. Petrarch's list, like both those of Chaucer and Boccaccio, embraces several times the number, six, included in the German scholar's parallels. In no two of the four works are the names presented in the same order. In Petrarch's list we find that the great Humanist, just like Chaucer and Boccaccio, "expresses himself in a few words" in regard to the masterpieces of the several poets. Facts such as these convince me that there is no significance in Chaucer's and Boccaccio's similar act of celebrating the names of their stock poets with comment on the works of them. Especially am I inclined to discountenance these final parallels of Koeppel through knowing that the verbal resemblances in them are limited to the two words "Tolosa" and "Tholosan." And the latter epithet, we have seen, Chaucer could easily have derived from the *Purgatorio*, a work with which we know positively he was acquainted. It would be superfluous then to try to trace the origin of the epithet to the *A. V.* And on account of this one negligible and only verbal similarity in Koeppel's parallels, "Tolosa" and "Tholosan," it has seemed unnecessary to me to quote *verbatim* the long parallels prepared by the German scholar.

The resemblances between the *A. V.* and the *H. F.*, when carefully analysed, reduce themselves to this: both Chaucer and Boccaccio are presenting symbolical figures of Fame and of Glory. Each presents his figure as a queen royally clothed and seated upon a throne; and each mentions, as does also Petrarch in his Trionfo della Fama, among her surroundings the names of famous poets who by their writings have conferred fame or glory. Among the *x* poets mentioned by Chaucer and the *y* mentioned by Boccaccio 6 are identical; but these *six* are precisely the poets whom no mediaeval writer would think of omitting from such a list. In the absence of any striking verbal parallels or any unexpected agreements, we are not justified in assuming that these resemblances are anything more than inevitable, when two contemporary poets, working in the same *genre*, handle the same theme. In conclusion, then, we perceive that there is in Koeppel's parallels no testimony which really substantiates an indebtedness of either the *P. F.* or the *H. F.* to Boccaccio's *A. V.*

We may now proceed to a review of the work of Professor Child. In the beginning it is only relevant for me to state that as a result of the investigation just presented, I cannot agree with the observation which he makes prefatory to his own inquiry: "Koeppel's parallels (reference is here made only to the *House of Fame*) identify in a very interesting way the *Lady Fame* of Chaucer with Boccaccio's Gloria del popol mondano." Continuing, Professor Child says of the *H. F.* and the *A. V.*: "One of the features of similarity is the citation of stock examples in history and mythology of loving maidens left forlorn   These, with their stories told at various lengths, take up a

good part of the *Visione*; in Chaucer they are used to illustrate the
fact that Aeneas was not alone in his "greet trespas," and all but two
(Demophon and Phyllis, and Theseus and Ariadne) are dismissed in a
line or so. It is, of course, natural to refer such a list at once, as
Skeat, for example, does (notes on ll. 388-426) to Ovid's *Heroides*,
but in so doing, it is possible to be a bit hasty" (*Mod. Lang. Notes*, X,
190).

Now in regard to this inferential hastiness of Professor Skeat
several things are to be noticed. Chaucer himself refers us for further
information on Aeneas' desertion of Dido to Virgil's *Aeneid* and to
Ovid's *Epistles*, i. e., to the work otherwise known as Ovid's *Heroides*:

But al the maner how she [Dido] deyde,
And al the wordes that she seyde,
Who-so to knowe hit hath purpos,
Reed Virgile in Eneidos
Or the Epistle of Ovyde,
What that she wroot or that she dyde;
And nere hit to long to endyte,
By god, I wolde hit here wryte. (*H. F.*, 375-382)

And when we turn with the great English scholar to the *Heroides*, we
find that every one of the cited stock examples of "loving maidens
left forlorn" (*H. F.*, 388-426) appears in the Latin work, to tell the
sad story of her abandonment and to reproach her lover. In order
they appear as follows.

Dido	(*H. F.* 287—*Epistola*			VII)
Phyllis	("	390—	"	II)
Briseis	("	398—	"	III)
Oenone	("	399—	"	V)
Isiphile	("	400—	"	VI)
Medea	("	401—	"	XII)
Dyanira	("	402—	"	IX)
Ariadne	("	407—	"	X)

It is then, in view of Chaucer's own references and of these coinci-
dences, difficult to regard Skeat's action as hasty. If on the other hand
we turn to that section of the *A. V.* in which the stories of some of
these ladies are briefly repeated, and if we read the headings of the
capitoli XVI to XXVIII, inclusive, in which love themes are especially developed, we find that the stories of only six of these ladies are
told, viz.—those of Isifile and Medea (the two in one *capitolo*, XXI);
Ariadne (XXII); Deidamia, i. e., Dyanira (XXVI); Briseis (in part

of XXIV); and Dido (XXVIII). Furthermore we make a discovery more pertinent to our inquiry: *Their stories are scattered amid the tales of other lovers*; Jove and Europa (XVI); Jove and the "figliuola d'Inaco" (XVII); Jove and Semele (XVIII); Mars and Citherea (XIX); Bacchus and the daughter of Lycurgus, Pluto and Proserpina, Pyramus and Thisbe (all in XX); Pasiphae and the Bull (XXII); Orpheus and Eurydice, Achilles and Polyxena (XXIV); Biblis and her brother (XXV); Paris and Helen (XXVII); lovers whose *innamoramenti* are so varied that one cannot for a moment suspect that the inclusion, among theirs, of the histories of the forlorn maidens is significant. In fact the purpose of Boccaccio's work is by no means similar to that of Ovid's, which designs primarily to interpret the grief of "maidens left forlorn,"—if not all by reason of treachery, as those cited in Chaucer's list, at least by reason of fortune's general vicissitudes. We are not, then, warranted in drawing leading inferences from the fact that the stories of six of these damsels "told at various lengths, take up a good part of the *Visione*." There is nothing in the sequence of Boccaccio's narratives of them to suggest them to Chaucer as a citative series of stock examples.

Professor Child is much impressed with his discovery that in certain minor details Chaucer's and Boccaccio's versions of the stories of Ariadne and Theseus, Phyllis and Demophon, Dido and Aeneas offer resemblances.

In both poets' accounts of the desertion of Ariadne that luckless lady's sister, Phaedra, is mentioned by name, although in Ovid's account (*Epistle* X) she remains nameless. The method and manner of the English and the Italian versions are similar. And there are some brief verbal parallels. In his study of the matter Professor Child quotes as follows from the *A. V.*:

> Io che andava avanti riguardando
> Vidi quivi Teseo nel Laberinto
> Al Minotauro pauroso andando
> Ma poichè quel con ingegno ebbe vinto,
> Che gli diede Arianna, quindi uscire
> Lui vedev' io di gioia dipinto;
> Al quale appresso Arianna venire,
> E con lei Fedra salir nel suo legno
> E quindi forte a suo poter fuggire.
> Nel quale avendo gia l'animo pregno
> Del piacer di Arianna, *lei lasciare*
> *Vedea dormendo, e girsene al suo regno.*

> Gridando desta la vedeva stare
>   E lui chiamava piangendo, *e soltetta*
>   *Sopr' un diserto scoglio in mezzo al mare.*
> Oimè, dicendo, deh, perchè s'affretta
>   Si di fuggir tua nave? Abbi pietate
>   Di me ingannata, lassa, giovinetta.
> Segando se ne gìa, l'onde salate
>   Con Fedra quegli, e Fedra si tenea
>   Per vera sposa per la sua biltate.   (XXII, 4-24)

Let us take up the several items of similarity Professor Child detects in the order of their presentation. There is nothing strange about Chaucer's mentioning Ariadne's sister Phaedra by name. Familiar as the English poet was with the *Heroides*, he must have known from *Epistle* IV, containing the lament of Phaedra to Hippolytus, the name of Ariadne's sister (if indeed he did not know it through his general reading). In that *Epistle* Phaedra tells her family's history briefly:

> Jupiter Europen, prima est ea origo,
> Dilexit, tauro dissimulante deum.
> Pasiphae mater, decepto subdita tauro,
> Enixa est utero crimen onusque suo.
> Perfidus Aegides, ducentia fila secutus,
> Curva meae fugit tecta sororis ope.
> En ego nunc, ne forte parum Minoia credar,
> In socias leges ultima gentis eo.
> Hoc quoque fatale est: placuit domus una duabus.
> Me tua forma capit, capta parente soror.
> Thesides Theseusque duas rapuere sorores. (*Ep.* IV, 55-65)

There is in the similarity in manner and method of the two versions, a similarity which Professor Child does not pause to define, nothing that can, except with very special pleading, argue literary relations between the *A. V.* and the *H. F.* Nor are the verbal parallels which Professor Child cites significant when one appends to them the passages from the *Heroides*. The parallels are quoted here *verbatim*:

. . . avendo gia l'animo pregno	For after this, within a whyle
Del piacer di Arianna, *lei lasciare*	He lefte hir slepinge in an yle,
Vedea dormendo, e girsene al suo regno.	Deserte alone, right in the se,
Gridando desta la vedeva stare	And stal away, and leet hir be;
Elui chiamava piangendo, e *soltetta*	And took hir suster Phedra tho
Sopr' un diserto scoglio in mezzo al mare.	With him, and gan to shippe go.
(*A.V.* XXII, 13-18)	(*H. F.* 415-420)

The Chaucerian passage Professor Child left without italicization.
Compare now both the Italian and the English passage with the following lines from Ariadne's lament in the tenth *Epistle* of the *Heroides*:

Quae legis, ex illo, Theseu, tibi littore mitto,
Unde tuam sine me vela tulere ratem.
In quo me somnusque meus male prodidit, et tu,
Per facinus *somnis* insidiate meis.
Tempus erat, vitrea quo primum terra prima
Spargitur, et tectae fronde queruntur aves.
Incertum vigilans, a *somno* languida, movi
Thesea pressuros semisupina manus.
Nullus erat: referoque manus, iterumque retento,
Perque torum moveo bracchia: nullus erat.
Excussere metus *somnum.*   (*Ep.* X, 3-13)
Aut mare prospiciens *in saxo frigida sedi.*   (49)
Quid faciam?   *quo sola ferar? vacat insula cultu.*   (59)
Omne latus terrae cingit mare.   (61)
Nunc quoque non oculis, sed, qua potes, adspice mente
(*Me*) *haerentem scopulo,* quem vaga pulsat acqua.   (135-36)

Comment seems hardly necessary.   It is, to be sure, true that the
"Deserte alone, right in the se" is nearer to the Italian, "diserto
scoglio in mezzo al mare," than to the phrases of lines 49, 59, 61, and
135 of the Latin text; but the similarity is too brief an instance to
argue weightily.   For certainly there is no great reason why Chaucer,
like Boccaccio, should not have been able to summarize in the six
lines of the *H. F.*, which Professor Child quotes, these details from
the tenth *Epistle* of Ovid, without the intermediary assistance of the
Italian poet.   Really nothing of weight in Chaucer's brief version
of the Ariadne story in the *H. F.* accounts for a possible influence of
the A. V.

We turn to the citation of Demophon and Phyllis.   Professor
Child assures us vaguely that "Chaucer's treatment of the story of
Demophon likewise in general method suggests Boccaccio's, even
though unlike Boccaccio he specifies the method of her death," but
again Professor Child fails to describe this "general method."   As
a matter of fact the two versions of the Demophon and Phyllis story
resemble each other only in brevity.   Later he avers that "Ovid's
single reference to Demophon's perjured lips,

Jura, fides ubi nunc, commissa dextera dextrae,
Quique erat in *falso* plurimus ore deus (*Ep.* II, 31-32),

does not so much resemble Chaucer's

> How he forswar himself ful *falsly* . . .
> . . . he had do hir swich untrouthe
> Lo! was not this a wo and routhe?   (*H. F.* 389,395-6)

as Boccaccio's

> . . . . .com' ora
> A lei *fallita* la promessa fede
> Per troppo amor dolor greve l'accora (*A. V.*, XXV, 67-69)

In other words Professor Child would have us believe that the words, *"com' ora A lei fallita la promessa fede,"* are more like the words, *"he forswar himself ful falsly,"* than are the words, *"in falso plurimus ore deus"*; or in brief he would have us believe that *fallita* is more like *falsly* than *falso*! Furthermore he would have us believe that the thoroughly Chaucerian lines,

> . . . he had do hir swich untrouthe
> Lo! was not this a wo and routhe?

which may be paralleled again and again in the *H. F.* itself (see 296-7, 331-33, 383-4, etc.), are influenced by Boccaccio's

> Per troppo amor dolor greve l'accora!

Exclamation points provide the only satisfactory punctuation for such statements. Yet it is upon these that Professor Child rests his belief that Boccaccio's version of the Demophon and Phyllis story influenced Chaucer's. It is indeed a poor case which the scholar is drawing up.

In the story of Dido and Aeneas as given in the *H. F.* Professor Child again believes "suggestions of direct indebtedness" to the *A. V.* are not lacking," despite the assertion which the poet himself makes,

> "Non other auctour alegge I" (*H. F.*, 314),

at which he is inclined to scoff because of his suspicion that Chaucer deliberately obscured the name of Boccaccio in other works, which he derived from the Italian writer,—a suspicion which a study of the "Lollius" problem, to be printed on later pages of this work, has convinced me is entirely unfounded. He quotes as follows in reference to Dido:

> Oimè, Enea, or che t'avea io fatto
> Che fuggendo disii il mio morire?
> Non è questo servar tra noi quel patto
> Che tu mi promettesti: or m'e palese
> L'inganno c'hai coperto con falso atto.

> Deh, non fuggir, se l'esser mi cortese
> Forse non vogli, vincati pietate
> Almen de tuoi. (*A. V.*, XXVIII, 65-72)

This passage he thinks is generally similar to the *H. F.* 315-18, 325-31; but he admits that lines 321-24 of the *H. F.* are a direct translation of the *Aeneid* (Lib. IV, 307-8); and then continues, "It is Boccaccio, not Virgil, that we have in Dido's prayer for pity as well as in her plea that she is guiltless of injury towards him." The statement contains a half truth, but it begs the question at the same time. Dido's prayer and plea in the *H. F.* do not come from Virgil to be sure, but there is another source for them, which it is a little more than hazardous to ignore. That source is *Epistle* VII of the *Heroides*, in which, throughout 195 lines of Latin poetry that we can unfortunately not take space to print here, Dido pleads her guiltlessness and craves the pity of Aeneas. Of this *Epistle* Professor Child has made no mention.

In closing our discussion of the *A. V.* and the *H. F.* then, it seems unnecessary to quote anything more than Chaucer's own injunction to him who would know what Dido wrote or by what means she died.

> Reed Virgile in Eneidos
> Or the Epistle of Ovyde (*H. F.* 378-9)

Does it not on the whole seem fantastic to belie Chaucer's own words, and seek a third source for the stories of Ariadne, Phyllis, and Dido?

Koeppel and Professor Child have both, beyond question, gone astray. They have at any rate furnished us with no really satisfactory evidence that Chaucer knew the *Amorosa Visione*, much less that the Italian poem had an influence in the *Parliament of Fowls* or the *House of Fame*.

CHAPTER III

CHAUCER AND THE *Ameto*

Until very recent years no scholar had ever suggested that Chaucer was acquainted with Boccaccio's prose pastoral romance and allegory, the *Ameto* (*Opere Volgari*, Vol. XIV); but in a very interesting article, published in *Anglia* for 1913 (pp. 69-117), Professor John S. P. Tatlock came forward with a theory that acquaintance with it, as well as with the *Filocolo*, may have aided the poet in devising the framework of the *Canterbury Tales*. While this article was designed primarily, as Professor Tatlock tells us (pp. 108-9), to show that Professor Morsbach had not proved his case in regard to Chaucer's acquaintance with the frame-work of the *Decamerone* (see Lorenz Morsbach: *Chaucers Plan der Canterbury Tales und Boccaccios Decamerone*; *Englische Studien*, 42, 43-52), it proposed so many resemblances between Chaucer's work and Boccaccio's that consideration of them must be taken here.

Professor Tatlock, satisfied (p. 70) that Professor Young had demonstrated his case for Chaucer's knowledge of the *Filocolo*, begins with that as a premise, and shows, first, that Professor Morsbach's four main points for Chaucer's use of the *Decamerone* are equally applicable when applied in an argument that he may have been influenced in the building of the frame-work of the *C. T.* by an "episode" in the *Filocolo*, and then even in an argument that Chaucer could have been influenced by the frame-work of the *Ameto*, wherein various anecdotes or stories are told as stories within a story.

Professor Morsbach presents his case as follows: 1. The separate stories of the *Decam.* and the *C. T.* are told in their totality not by one or by several individual persons, but by a company of persons. 2. The individual persons are together as a company not by chance, but their meeting has been due to a common occasion, a purely external event. 3. In both works the separate stories are interrupted, and bound together by links. 4. The idea of having an authority exercised over the telling and order of the stories by a person who appoints the speakers, is common to both works.[1]

---

[1] I. Morsbach: *Chaucers Plan der Canterbury Tales und Boccaccios Decamerone*: *Eng. Stud.* 42, 45-46, I. "Die einzelnen, im inhalt verschiedenen geschichten (nur die *Parson's Tale* ist keine erzählung, sondern eine predigt) werden in ihrer gesamtheit nicht von einer oder mehreren einzelpersonen, sondern von einer gesellschaft erzählt. Das finden wir in keiner der älteren rahmenerzählungen vor

As Professor Tatlock adduces no new evidence for Chaucer's having known the episode of the story-telling in the *Filocolo* (*Opere Volgari*, Vol. VIII, 27-120), we shall not consider further his application of Professor Morsbach's points to that work.   Possible relations between the plan of the *C. T.* and that of the *Ameto* Professor Tatlock sees on the following grounds:

1.   There are passages apropos of the spring season and of religious observance, either at or on the road to a shrine, in both the *Am.* and the *Prologue* to the *C. T.* (*Anglia*, 1913, 86-90), which reveal occasional verbal parallelism.

2.   Professor Morsbach's four points in regard to frame stories are applicable to the *Am.*

a.   The narratives are related by a company of persons.

b.   An external event (äusseres ereignis), here a religious observance, is the cause of the assembling of the company.

c.   The narratives are connected by links.

d.   As in the *Filocolo*, the *Decam.*, and the *C. T.* "there is a head," who appoints the speakers (90-91).

3.   There are in both the *Am.* and the *C. T.* a number of minor miscellaneous resemblances in construction or characterization.   These Professor Tatlock admits to be "of varying importance" (91).

a.   In both works, at the temple of Venus or at the Tabard Inn, "people arrive in troops at the resort, which is in each case in the outskirts of a large city, and in the sociable part of the day ('noon in

---

Boccaccio äusser bei Ovid, der vielleicht dem Italiener die erste anregung gegeben hat.   Der Gesellschaft von zehn jungen Florentinern beiderlei geschlechts steht die "Company" von Chaucers Pilgerfahrern gegenüber.   In beiden werken erzählen die mitglieder der gesellschaft sich die einzelnen geschichten.

II.   Die einzelnen personen finden sich zwar als solche zufällig zusammen, aber das zusammentreffen wird sowohl hier wie dort eingehend motiviert.   In beiden dichtungen ist ein äusseres ereignis, eine begebenheit die verlassung, bei Boccaccio die pest und die damit verbundene flucht au der stadt, bei Chaucer die Pilgerfahrt zum schrein des hl. Thomas à Becket.

III.   In beiden werken sind die einzelnen geschichten durch zwischen- und bindeglieder unterbrochen.   Bei Boccaccio schildern sie das tägliche leben und treiben der auf zehn tage in einem landhause vereinigten gesellschaft und verknüpfen zugleich die einzelnen erzählung miteinander, wobei die empfindungen der zuhörer geschildert werden.   Bei Chaucer berichten die bindeglieder über die einzelnen etappen der pilgerfahrt, wobei der wirt (Host) und andere personen in wortwechsel geraten und über die jeweilig erzählten geschichten sich äussern. Die grundgedanken (trennung und verknüpfung, bericht und äusserung) sind also in beiden werken dieselben, obwohl inhalt und ausführung den umständen

Tuscany . . . sundown in Kent'), there is talk, eating and drinking."

    b. Each narrative is given from a personal point of view.

    c. The nymphs, joining the party, "are, like Chaucer's pilgrims, fully described one at a time at the outset."

    d. "The variety and free democracy of Chaucer's pilgrims . . . is found among the other visitors to the temples"—but not, as Professor Tatlock admits, among the narrators of the stories or the anecdotes of the *Am*.

    e. In both works there is an idea of competition in story-telling and of a prize.

    f. There is a confession motive apparent in the links both of the *Am*. and the *C. T.*

    g. The "marriage group" of the *C. T.* and "the whole of the *Am.*" deal both "with varieties of love and marriage." The nymph Agapes, of the *Am*. (pp. 121-137), in her confession, describes a senile husband, who reminds Professor Tatlock of certain scattered passages in the *Merchant's Tale*. (*Anglia*, 1913, pp. 91-105)

Professor Tatlock is prone to discount the value of all these grounds. He says, "Few of these parallels are actually verbal, or exceedingly striking singly" (105). "But," he adds later, "the chief thing is the number of them and the fact that Chaucer's great innovation in the pear-tree story, the husband's repulsive senility and all it involves,

---

entsprechend durchaus verschieden sind. Demgegenüber kommt die völlig abweichende art der verbindung) der fünfzehn chronologisch geordneten meta-, morphosen-bücher Ovids, noch auch das vierte buch desselben (siehe oben unter I und die anmerkung dazu) für Chaucer als vorbild kaum in frage.

IV. Gemeinsam ist schliesslich beiden werken auch die idee, dass über die reihenfolge der geschichten eine kontrolle geübt und überhaupt die gesellschaft einer gewissen autoritativen ordnung unterstellt wird. Bei Boccaccio wird für jeden der zehn tage ein anderer zum könig oder zum königin gewählt; diese führen den vorsitz und sorgen, dass das erzählen in strenger ordnung geschicht, indem jedes mitglied der gesellschaft täglich mit einer novelle an die reihe kommt. Bei Chaucer finden wir denselben gedanken, aber das motiv ist insofern variiert, als nur einem und zwar dem "Host" die leitung des ganzen übertragen wird. Das ändert aber nichts an dem kern der sache. Ja, ich möchte gerade diesen punkt, den man oft genug beiseite geschoben hat, für einen der beweiskräftigsten halten, weil er am charakteristischen ist und auch andere möglichkeiten dem dichter gegeben waren. Dass aber Chaucer das motiv nicht nur variiert, sondern auch nach seinen intentionen künstlerisch fort entwickelt hat, indem der "Host" am schluss der pilgerfahrt auch der urteilspruch über die beste geschichte fällen soll, nimmt der parallele nichts von ihrer beweiskraft.

occurs in even more memorable form in the *Am.*" (106),—a statement the latter part of which is decidedly misleading. It refers, of course, to the *Merchant's Tale* and the senility of January, but one must remind Professor Tatlock that the repulsive senility of the husband, described by Agapes, does not appear in the case of the husband of the lady, Adiona, who plays the part of May in Boccaccio's version of the salacious pear-tree story (*Am.* 84-105). He himself admits that Adiona "speaks well of her parents and of her husband Pacifico, the son of a pear-tree" (*Anglia*, 1913, 83). Moreover nothing could be more different than is the Chaucerian from the Boccaccian version of the pear-tree story. In a word Chaucer's "innovation" in this story, "the husband's repulsive senilty," parallels no similar innovation in Boccaccio's work. There may be "repulsive senility" from time to time in the *Am.*, but it is not found in the Italian version of the pear-tree story as it is found in Chaucer's.

"The chief thing," then, we may agree with Professor Tatlock, "is the number" of his cited parallels. Unfortunately he is inclined to support his view by reference to Professor Young's study of the *Filocolo* and *Troilus and Criseyde.* "The minute care and skill with which, as Young has shown, Chaucer wove details from the *Filocolo* into *Troil.*, a poem mainly based on another story, will make us the readier to believe that here he may have done the same with details from one or more narratives in another work of Boccaccio's," he observes (*Anglia*, 106). In this regard it need only be remarked here that the tenuity of Professor Young's study was demonstrated in the first chapter of the present work. It will be seen in consequence that evidence for Chaucer's knowledge and possible use of the *Am.* rests wholly, up to the present time, upon Professor Tatlock's parallels. My own investigation of the *Am.* has revealed to me nothing further in it that is suggestive of the *C. T.* The conscientious care of Professor Tatlock in gathering his material leaves me nothing to glean.

Before a discussion in detail of the parallels between the two works, it is necessary to offer a summary of the *Am.* As previously stated, the work is a prose pastoral and allegory, with long songs in *terza rima* inserted at regular intervals. The narrative of it is as follows:

Ameto, a young and rugged Tuscan huntsman, is interrupted in his playing with his dogs one evening by the singing of several nymphs, whom he subsequently in timidity approaches. He is received cordially by the group and presently becomes enamoured of one of them, Lia, a nymph who follows the chase. Soon separated from her, he spends the winter in unceasing thought of her, and in the spring-time he courses through the woods seeking her. In his quest he is successful (*Am*. 23), and the two dally with one another amid "coloured flowers" along the clear streams (24). Later Lia strays a second time from his side, and some time passes before they meet again (29) at the temple of Venus for the spring festival. Ameto joins her band of companions and all seat themselves near a clear fountain beneath branches laden with new foliage. Here they are joined by two more nymphs described in typically voluptuous Boccaccian fashion. Presently the party, on hearing a shepherd sing, rise and draw near to him to listen. While they are enjoying his song, they are again joined by two more nymphs. As Ameto stands rapt in wonder at the latter's beauty, the shepherd finishes his song and receives the thanks of Lia's party (43). At this point two other shepherds approach and engage in a singing contest, the winner to be rewarded by the first shepherd by a garland (43). The contest results in a quarrel; and after it has been adjusted, the party return to their meadow ("al prato loro," 48) and again seat themselves beneath a blooming laurel in a circle (48). Here they are joined by a third pair of nymphs, whose aspect moves Ameto to sing (54-57).

While they are sitting under the laurel, Lia proposes that since, on account of the heat of the sun ("il sole tiene ancora il dì librato, perchè la sua calda luce ne vieta di qui partirci" 58), they cannot leave this spot, they divert themselves, while the shepherds sleep, by narrating to one another the history of their several *innamoramenti*, for, as she assures them, none of them seems "to have lived or to live without having felt or without feeling the flames of the goddess revered in the temples visited by us to-day ("d'essere vivute o di vivere senza avere sentito o sentire le fiamme della riverita Dea ne' templi visitati oggi da noi" 58). The ladies agree, and Ameto being put into the middle of their circle the tales are begun (59).

In all, the nymphs tell seven stories, six of them being brief narratives of the illicit love of a disappointed wife for a youthful lover— although the sixth of these presents a lady who has had many *amours*— and one, the seventh, told by Lia, being an account of the origin of the city of Florence (59-185). It should be observed that this account is given by a nymph who has been twice married, the second time happily (181), and who is now herself carrying on an *amour* with Ameto. As all the others have done, Lia concludes her narrative by singing a song (182-85).

This hymn, we are surprised to discover, contains a summary of Christian doctrine, somewhat allegorized; and we are again astonished to find, in the conclusion of the work, that the erotic love of the whole of it is but symbolical of ideal Christian love. The Venus who has been celebrated is suddenly perceived by Ameto to be divine love. One by one the hitherto fleshly nymphs are transformed into effulgent light; and, on realizing what is their real nature, Ameto becomes ashamed of his former concupiscence, returns repentant to his home, and sings of the newly awakened divine love as he goes.

Turning from this summary we may examine Professor Tatlock's points and parallels more closely, first of all the passages in the *Am.* and the *Prologue* of the *C. T.* regarding the beauty of spring. In these passages he has italicized a number of words expressive of the most common phenomena of spring (*Anglia*, 86-90), the new flowers, fresh leaves, singing birds, and verdant roadsides, zephyrs, and the "yonge sonne." In none of these does the parallelism extend beyond two words, noun and adjective; and the only epithets paralleling strikingly are *yonge* and *giovane* (*Am.* 24), as applied to the sun. The epithet *yonge* is used on at least one other occasion by Chaucer, in the *Squire's Tale* (385), a fact which minimizes rather than magnifies the negligible significance of its use in the *Prologue* (7). Further the aspects of spring, mentioned above as employed by Chaucer, can be as readily paralleled by reference to others of his own works as by reference to Boccaccio's. A glance at lines 49 to 90 of Chaucer's *Romaunt of the Rose* reveals a full quota of them.

Hardly more significant than these aspects are the two brief clause passages which Professor Tatlock parallels:

per la qual cosa i templi con sollecitudine visitati suonano (*Am.* 28)	Than longen folk to goon on pilgrimages. (*Pro. C. T.* 12)
a questo (templo), come a più solenne, concorre ciascuno (*Am.* 28)	And specially, from every shires ende, ... they wende (*Pro. C. T.* 15-16)

One observes in them no verbal parallelism; and only the most precarious suggestion would maintain that the ancient pagan springtime prompting to worship, as here briefly mentioned by Boccaccio, may have induced Chaucer's pilgrims to undertake the journey to the shrine of Thomas à Becket!

The points of Professor Morsbach, applied to the *Am.* by Professor Tatlock, may not be so lightly dismissed. Of the first of these the latter says, "The narratives in the *Am.* are related by the various

members of a company of pilgrims (as they are not in the *Decam.*)."
But in fact the narratives of Boccaccio's work are not related by
pilgrims (no word in the *Am.* gives Professor Tatlock sanction for the
use of that term), but all of them are related by *nymphs*, who are
resting, not from a pilgrimage, but after worship, at the temple of
Venus. There is, too, no cosmopolitan variety among the narrators
of the stories of the *Am.*

Of Professor Morsbach's second point Professor Tatlock observes:
"The season and occasion on which the company have come together
and give their narratives have been seen not only to be far nearer those
in the *C. T.* than those in the *Decam.* are, but to be curiously parallel.
It is a religious observance in April; the devout visit various shrines,
but one of especial eminence." In brief the season and the occasion
of the *C. T.* and of the tales of the *Am.* are religious observances in
April. It should be observed, however, that, whereas Chaucer dates
his tales very specifically by his line,
      "Whan that Aprille with his shoures soote,"
and a reference to the Ram (*Pro. C. T.* 8), Boccaccio dates his only
vaguely by a reference to the Bull, termed by him the "rubatore di
Europa" (*Am.* 28). Surmise that the briefly described spring festival
of the *Am.* had in some way influenced the season of the Canterbury
pilgrimage would be much easier at this point if Boccaccio's dating
had been more specific and similar to Chaucer's. I cannot believe
that any significance attaches to the coincidence of the seasons of the
two works. As for the occasion of the meeting of the two parties of
persons, it must be observed that Chaucer's pilgrims take lodging at
an inn, and fall into ways of companionship no more because they
are going to Canterbury than because they are wayfarers in need of
rest and shelter, whereas the company of nymphs in the *Am.* gather
not to go to worship in unison, but assemble to rest after their devotions
and to avoid the burden of the noon heat. And nothing could appear
more fortuitous than this gathering of the nymphs in the *Am.* (29-30).
Moreover, the dissimilarity of the meetings in an *inn* and under a
laurel-tree more than obviate, as an argument for the possible relationship of the *C. T.* and the *Am.*, any similarity that may lie in the indirect occasion of their meetings, a religious observance in one case
Christian, and in the other pagan. If Professor Morsbach's "external
event" does not conclusively argue a relationship between the *C. T.*
and the *Decam.*, the application of it in an argument for a possible
relationship between the former work and the *Am.* proves far from

convincing. The question remains, too, if any real application of it may be made here.

Of Professor Morsbach's third point Professor Tatlock observes; "The narratives are connected by links; though far less varied and vivacious than the links in Chaucer, less so even than the nine longer ones in the *Decam.*" The links are indeed no less tediously similar than are the stories of the *Am.* From their lifelessness to the animation of Chaucer's links relationship could be argued only with temerity.

Professor Tatlock himself admits the occurrence of a striking dissimilarity in the application of Professor Morsbach's fourth point. Of it he says: "As in the other three works, there is a head (Ameto himself) who appoints the speakers. Before and after (185) the narrating, Lia takes the lead. *Neither, however, wields the authority of the heads in the other three works*," i. e., the *Decam.*, the *Filocolo*, and the *C. T.* There is in fact only an impotent form of authority in Boccaccio's head. This is Ameto, who gazes delightedly at each narrator at the conclusion of her tale in turn, and then gently calls upon the next nymph, who as gently complies.

In the end one must admit that Professor Morsbach's points offer nothing really cogent when applied to the *Am.* in connection with the *C. T.* That is to say neither Professor Morsbach's points nor verbal parallelisms offer any convincing evidence of a relationship.

To argue a possible relationship there remain only the miscellaneous minor resemblances in construction or characterization, pointed out by Professor Tatlock in the third general division of his evidence, and admitted to be "of varying importance." The first of these, it will be remembered, consists in the arriving in groups of persons at the temple of Venus and at the Tabard Inn in the outskirts of a large city and in the sociable part of the day, noon in Tuscany and evening in Kent, and in talking, eating, and drinking. Of this resemblance, remote as it is, little need be said. *The groups who arrive at the temple of Venus are not the narrators of the stories of the Ameto*; and so the place of their arrival is in no sense pertinent. The Canterbury Pilgrims seek the Tabard Inn in the evening, not because that is the sociable part of the day, but because at that hour the "lated traveller" spurs apace; and the nymphs of the *Am.* seek the shade of the laurel for refuge from the heat, not because they are bent upon a picnic and story-telling (*Am.* 58).

Of the second resemblance, consisting in the fact that each narrative is given from a personal point of view, it need only be remarked that although the C. T. are told very well *en caractère*, the stories of the *Am.* are told by seven nymphs, all made by Boccaccio of precisely the same pattern. And in their narratives they offer no variety. The charm of the variety of the *personnel* of Chaucer's pilgrims is that it is infinite.

As a third resemblance Professor Tatlock pointed out that the nymphs joining the party "are, like Chaucer's pilgrims, fully described one at a time at the outset." Rather they are described two at a time (cf. *Am.* 30-33), and always in the same voluptuous fashion. Furthermore, unlike the descriptions in the *Prologue*, the three descriptions in the *Am.* of the three pairs of nymphs, have long intervals of narrative between them. Chaucer's pilgrims are described in succession.

As for Professor Tatlock's fourth resemblance "the variety and democracy" of the devotees at the temple of Venus and on the road to Canterbury, it is enough to reiterate here the fact that not the great body of worshippers in the *Am.* (28), but seven unvarying nymphs are the narrators of Boccaccio's illicit love tales.

In the fifth resemblance cited by Professor Tatlock, too, there is nothing pertinent. The idea of a competition in story-telling and of a prize appears to be sure in the *C. T.* and in the *Am.*; but in the *C. T.* the reward is to be assigned to one of the pilgrims, one of the actual narrators of the main group of tales. In the *Am.* (43-48) the reward of a garland is proposed for, and won, in a singing contest by a shepherd *who does not tell any one of the Ameto stories.* There is no reward nor prize of any sort proposed for any one of the nymphs who tell the seven stories. *And in their story-telling there is no competition.*

The sixth general resemblance Professor Tatlock perceived was in the confessions made by several of the Canterbury pilgrims in the links of the *C. T.* and by six of Boccaccio's nymphs in their tales (but not in the links!). Of this resemblance I believe nothing can, and that nothing need be made. The confessions of the nymphs, of unvarying amorous nature, are made in praise of Venus; the confessions of Chaucer's pilgrims are made for several various reasons, discussion of which may not be attempted here.

Professor Tatlock pointed out a seventh and last general resemblance in the "varieties of love and marriage" dealt with in the *Am.* and in the "marriage group" of the *C. T.* Had the other resemblances been convincing, this one might have some weight. What weight it does possess is reduced infinitesimally when Chaucer's familiarity with Deschamps's *Miroir de Mariage*, St. Jerome's *Adversus Jovinianum*, and the *Roman de la Rose*, furnishing him with more than ample material for the discussion of marriage problems, is recalled. For a careful study of the matter one has only to consult the two excellent articles on *Chaucer and the 'Miroir de Mariage' by Eustace Deschamps*, by J. L. Lowes in *Modern Philology* for 1910-11 (pp. 165-86; 305-34). It is true besides that Boccaccio's nymphs are not so much concerned with marital duties, as Chaucer's pilgrims so often are, as with their dissatisfaction with physically repulsive husbands. The scattered parallels, not verbal, of passages in the *Am.* and in the *Wife of Bath's Prologue* and the *Merchant's Tale*, cited by Professor Tatlock and admitted to be weak, do not require further comment. We have already seen[1] that the only one of them which he considered significant was valueless, viz.—the senility of the husband of Boccaccio's nymph, Agapes, a senility which does not appear in the story of Adiona, the heroine of the *Am.* version of the pear-tree story, i. e., the story of the *Merchant's Tale*. And the handling of that common story, be it further recalled, by Boccaccio was very different from that by Chaucer in the *Merchant's Tale* of January and May.

A review, then, of Professor Tatlock's tentative evidence for Chaucer's possible knowledge of the *Am.* leaves us with the conviction that it is quite insufficient to establish a relationship. To do that was, of course, not primarily his purpose. My own investigation of his work has been due only to a sense of caution, and to a desire to save more incautious Chaucerians from unstable inferences that Chaucer really knew the *Am.* I believe that I have incidentally, however, much aided Professor Tatlock in showing the weakness of Professor Morsbach's points, if those points may be applied with hardly less conviction to two of Boccaccio's frame-stories, with which we have no trustworthy knowledge that Chaucer was acquainted, than to the *Decamerone*.

[1] See page 36 of this text.

CHAPTER IV

The "Wyf of Bath" and the "Vedova" of the *Corbaccio*

We have seen that we have no adequate reason for believing that Chaucer was acquainted with Boccaccio's *Filocolo* or the *Amorosa Visione* or the *Ameto*. It becomes our duty now to investigate his possible knowledge of another little known work of the Italian poet, the *Corbaccio* (*Opere Volgari*, Vol. V), with which Professor Rajna was, in 1903, inclined to believe the English poet was acquainted. Summing up the number of Boccaccio's works, with which he considered Chaucer familiar, the Italian scholar remarked, "Something of the widow—a widow, one may note, of two husbands—so vehemently reviled by Corbaccio, appears to me discernible in the Wyf of Bath, in whose mouth, besides the impudent confession of her life and her appetites, might also have been put something of the *Ruffianella*, i. e., a composition attributed to Boccaccio with much insistence. One might easily prophesy that new relations will be discovered from later studies."[1]   No one hitherto has examined Professor Rajna's conjecture. It is my purpose to examine it only with with reference to Chaucer's possible knowledge of the Corbaccio.

Let us look into this work, which contains Boccaccio's most bitter arraignment of woman (Vol. V, 155-255). The writer announces his purpose to express certain facts that he has learned only through especial grace, in the hope that others may profit by the revelation to himself of the errors into which he was falling. Spending his time one day in his room, thinking disconsolately of his mistress, and indulging suspicions of her fidelity, he falls into a sweet slumber, and, beginning to dream, is surprised to find himself entering a pleasant and beautiful path amid unfamiliar scenes, whose rare beauties inspire in him so fervent a desire to hurry forward that his feet seem

---

[1] Pio Rajna: *Le Origini della Novella narrata dal "Frankeleyn," Romania,* 1903, 247-48. "Quanto al concetto generale il *Monkes Tale* vuol essere ricondotto al *De casibus virorum illustrium,* donde esso anche ripete taluna delle "tragedie" di cui si compone, mentre poi un' altra ne deve al *De mulieribus claris,* suscitatore alla sua volta della *Legend of Good Women*; parecchi riflessi dell' *Amorosa Visione* ha segnalato il Koeppel; qualcosa della vedova—vedova, si noti di due mariti—così sanguinosamente vituperata dal *Corbaccio,* pare a me di sentire nella Donna di Bath, sulla bocca della quale d'altronde la confessione sfacciata della sua vita e de' suoi appetiti potrebbe fors'anche essere stata messa dalla *Ruffianella,* cioè da una composizione attributa al Boccaccio con molta insistenza. Facile profezia il presagire che nuovi rapporti resulteranno dagli studi ulteriori."

to have taken wings and to carry him through the air. The road changes its appearance as he flies through space, and suddenly his progress is arrested. In another moment he finds himself in a dreary solitude—the scenes of which reflect Dante's *Inferno*. While he stands mystified by the terrible lamenting, with which the air is filled, and at a loss to know whither to turn or whether to pray to God, he beholds coming toward him slowly a man, companionless, of great stature, dark of skin and hair, although the latter is in part whitened by years, apparently sixty years or more of age, weazened and nervous, of no pleasing aspect, and clothed in a long and flowing vestment of vermilion hue. The dreamer masters his horror and exchanges greetings with the man, who, he is astounded to perceive, is not flesh but a shade, a spirit sent by the Virgin Mary herself to instruct the youth. Two things, he learns, are the occasion of the spirit's present discomfiture in the sombre valley, the Laberinto d'Amore; one the "insatiable craving which I had for money while I lived, and the other the indecent patience with which I endured the criminal and dishonourable conduct of her," i. e., the lady who had been the spirit's wife.

A long dialogue ensues, in which it devolves that the woman with whom the author, or dreamer, is now in love is the very widow of the spirit. The dreamer in a long peroration finally admits to the spirit his dissatisfaction in his *amour*, and becomes attentive to the arraignment of the woman which the latter initiates. For two reasons the spirit is induced to speak, one being the age, the other the studies of the young dreamer. He will explain the perfidy of the woman, whose gentle manners the young man has so highly praised. He begins with a thorough castigation of her entire sex. "La femina è animale imperfetto, passionato da mille passioni spiacevoli, e abominevoli pure a ricordarsene non che a ragionarne" (186). They set traps and ensnare the liberty of men; dissatisfied with whatever of beauty or appearance nature has furnished to them, they paint themselves with a thousand unguents and colours; with soap or manufactured waters or especially with the rays of the sun they strive to make their dark black hair similar to threads of gold, and then arrange it to appear most beautiful either in long tresses flowing over their shoulders or in braids gathered about their heads. They delight then to be heard singing or to be seen at balls and dances. By such means they succeed in becoming men's wives or mistresses. And once they have achieved such a position, the spirit continues, "Although they know they were born to be servants, they incontinently take hope, and sharpen their desires for mastery ("aguzzano i desiderii alla signoria" 187) "employing every conceivable blandishment of humility and the wearing of beautiful apparel and jewelry to attain their end. And so soon as they have attained it, their conduct becomes intolerably arrogant, and then flagrantly wanton. They become shameless in their behaviour as prostitutes; they pretend to be diligent in saving their husbands' patrimony, but wilfully dissipate it; they quarrel with their husbands' friends and relatives. Faithless themselves, they keep their husbands awake at night with querulous charges, "saying each one to her husband, 'I see well how much you love me: I should be blind if I did not perceive that another is more in your mind than I am. Do you imagine that I am so deceived that I do not know to whose house you go by the back door, whom you so much esteem, to whom you prate all day? I know it well enough; I have better spies than you suspect. Poor me, for as often as I have come hither, you have not so much as one time said, "My Love, you are welcome." But by the Rood, I will do to you what you are doing to me. . . . Am I not so fair as such a woman? . . . Make yourself off to her; as God helps me, you shall not touch me.' " (189) And so the imagined tirade continues, the woman declaring it a shame that one of her parentage, one who brought so fine a dowry to her husband, should be so inconsiderately treated.

At this point the spirit brings to an end the importunities of his hypothetical woman, and resumes his own arraignment of her sex, which covers forty pages of closely printed prose (188-228). He impugns her luxuriousness (190), her feigned timidity (190), her desire for mastery (192), her receiving of letters from lovers (195), her callous ambition not to have daughters better than herself (195), and her greed, envy, wrath, and imperiousness (199). He claims that man, made in the image of God, is born to govern and not to be governed; he proclaims the exalted origin and destiny of man, and explains what are the duties of the dreamer to literature and the muses (199-202). His attention he then turns to his own former wife, who entered his house like a dove and soon proved herself to be a serpent (202-4). When he attempted to curb the indomitable animal, i. e., his wife, it was like adding wood and oil to the flames (204). He tells of her extravagance, of his being compelled for the sake of peace to avoid his own house (205), his wife's gradual assumption of complete control in all things (206), her accusation that he was unfaithful (206), his own forced submission (206), then of his wife's indulgence in expensive foods and liquors to preserve her beauty (208), her associations with other women (209), of her further precautions to preserve her beauty by avoiding the sun and air (210), her rage over the bite of a fly or her disturbance of the whole household in the pursuit of a gnat (210), her pretenses about her age (211), of her vanity and the details of her toilet (211-12), her false assurances of her solicitude for her husband's welfare (213), of her amorous dalliance with this youth and that (213), of her vanity when her beauty has been praised (214), her assumption of the manners of *la grande dame* loved of many men (215), of her inordinate lust (215); etc., etc. Then momentarily the spirit, who, although he is a shade, has cognizance of affairs in the world he has left, pauses to inform the dreamer of the widow's treacherous conduct to the latter in showing his letters to other men (216). Then he once more denounces her sex for being indifferent to the nobler qualities of men and interested only in them as the objects of their passion (219). Woman's garrulity falls under his indictment next (220-21).

As a final section of his general arraignment, the spirit feels constrained to discuss the physical indecencies of a woman's person, and five pages of Boccaccio's text are devoted to a revolting description of the female body (224-28).

Henceforth his discussion is confined to the conduct of his own wife after his death. Regardless of his children's claims she seized her husband's property (230); she lamented his death "con altissimo rumore" in public, and in her heart cursed him for having lived so long (230); pretending to wish to spend the rest of her life in mourning, she moved from her husband's house and took residence in a tiny cottage near a church, only that, under the guise of religious meditation, she might conceal the approaches of men to her (230-31). In the church her alluring manner of saying the *pater-nosters* aroused the gallantries of young men (231-32). In private she read lascivious romances, such as that of *Florio and Biancofiore*, and to satisfy her lusts she kept "certi animaletti" in the house (233). She entered into relations with a lover Ansalone (233-34); and she was still receiving attentions from the latter when the dreamer became acquainted with her (234).

The spirit then describes to the young man a visit he had made to his widow's house, during which he discovered the lady in the embraces of her other lover, with whom she was exchanging jokes about the dreamer (234-35); and, angry that the latter should be so abused, he

determined to expose the absolute depravity of the woman to him
(236-37), and protect him from further deception and calumny.

He adds then many words of advice to the youth about the pursuit
of such a woman, and enjoins him to devote his interest to letters and
to things divine (239-41). The dreamer acknowledges his sin (246)
and resolves to follow the spirit's counsel, whereupon the spirit disappears and the young man awakes (253-54).

Boccaccio ends his work with an injunction to it to reveal its truths
to young men, and above all to keep itself from falling into the hands
of the vile woman who has been the occasion of it (255).

Such, then, are the contents of Boccaccio's fiercest polemic on woman,
the *Corbaccio*. If we examine the conduct and experiences of either
the generic woman or the particular widow described therein, we find
in them certain general resemblances to the conduct and experiences
of the Wyf of Bath, discernible in her *Prologue* and *Tale*. The
woman described by Boccaccio resembles the Wyf in her exceeding
lustfulness of temperament; in the cunning with which she manages
her husbands; particularly in her sly upbraiding of her husband for
pretended relations with other women (cf. *W. B. Pro.* 587-92, and
Corbaccio, 231-32); in her desires for amorous relations with young
men (cf. *W. B. Pro.*, 596-626, and *Cor.* 231-32); and finally in her
belief that to her should belong sovereignty or mastery over her husband (cf. *W. B. Pro.*, 813-28, and *Cor.*, 187-88). A minor similarity
appears in the careless disposition of the two women to expend the
worldly goods of their husbands.

I have been able to detect no noteworthy resemblances in the general
structure of the two complete works, i. e., in the *Wyf of Bath's Prologue*
and *Tale* as one unit and in the *Corbaccio* as the other, beyond the
satirical attitude of the two authors, the one expressing himself
through the lips of a wanton dame, the other through the utterance
of an offended spirit, and a discussion in each work of "true gentility,"
in Boccaccio by the spirit and in Chaucer by the faery dame of the
Wyf of Bath's Tale (cf. *W. B. Tale*, 1124-1212, and *Cor.* 244-45). But
the lack of verbal resemblances and the difference of method in the
two discussions, one of which, Chaucer's, we know to have been
largely affected by Boethius and the *Romance of the Rose*, make it
precarious to draw, from this one detail, inferences in regard to the
actual existence of relations between the Italian and the English work.

Let us then return to an examination of the several details in conduct, in which Chaucer's woman resembles Boccaccio's. The lust-

fulness of the latter is that of a wanton who craves the embraces of all men, while the lustfulness of the Wyf of Bath is that of a woman who prudently limits the indulgence of her passion to relations with the particular husband with whom she is joined in wedlock at any one time in her career of frequent marriages. At no time, disgusting though her code of morality cannot but be to us, does she prove herself guilty of deliberately breaking any one of her wedding vows. She is apparently faithful to each of her five husbands in turn.

The cunning in wifely upbraidings is a more significant detail of similarity. But Professor J. L. Lowes in an article on *Chaucer and the 'Miroir de Marriage' of Eustache Deschamps (Modern Philology,* VIII, 305-34) has demonstrated clearly (p. 307) that the upbraiding in the *Prologue* has its origin in lines 1,589-1,611 of Deschamps's work. (Eustache Deschamps: *Oeuvres complètes. Société des anciens textes français,* Vol. IX). In the Chaucerian passage,

> . . . but herkneth how I sayde
> 'Sir olde kaynard, is this thyn array?
> Why is my neighebores wyf so gay?
> She is honoured over-al ther she goth;
> I sitte at hoom, I have no thrifty cloth.
> What dostow at my neighebores hous?
> Is she so fair? Artow so amorous?
> What rowne ye with our mayde? ben'cite!
>   (*W. B. Pro.,* 235-241),

the neighbor's wife and the maid, the alleged correspondents of the husband, are derived directly from the French verses. The person accused by the Italian virago (*Cor.* 189) is never defined more definitely than with the relative and demonstrative pronouns, *a cui* and *cotale.* It seems then altogether unlikely that the reproof, unfairly administered by the Wyf of Bath, could have been affected by that administered by the wanton in the *Corbaccio.*

The sham grief of the Wyf of Bath at the death of her fourth husband (*W. B. Pro.* 587-592) and her looking, as she walks in the funeral procession, at the sprightly figure of Jankin, are also paralleled in the *Miroir (Mod. Phil.,* VIII, 315) whereas in the Boccaccian passage (*Cor.* 230-31) no such funeral details are presented, but there occur only a false extravagance of grief, and, after the burial, complete lewdness on the part of the woman, disguised under the cloak of religious vows.

The resemblance, as it is never verbal, in the expression of the predilection of the Wyf of Bath and of Boccaccio's woman for young lovers, is not significant in the field of mediaeval literature, wherein there was never a wanton who did not cast her passionate eyes upon some fair youth.

As for the resemblance of the two women in craving sovereignty over their husbands, that was a much discussed mediaeval topic, and was, moreover, the essential theme of the *Wyf of Bath's Tale*, while no story to illustrate it was told in the *Corbaccio*. The spirit merely reviles woman for craving *signoria*, while the Wyf of Bath, in the end, acquires with Jankin the *maistrie* and *al the soveraynetee* (*W. B. Pro*. 817-22), to such good purpose that debate is ruled out of the household. The presence of this common theme of mastery in the two works, interesting though it is, indicates no relation between them. And further, the lack of verbal similarities as well as the very undeveloped treatment of *signoria* in Boccaccio's work and the general difference in the presentation of it precludes the likelihood of such a relationship. In this matter Boccaccio has only to say:. "E parendo loro essere salite un' altro grado, quantunque conoscano sè essere nate a essere serve, incontanente prendono speranze *e aguzzano i desiderii alla signoria*" (*Cor*. 187), and later, "Con ogni studio la loro signoria s'ingegnano d'occupare (188)."

It is after all, very doubtful if Chaucer knew at all the *Corbaccio*. The best evidence we can present for his knowledge of it proves flimsy. I can see no objection to our coming to a conclusion that he was entirely unacquainted with it. That conclusion, I believe, will in the long run prove to be sound. The Wyf of Bath is not entirely of Chaucer's creation, but she can hardly trace her origin back to the formative hand of Boccaccio. I feel that Professor Rajna's conjecture is groundless.

CHAPTER V

Chaucer's Use of the *Filostrato*

A. A Summary of the Sources of Troilus and Criseyde

In the Prefatory Remarks of his parallel edition of *Troilus and Criseyde* and the *Filostrato* translated into English (Chaucer Society, 1873), W. M. Rossetti presents, in a brief table, a scheme of the poet's indebtedness to Boccaccio which is no longer altogether satisfactory. Its tendency, no matter how legitimate its original aim was, is now to make the student of Chaucer-Boccaccio relations accredit the Italian poem with less than its full and proper amount of contributions to *Troil.* As we note that only 2,730 lines of *Fil.* were adapted into Chaucer's poem and there condensed into 2,583 lines, or something less than a third of the total lines of *Troil.*, we are prone to infer that Chaucer is indebted to Boccaccio for less than one third of the material of his romance. Such an inference is very far from being the truth. Besides the material, borrowed line for line from Boccaccio, there is of course in *Troil.* much in the way of episode, plot, or characterization, which is taken over into the English work by a less direct method than verbal translation, and which constitutes a far greater indebtedness to *Fil.* than the actual use of a number of Italian lines, however great. It is really impossible to over-estimate Chaucer's debt in this regard.

In order that it may be more conveniently seen how much of the material and how much of the spirit of Boccaccio's work the English poet actually borrowed, it is my desire to submit as a supplement to Rossetti's parallels a number of notes, accounting in a more concise way for the sources of *Troil.* These notes will not only reveal further indebtedness to *Fil.* in spirit and, at times, in instances of actual translation, not hitherto pointed out, but will attempt to summarize Rossetti's work. All references to *Fil.*, not otherwise commented upon, will be taken immediately from the latter's parallels. In addition it shall be my aim, so far as it is possible, to point out the sources of such lines in *Troil.* as are known to be derived from other works than *Fil.* To do this I shall draw largely upon the work of Professor Young, who has pointed out many of the lines which Chaucer derived from the *Roman de Troie*, and upon the work of other commentators who have studied the indebtedness of the poet to the works of Boethius, Ovid, Statius, Guido delle Colonne, and Joseph of

Exeter, as well as his indebtedness to a second poem of Boccaccio, the *Teseide*, and to minor sources.

Comment, too, will be made from time to time on Chaucer's own contributions to the Troilus story and on his particular methods of developing a suggestion he receives from one or another of his several sources. All passages abbreviated, "C.", are to be ascribed to the invention of Chaucer himself, unless further remarks are submitted.

It should, of course, be remembered that increase is an inevitable result in translation. When material is translated from one language to another, the vocabulary interpreting it always grows. It would have been an impossible feat for Chaucer to make of the *Filostrato* a translation into a poem containing less words than its Italian original, unless primarily he set out with the purpose of summary and reduction, the method he employed in Englishing the *Teseide*. This principle of increase will be observed in many of the passages about to be cited.

A
Notes on the Sources of Troil.
Book I

1-20. C. Cf. invocations with Statius, *Theb.* I, 58-60, 80, 85; VIII, 65-71, 686.[1]

21-3. *Fil.* I, 5, 6.

24-8. C.

29-30. *Fil.* I, 6.

31-56. C. But cf. Chaucer's address to young lovers with *Fil.* I, 6; VIII, 29-33. In the latter passage Boccaccio addresses his entreaty to the "giovanetti" that they curb amorous desires within themselves, and profit by the example of Criseyde's betrayal of Troilus. He fills three stanzas with an arraignment of women, and in the concluding one he counsels "giovanetti" to be "avveduti" (cautious), to have compassion upon both Troilus and themselves, and requests that they make prayer to Amor "pietosamente" that he will establish Troilo in peace in the region where now he dwells. Furthermore he hopes the "giovanetti" may not themselves be slain "per ria donna."

57-140. *Fil.* I, 7-16.

---

[1] See B. A. Wise: *The Influence of Statius upon Chaucer*; Johns Hopkins University dissertation, 1911. This similarity as well as all other similarities to Statius, yet to be pointed out in my notes, came first to my attention in the dissertation of Dr. Wise.

141-7.   C.   Author's comment.

148-213.   *Fil.* I, 17-25.   Line 171, "Right as our firste lettre is now an A,"[1] is Chaucer's.

214-66.   C.   The poet's counsel to his readers, etc.

267-73.   *Fil.* I, 26.

274-80.   C.

281-329.   *Fil.* I, 27-32.

330-50.   C.   Troilus apostrophizes Love and lovers.

351-92.   *Fil.* I, 32-7.

393-9.   C.   "Myn auctor called Lollius."

400-20.   Petrarch. Sonnet 88.

421-53.   *Fil.* I, 38-51; 53-57; II, 1.

554-67.   C.

568-630.   *Fil.* II, 2-10.

631-51.   C.   Koeppel however assigns most of these lines to the *Roman de la Rose*[2]   635-6 to 8,041-2; 637-45 to 21,819-35.

652-65.   C.   Classical allusions.

666-75.   *Fil.* II, 13, 11.

676-79.   C.   Cf. however these four lines,

> Ne, by my trouthe, *I kepe nat restreyne*
> *Thee fro thy love, thogh that it were Eleyne*
> *That is thy brotheres wyf*, if ich it wiste;
> Be what she be, and love hir as thee liste. . . .

with *Fil.* II, 16.

> . . . . lascia il tapino
> Pianto che fai, *che io non sia ucciso*;
> *Se quella ch'ami fosse mia sorella,*
> *A mio potere avrai tuo piacer d'ella.*

680-86.   *Fil.* II, 12.

687-700.   C.   Proverbs.

701-28.   *Fil.* II, 13, 15.   Lines 715-21 are Chaucer's enlargement of 708-9 from *Fil.* II, 13.

729-859.   C. Lines 738-9, 755, 806, etc., expressive of Troilus's grief come from similar lines in *Fil.* II, 1, 6, 13, 16, 19, etc.

---

[1] By means of this line Professor J. L. Lowes dates the composition of *Troil.* to a time after the marriage of Richard II of England to Anne of Bohemia.   See *The Date of Chaucer's Troilus and Criseyde: Publ. Mod. Lang. Assoc.* XXIII, no. 2, 285-306.

[2] For this and later assignments to the *Rose* see E. Koeppel: *Chauceriana, Anglia,* 1891-92. pp. 241-44.

860-89.   *Fil.* II, 16-17, 20-22.
890-6.   C.
897-903.   *Fil.* II, 23.
904-66.   C.   But cf. 904-31 with *Troil.* I, 197-205, and *Fil.* I, 23-26; 932-8 with *Troil.* I, 421-7.
967-1001.   *Fil.* II, 24, 25, 27. 28.
1001-8.   C.   Author's comment.
1009-64.   *Fil.* II, 29-34.
1065-92.   C.   But lines 1065-71 enlarge 1058-64; 1072-78 look forward to *Troil.* II, 155-210, 610-44; III, 1772-8.   These passages all portray the valour of Troilus, and the last of them comes directly from *Fil.* III, 90.
Cf. ll. 1072-4

> But *Troilus lay tho no lenger doun,*
> But up anoon upon his stede bay,
> And in the feld *he pleyde tho leoun.*

with *Fil.* VII, 80.

> *Quale lion famelico,* . . .
> Subito *su si leva* i crin vibrando
> . . . .
> Tal Trolio udendo la guerra dubbiosa
> Ricominciarsi, subito vigore
> Gli corse dentro all' infiammato core.

The conventional theme in romances of courtly love of men made gentle by their submission to Love in ll. 1079-85 may be compared with *Fil.* III, 90.

> . . . e questo spirto tanto altiero
> Più che l'usato gli prestava Amore,
> Di cui egli era fedel servidore.

In 1086-92 is further author's comment.

Book II

1-7.   C.   Dante, *Purg.* I, 1-3, is often assigned as the origin of these lines; but the comparison of a poem or a poet to a bark at sea is a common one in Italian poetry.   Cf. Petrarch, Canzone VIII (*Vergine bella.*), 66-71; Boccaccio, *Ninfale Fisolano,* VII, 65; *Sonnetto 95; La Teseide,* XI, 12; *Fil.* IX, 3.

8-49. C. Cf. invocation to Clio, l. 8, with Statius, *Theb.* I, 41; X, 630. Cf. 19-21 with the Italian poem, *L'Intelligenza*, st. 5, and with the *Confessio Amantis*, 2489-90.[1]

50-224. C. Lines 64-70, which picture the wakin of Pandarus as he hears the lament of the swallow, Proigne, telling the story of Tereus and Philomena, should be compared with *La Teseide*, IV, 73.

> Allor sentendo cantar Filomena,
> Che si fa lieta del morto Tereo,
> Si drizza, e 'l polo con vista serena
> Mirato un pezzo lauda Penteo
> La man di Giove d'ogni grazia piena,
> Che lavoro sì grande e bello feo.

Cf. also 64-6 with *Purg.* IX, 13-15.

The references to Oedipus, Laius, and Amphiorax, ll. 99-105, may come from the *Thebaid*. See Wise, pp. 8-9. Young assigns 157-61 to *R. de T.* 3991-2, 5393-6, etc.;[2] Koeppel, 167-8 to *Rose* 5684-6.

The mental attitude of Criseyde, ll. 113-9, should be compared with that of Griseida, *Fil.* II, 49. It must be remembered, too, that Pandarus's visit to Criseyde is a scene borrowed from *Fil.* II, 108.

225-73. C. Rossetti assigns four lines of this passage to Boccaccio; 225-6 to *Fil.* II, 37; 265-6 to *Fil.* II, 35.

274-82. *Fil.* II, 36.

283-92. C. An enlargement of 281-2.

293-308. *Fil.* II, 37-45.

309-15. C. A query rising naturally from 302-8.

316-22. *Fil.* II, 46.

323-90. C. The suggestion for the possibility of Troilus's death, so much harped upon by Pandarus, comes from *Fil.* II, 2,

> . . . qual fortuna
> T' ha qui condotto a vedermi morire?

The suggestion for 344-50 is in *Fil.* II, 43,

> Ben è la gemma posta nell' anello.

Pandarus's grief and fears for his own death are due to *Fil.* II, 44,

> Lascia me pianger, che'n mal'ora nacqui,

[1] See G. L. Kittredge: *Chauceriana Mod. Phil.*, VII, 477-8.

[2] For assignments to the *R. de T.* see Professor Karl Young: *The Origin and Development of the Story of Troilus and Criseyde*, Chaucer Society, 1908, pp. 105-139.

Benoit de Sainte-More.: *Le Roman de Troie.* L. Constans, Paris, 1904-1906, 3 vols. In all references to this text I have used the line numbers in italics placed at the right of the page, i. e., the line numbers employed earlier by Aristide Joly in his edition of the *Roman*, Paris, 1871.

Ch'a Dio, e al mondo, ed a fortuna spiacqui.

as well as to *Fil.* II, 16;

. . . . orsu lascia il tapino
Pianto che fai, che io non sia ucciso.

Pandarus's insistence, too, that as her uncle he can never seek Criseyde's shame (355-7) is due to the query of Griseida in *Fil.* II, 48,

Che faran gli altri, poi che tu t'ingegni
Di seguir farmi gli amorosi regni?

391-4.   *Fil.* II, 43, 54.

395-406.   C.   An enlargement of 393-4.   Cf. also 398-9,

"To late y-war," quod Beautee, whan it paste;
And elde daunteth daunger at the laste.

with *Fil.* II, 54,

Non perder tempo, *pensa che vechiezza*,
O morto, torrà via la tua bellezza.

407-20.   *Fil.* II, 47-8.

421-7.   C.

428-500.   C.   Cf. lines 435-6,

O cruel god, O dispitouse Marte,
O Furies three of helle, on yow I crye!

with the *Teseide*, I, 58,

O fiero Marte, o dispettoso Iddio.

and III, 1,

Marte nella sua fredda regione
Colle sue furie insieme s'è tornato.

Cf. 447-8,

And up he sterte, and on his wey he raughte,
Til she agayn him by the lappe caughte.

with *Fil.* II, 52,

E per partirsi quasi fu levato;
Poi pur ristette, rivolsesi ad ella.

Lines 449-67 are but the natural response for Criseyde to make to Pandarus's prophecy that, without her love, Troilus will die and he will follow his friend to death in grief. Ll. 468-98 continue the same theme. Cf. Criseyde's desire to preserve her honour, ll. 468 and 480, with *Fil.* II, 66,

Ma per fuggir vergogna, e forse peggio,
Pregalo che sia saggio, e faccia quello
Che a me biasmo non sia, ne anchè ad ello.

and with II, 121,

Griseida, salvato il suo onore,

. . . .

. . . . dove sia

L'onestà salva, e la castità mia.

501-9. *Fil.* II, 56.

510-18. C. The contents of the lines merely anticipate the following stanza, which comes from *Fil.*

519-25. *Fil.* II, 56-7.

526-539. C. This song of Troilus is of various origin. Skeat[1] assigns 526-8 to Boethius, *Cons.* IV, pr. 6. Lines 533-9 should be compared with *Fil.* II, 59.

540-1. *Fil.* II, 61.

542-53. C.

554-88. *Fil.* 62-64, 43.

589-95. C.

596-603. *Fil.* II, 68.

604-44. C. Ll. 604-10 enlarge upon 601-2. Cf. 615,

A! go we see, caste up the latis wyde.

with *Fil.* II, 82.

Ella si stava ad una sua finestra.

This passage, 604-44, contains one of Chaucer's finest artistic additions to the Troilus story, viz.—the figure of Criseyde at the window watching her hero ride by in triumph. Young assigns lines 611-18, 631-2, 638-44 to *R. de T.* 3133-4, 10139-56, 10221-5, 20591-602, 20607-14. The main incident is, however, Chaucer's.

645-65. *Fil.* II, 82-88, 71-78, 72.

666-703. In 666-79 Chaucer forestalls the criticism of his readers. Ll. 687-93, except for brief descriptive touches, resume the contents of 603-9.

704-7. *Fil.* II, 72.

708-32. C. Koeppel assigns 715-18 to *Rose.* 5765-9: Comparisons may be made too with *Fil.* as follows:

1. 708,

And *sith he hath to see me swich delyt.*

with II, 121,

A te amico discreto e possente,

Il qual forte di me t'inganna amore,

Com' uom preso per me indubitamente.

---

[1] See W. W. Skeat, (*The Complete Works of Chaucer.* Vol. II, xxix-xxx,) for this and other assignments to Boethius.

ll. 719-21,
>
> Eek sith I woot for me is his distresse
> I ne oughte not for that thing him despyse,
> Sith it is so, he meneth in good wyse.

with II, 125,
>
> . . . . .e che contento
> . . . . tu sarai,
> E porrai modo al tuo grave tormento,
> Che nel cor mi dispiace e noia assai.

ll. 722-8,
>
> And eek I knowe, of longe tyme agoon,
> His thewes goode, and that he is not nyce.
> Ne avauntour, seyth men, certein, is he noon;
> To wys is he to do so gret a vyce;
> Ne als I nel him never so cheryce,
> That he may make avaunt, by juste cause;
> He shal me never binde in swiche a clause.

with II, 123,
>
> Ed ogni cosa con ragion pensando,
> E l'afflizione e 'l tuo addomandare,
> La fede, e la speranza esaminando,
> Non veggio com' io possa soddisfare
> Assai acconciamente al tuo dimando,
> Volendo bene e intiero riguardare
> Ciò che nel mondo più è da gradire
> Ch' è in onestà vivere e morire.

and with II, 125,
>
> Ma è sì grande la virtù ch'io sento
> In te. . . .

733-5. *Fil.* II, 70.

736-42. C.

743-9. *Fil.* II, 69, line 1. Rossetti assigns only 746 to this Italian line, but in truth Chaucer's whole stanza is built up from it.

750-6. *Fil.* II, 69, line 2; 73-75.

757-84. *Fil.* II, 68, 69, 75, 73-75, 75-78. Skeat assigns 766-7 to Boethius, *Cons.* I, met. 3, 8-10.

785-810. C. Chiefly a digression on the part of the poet to decry the practice of betraying women.

813-931. C. The garden scene and Antigone's song are new effects added by Chaucer to the story. Both are common devices

in Boccaccio's works. For the nightingale, 918, to whose song
Criseyde lies abed listening, cf. note on *Troil*. I, 64-70.

932-6. C. Author's comment.

937-38. *Fil*. II, 79.

939-59. C. Cf. however line 939,

> This Pandarus com leping in at ones.

with *Fil*. II, 79,

> Pandaro . . . .
> A Troilo dritto se n'era ito.

960-6. *Fil*. II, 79, lines 7-8. Chaucer, as ever, builds upon the
suggestion of Boccaccio, analyzing "il fatto" and enumerating the
things done.

967-981. *Fil*. II, 80-81, 89. Cf. also *Inferno*, II, 127-9.

982-994. C.

995-1010. *Fil*. II, 90-91.

1011-43. C. Lines 1011-22 are built upon ll. 615-6 and 645-658.
Lines 1023-9, the suggestion that Troilus write a letter, look to *Fil*.
II, 91,

> S'io fosse in te, intiera scriverei
> Ad essa di mia man la pena mia.

The figures of speech in 1030-43 are Chaucerian; cf. their proverb
form with *Troil*. I, 631 ff.

1044-64. *Fil*. II, 93-95.

1065-70. C. Author's comment in anticipation of the following
lines, which spring from *Fil*.

1071-94. *Fil*. II, 96-98, 103-106, 100, 102, 107.

1095-99. C. But cf. these lines, wherein Pandarus speaks of the
smarting in his own heart, with *Fil*. II, 11,

> Io ho amato sventuratamente,

and II, 13,

> Ed io, . . ., contra mia voglia
> Amo, nè mi può tor nè crescer doglia.

1100-6. *Fil*. II, 108-109.

1107-24. C. Another garden in lines 1114-17. Cf. lines 813-14.
Cf. also Pandarus's delivery to Criseyde of Troilus's letter, 1120-24,
with similar scene in *Fil*. II, 109.

1125-62. *Fil*. II, 109-113.

1163-72. C.

1173-76. *Fil*. II, 114.

1177-94. C. But of course the act of reading the letter comes from *Fil.* II, 114.

1195-97. *Fil.* II, 118.

1198-1200. *Fil.* II, 118.

1201-4. C.

1205-7. *Fil.* II, 119.

1208-11. C. Another plea to Criseyde to have mercy on Troilus before he die of grief. Cf. ll. 316-36, and *Fil.* II, 109,

> Di colui, che per te mi par vedere
> Morir, se poco te ne è in calere.

1212-26. *Fil.* II, 120-28. Greatly abbreviated. Observe, too, the similarity in Criseyde's desire to please Troilus "as his suster" (l. 1224) to Griseida's promise to love Troilo "come fratel" (*Fil.* II, 134, 7-8).

1227-38. C.

1239. *Fil.* II, 129, Rossetti.

1240-1304. C. Pandarus moralizes, lines 1240-46. Chaucer again pictures Troilus riding by Criseyde's window, 1247-74.

1305. *Fil.* II, 128.

1306-16. C. Another picture of the despondent Troilus. Cf. again *Fil.* II, 1-17, etc.

1317-72. *Fil.* 128, 129; 130-143. Italian passages somewhat modified.

1373-1757. C. A long and notable passage, of Chaucer's invention. Ll. 1373-9 are reminiscent, in their references to "daunger," of the *Rose.*

It is interesting to observe the relations of Troilo and Deifebo in *Fil.* as compared with those of Troilus and Deiphebus in Chaucer's poem. In the Italian work the only friend besides Pandaro to whom Troilo ever goes is Deifebo. It is thence, very probably, that Chaucer derives the idea of making Deiphebus the best loved brother of Troilus. (II, 1396-98). Observe in comparison with these lines of *Troil.* the particular solicitude of Deifebo for Troilo as expressed in *Fil.* VII, 77, 78, 82.

Cf. the hospitable reception of Deiphebus to Troilus (II, 1541-43) with the kindliness of Deifebo to Troilo in *Fil.* VII, 78, 82.

Cf. the sympathy and interest of Deiphebus and Helen in the feigned illness of Troilus and their presence at his bedside (II, 1571-86, 1665-73) with those of the group of friends and relatives, including Deifebo and Elena, who gather around the invalid Troilo to comfort him in *Fil.* VII, 83-85, i. e., in scenes near the end of the Italian poem, which are not otherwise made use of by Chaucer.

The idea of Criseyde's insecurity in Troy, lines 1415 ff., used as a pretext by Pandarus for his feigned intercession for her with Deiphebus, Helen, Troilus and Hector, is, it would appear, suggested to Chaucer by Griseida's supplications to Hector. Cf. *Troil.* I, 106-26, and *Fil.* I, 1-13. A fuller description of this scene in *Fil.* will be given on a later page of the present work.[1] It should be remembered however that so precarious a position as that in which Griseida was left, was no unusual situation in the middle ages, when feudal lords vacillated in their fealty. Chaucer may have seen the picture in life.

The brief interview of Pandarus and Troilus, 1492-1536 suggests earlier interviews.

The first secret interview of Troilus and Criseyde, so craftily arranged for by Pandarus, at the house of Deiphebus, should, of course, be compared with arrangements for secrecy in *Fil.* Cf. especially II, 140-143,

> Ma se alcun prego val nel tuo cospetto,
> Ti prego, dolce e caro mio fratello
> Che tutto ciascun nostro fatto o detto
> Occulto sia; tu puoi ben veder quello
> Che seguir ne potria, se tale affetto
> Venisse a luce, deh parlane ad ello,
> E fannel savio, e come tempo fia,
> Io farò ciò che 'l suo piacer disia.

> Rispose Pandar: guarda la tua bocca,
> Che el per sè, nè io, mai il diremo.
> . . . .
> . . . .
> Pandar disse: di ciò non dubitare,
> Che in ciò avremo ben buona cautela.
> . . . .
> . . . .
> Tu sai, disse Griseida, che in questa
> Cosa son donne ed altra gente meco,
> Delle quai parte alla futura festa
> Devono andare; ed allor sarò seco.

[1] See page 84.

Questa tardanza non gli sia molesta;
Del modo e del venire allora teco
Favellerò; fa' pur ch'egli sia saggio,
E sappia ben celare il suo coraggio.

N. B. Griseida in the last quoted stanza promises to talk with Pandaro of a way of coming to Troilo with him.

The dinner party at the house of Deiphebus is a prototype for the later dinner party at the house of Pandarus.

In lines 1734-50 is again repeated an appeal to Criseyde that she have mercy upon Troilus and spare his life.

In 1751-57 we find again the comment of the author.

Book III

1-49. *Fil.* III, 74-79. Cf. invocation to Calliope, l. 45, with Statius, *Theb.* IV, 34.

50-238. C. Cf. Troilus waiting for the first meeting with Criseyde to Troilo with similar anticipations in *Fil.* III, 25, "in certo luogo rimoto ed oscuro."

Cf. Pandarus's accompanying Criseyde to Pandaro's accompanying Troilo to the latter's first meeting at night with Griseida, *Fil.* III, 23,

Con Pandar solo il suo cammin suo prendea
In ver là dove Griseida stava.

Cf. the picture of the feigning invalid Troilus's rising, 69-71, with Troilo's rising to meet Griseida, *Fil.* III, 27,

Il qual, com' egli la sentì venire,
Drizzato in piè, . . .

Cf. also the greetings of Troilus and Criseyde with those of Troilo and Griseida, *Fil.* III, 28-29.

The timidity of Troilus in Criseyde's presence is Chaucer's development of Troilo's self-disparagement in the presence of Pandaro, *Fil.* II, 1-3. Cf. too Pandarus's weeping, 115, with the grief of Pandaro present at a similar scene in *Fil.* II, 4, line 1.

Observe in 120-26 another appeal to Criseyde, not, by her indifference, to do Troilus to death.

The vows of Troilus, 127-47, should be compared with passages in the letter of Troilo to Griseida in *Fil.* II, 96-107. Cf. passages as follows:
129-35,

That, with the stremes of your eyen clere,
Ye wolde som-tyme freendly on me see,
And thanne agreën that I may ben he,
With-oute braunche of vyce in any wyse,
In trouthe alwey to doon yow my servyse
As to my lady right and chief resort,
With al my wit and al my diligence.

with *Fil.* II, 98,

L'onestà cara e'l donnesco valore,
I modi e gli atti. . . .
Nella mia mente hanno. . . .
. . . *te per donna in tal guisa fermati,*
Ch'altro accidente mai fuorchè la morte,
A tirarline fuor non saria forte.

and III, 83,

E benedico il figliuol. . . .
. . . che m'ha fatto *a lei servo verace,*
Negli occhi suoi ponendo la mia pace.

and II, 101,

Tu sola puoi l'afflizion pensose,
Madonna, porre in riposo verace;
Tu sola puoi con l'opere pietose
Tornir il tormento che si mi disface.

136,

And *I to han*, right as yow list, *comfort*.

with II, 101,

Tu sola puoi queste pene noiose,
Quando tu vogli, *porre in dolce pace.*

134-40,

As to my lady right and chief resort
With al my wit and al my diligence
And I to han, right as yow list, comfort,
Under your yerde, egal to myn offence,
As deeth, if that I breke your defence;
And that ye deigne me so muche honoure,
Me to comaunden ought in any houre.

with II, 102,

Dunque, se mai per pura fede alcuno,
Se mai per grande amor, se per disio
Di ben servire ognora in ciascheduno

> Caso, qual si volesse o buono o rio,
> Meritò grazia, fa' ch'io ne sia uno,
> Cara mia donna; fa' ch'io sia quell' io,
> Che a te ricorro, sì come a colei
> Che se' cagion di tutti i sospiri miei.

141-47.

> And I to be your verray humble trewe,
> Secret, and in my paynes pacient,
> And ever-mo desire freshly newe,
> To serven, and been y-lyke ay diligent,
> And, with good herte, al holly your talent
> Receyven wel, how sore that me smerte,
> Lo, this mene I, myn owne swete herte.

with II, 103,

> Assai conosco, che mai meritato
> Norí fu per mio servir quel per che vegno;
> Ma sola tu che m'hai il cor piagato,
> E altro no, di maggior cosa degno,
> Mi puoi far, quando vogli; o disiato
> Ben del mio cor, pon giù l'altero sdegno
> Dell' animo tuo grande, e sii umile
> Ver me, quanto negli atti se' gentile.

Lines 148-168, with their central thought,

> And myn honour, with wit and besinesse,
> Ay kepe,

look again to *Fil.* See comment on *Troil.* II, 468 and 480.

Criseyde's views as to the proportion of "soverainetee," 169-175, Troilus shall have in his love are a common Chaucerian expression. Perhaps in them, as in the *Franklin's Tale*, is the solution Chaucer would offer for the problem of marriage. See G. L. Kittredge on the marriage problem in Chaucer, *Modern Philology*, April, 1912.

The arrangement made by Pandarus for a second secret interview of the lovers points again to the general secrecy of *Fil.* Cf. *Troil.* III, 193-200.

The farewells of Helen, Criseyde, etc., 204-233, are purely Chaucerian.

The figure of Pandarus at the bedside of Troilus, 234-38, should be compared with that of Pandaro in a like position, *Fil.* II, 1, 16.

239-87. *Fil.* III, 5-10. Rossetti does not assign 246-52 to Boccaccio, but the contents of the lines are anticipatory of those following, the material of which is derived from *Fil.*

288-329. C.   Further moralizing and proverbs of Pandarus.

330-36. *Fil.*   According to Rossetti only l. 336 is due to *Fil.* III, 10, l. 1; but cf. 330-32,

> But now to purpos; leve brother dere,
> Have al this thing that I have seyd in minde,
> *And keep thee clos,* and be now of good chere,

with *Fil.* III, 9,

> Perch' io ti prego tanto quant' io posso
> *Che occulto sia tra noi questo mestiero.*

and 333-35,

> For at thy day thou shalt me trewe finde.
> I shal thy proces sette in swich a kinde,
> And god to-forn, *that it shal thee suffyse.*

with *Fil.* III, 9,

> . . . . ed ho'l tanto percosso
> Col ragionar del tuo amor sincero,
> Che ella t'ama, ed è disposta fare
> *Ciò che ti piacerà di comandare.*

337-43. C.   But Pandarus disconsolately sighing for death or "lysse," 342-43, reminds one of Pandaro's lament, *Fil.* II, 13,

> Ed io, come tu sai, contra mia voglia
> Amo, nè mi puo tor nè crescer doglia.

344-78. *Fil.* III, 11-15.

379-85. C.   An enlargement however of *Fil.* material in preceding stanza.

386-427. *Fil.* III, 16-20.

428-434. C.   But cf. Troilus's concealment of his love from the public with Troilo's conduct in *Fil.* II, 84,

> E per piacer non gli è cosa molesta
> Amor seguir, *mirar discretamente*
> *Griseida* . . . .

435-55. *Fil.* Rossetti only assigns 435-41 to *Fil.* III, 20, 442-48 are an enlargement upon the thought of these lines; cf. also the occasional meetings of the lovers, 449-55,

> But certeyn is, to purpos for to go,
> That in this whyle, as writen is in geste,
> *He say his lady som-tyme; and also*
> *She with him spak, whan that she dorste or leste,*
> And by hir bothe avys, as was the beste,
> Apoynteden ful warly in this nede,
> So as they dorste, how they wolde procede.

with *Fil.* II, 84,

> E per piacer non gli è cosa molesta
> Amor seguir, *mirar discretamente*
> *Griseida, la qual non men discreta,*
> *Gli si mostrava a' tempi vaga e lieta.*

456-83. C. But certain passages in this account of the growth of Troilus's and Criseyde's mutual infatuation should be compared with the Italian. Cf. stages in it as follows:

The lady begins to favour her lover's suit, 465-7 and *Fil.* II, 117, ll. 3-8; 468-9 and II, 85, ll. 1-4.

The lady finds pleasure in the knowledge that she is loved by the Trojan youth, 470-74 and II, 83.

The youth in the lady's "service," 475-76 and II, 98, ll. 4-6; 102; 103, ll. 1-2.

The discretion of the two lovers, 477, 481-82 and II, 84, ll. 5-8; 121, l. 1.

The "obeisaunce" of the Trojan lover, 477 and II, 105.

484-90. *Fil.* Rossetti attributes this stanza to Chaucer, but Pandarus's diligence and carrying of letters between the lovers looks to *Fil.* II, 130, 133, 134, 108, 128, etc.

491-511. C. Author's comment.

512-18. *Fil.* Rossetti assigns these lines to Chaucer; but the zeal of Pandarus described in them is everywhere evident in *Fil.* Cf. III, 17, 19, 20, 23, etc.

519-39. C. The idea of waiting for a suitable time for a meeting, however, is also present in *Fil.* Cf. III, 21,

> In questo mezzo il tempo disiato
> Da' dui amanti venne, . . .

540-46. C. The idea of Troilus's frequenting the temple, however, is found also in *Fil.* Cf. III, 4,

> Ch'egli il trovò in un tempio pensando.

It is interesting, too, to note that Troilus has recourse to the temple of Apollo for assistance in his suit, just as the lover Arcite makes appeal to that god in the *Teseide*, IV, 42-49.

547-553 *Fil.* According to Rossetti this stanza is C., but the conception of the moonless night, when the welkin is over-clouded, should be compared with *Fil.* III, 24,

> *Era la notte oscura e nebulosa*
> *Come Troilo volea.*

Observe also the phenomena of the second night in *Fil.* III, 64,

. . . . fu la notte bruna,

. . . .

Senza nel ciel vedere stella alcuna.

554-567. C. Cf. the arrangement for the supper at Pandarus's house with the earlier dinner at the house of Deiphebus, *Troil.* II, 1488 ff. The rain, 562, points again to *Fil.* III, 24.

568-81. *Fil.* The language only is Chaucer's. The assurance that Troilus would not be at Pandarus's house is due, beyond doubt, to the implicit statement, made in Griseida's presence by Pandaro, who, *Fil.* III, 21,

. . . .*dolessi*
Di Troilo, che 'l dì davanti andato
Era con certi, per bisogni espressi
Della lor guerra, alquanto di lontano,
Bench' el dovea tornare a mano a mano.

582-598. C. Criseyde's fears of public opinion, 582-88, look again to the secrecy of the *Fil.* Cf. II, 140.

599-602. *Fil.* These lines are not so assigned by Rossetti, but Troilus's hiding place, the "litel stewe," 601, can only correctly be compared with the hiding place of Troilo in *Fil.* III, 25,

E in certo luogo rimoto ed oscuro,
Come imposto gli fu, la donna attese.

603-693. C. The supper is modelled upon earlier scenes of *Troil.* The secrecy of line 603 points once more to *Fil.* Skeat assigns lines 617-19 to Boethius, *Cons.* IV, pr. 6, 60-71. The astrology of 624-630 is Chaucer's, but the suggestion for rain comes from *Fil.* III, 24.

The necessity for waiting until all of Criseyde's women are asleep and the house has become quiet, 666-93, looks to *Fil.* again. Cf. III, 27,

Poi che ciascun sen fu ito a dormire,
E la casa rimasa tutta cheta.

694-97. *Fil.* The characterization of Pandarus presented in these lines, that of the man who knew the "olde daunce" so well, must certainly be compared with Pandaro's self-characterization in *Fil.* II, 32,

A cui ridendo Pandaro rispose:
Niente nuoce ciò che tu ragioni,
Lascia far me, che le fiamme amorose
Ho per le mani, e sì fatti sermoni,

> E seppi già recar più alte cose
> Al fine suo con nuove condizioni,
> Questa fatica tutta sarà mia,
> E 'l dolce fine tuo voglio che sia.

698-799. C. Many elements of this passage however remind one of the *Fil.*

The secrecy of 698-700 suggests *Fil.* III, 23,

> . . . . .e poi tacitamente
> Con Pandar solo il suo cammin prendea
> In ver là dove Griseida stava.

The praise of Venus, 701-714, is reminiscent of *Troil.* III, 1-42, and *Fil.* III, 74-79.

The supplications and mythological allusions of 715-735, Chaucer seems to adapt from various sources. See Wise, pp. 11-12. They are a literary device rarely employed in *Fil.* but very commonly used in Boccaccio's *Teseide.* From the latter poem Chaucer, it is quite possible to believe, derived the idea of ornamenting *Troil.* with its numerous allusions.

The stealth of 743-49 reminds one again of *Fil.* III, 23; the appeals of Pandarus, 771-784, that Criseyde will pity Troilus, of *Fil.* II, 125, 135, 137, etc. The rain, 788, and further secrecy, 785-91, point also to passages previously cited from *Fil.*

The jealousy of Troilus, pictured in 792-98, has a counterpart in *Fil.* Cf. specimens of Troilo's *gelosia* I, 49; IV, 139-145; VII, 18.

800. *Fil.* Not so assigned by Rossetti. Cf. the line however,

> *Gan sodeynly aboute hir herte colde,*

with *Fil.* II, 138,

> . . . *il sangue mi s'agghiaccia.*

801-12. C. Criseyde's surprise at learning of Troilus's jealousy.

813-33. Boethius. Assigned by Skeat to *Cons.* II, pr. 4, 86, 87, 56, 109-117.

834-837. C. Cf. 801-812.

848-917. C. The dialogue between Pandarus and Criseyde is a conventional situation in *Fil.* The points in the argument are Chaucerian, largely resumptive in character. The ring which Criseyde proposes to send to Troilus by Pandarus, 885, is a world-old pledge of constancy in love. Chaucer's use of it is probably independent of all source influences.

918-45. C. But Criseyde's final consent to see her lover, 920, 925-8, 941-5, her honour to be saved, is due to lines in *Fil.* Cf.

especially 945,

> For I am here al in your governaunce,

with II, 133,

> . . . i' non posso altro, io gli fo quello,
> Che m' imponesti, caro mio fratello.

Observe too II, 139,

> E che mi fia cagion dell' onor mio
> Perdere, o lassa, e d'infiniti guai;
> Or più non posso, poichè t' è in piacere,
> Disposta sono a fare il tuo volere.

and II, 121,

> Griseida, salvato il suo onore,
> Manda salute, e poi umilimente
> Si raccomanda al tuo alto valore
> Vaga di compiacerti, dove sia
> L'onestà salva, e la castità mia.

946-52. C. The praise of Venus resumes *Troil*. III, 1-42.

953-94. C. But the courtesy of Troilus's greeting, 955, should be compared with Troilo's gracious salutation, *Fil*. III, 29. Lines 981-994 are resumptive of various topics, Troilus's service of Criseyde, the futility of resistance to Love, etc., drawn largely from Troilo's letter, *Fil*. II, 96-106, and earlier passages in *Troil*. I, 421-539, etc., passages due to *Fil*. I, 38-55, etc.

995-1008. *Fil*. Not so assigned by Rossetti, but cf. the general sentiment of stanzas with that of *Fil*. II, 136, where Griseida speaking of Troilo, declares

> Ed io ti giuro per la mia salute,
> Ch'io son, da qual che tu dimandi in fuore,
> Sua mille volte più ch'io non son mia,
> Tanto m'aggrada la sua cortesia.

Observe also III, 28, . . . dolce mio disio.

1009-71. C. Criseyde's lament over Troilus's jealousy and his consequent grief. Observe, similarly, conversation in *Fil*. III, 40,

> Rassicurati insieme i due amanti,
> Insieme incominciaro a ragionare,
> E l'uno all' altro i preteriti pianti,
> E l'angosce e' sospiri a racontare.

1072-1127. C. Lines 1072-1092 however merely develop similar scenes of Troilo's despondency in *Fil*. II, 1-3, 62, etc. The swoon of Troilus, 1092, is paralleled by the swoon of Troilo after he has learned of the demands of Calcas for his daughter Griseida, *Fil.* IV, 18-21.

1128-34. C. The affectionate tenderness of these lines should, however, be compared with that of *Fil.* III, 30.

1135-48. C. The figure of Pandarus going to the "chimeneye" with the candle is original with Chaucer. The idea of love in association with gentleness, 1146-7, is a common theme in Italian poetry, especially in the sonnets of Petrarch.

1149-76. C.

1177-83. C. The endearments are merely English for "dolce mio disio" and kindred phrases in *Fil.*

1184-1253. C. Occasional lines should be compared however with *Fil.* Cf. 1205,

> This Troilus in armes gan hir streyne,

and 1230-2,

> And as aboute a tree, with many a twiste,
> Bitrent and wryth the sote wodebinde,
> Gan eche of hem in armes other winde.

with *Fil.* III, 32, line 7,

> E strignendo l'un l'altro con fervore.

Cf. 1221,

> For out of wo in blisse now they flete,

with *Fil.* III, 32, line 8,

> D'amor sentiron l'ultimo valore.

Troilus's praise of the gods is again resumptive, 1202-3.

The two beautiful classical similes of 1233-46, it should be noted, are Chaucer's. In the use of such devices the poet was probably influenced by such Italian poems as the *Teseide*.

Cf. 1252,

> And ther-with-al *a thousand tyme hir kiste*,

with *Fil.* III, 30,

> *Che mille volte insieme s'abbracciaro.*

1254-74. *Fil.* Not so assigned by Rossetti, but the passage is chiefly a *resumé* of the song in the proem of Book III, 1-42, which is derived from *Fil.* III, 74-89.

Skeat assigns 1261 to Boethius, *Cons.* II, met. 8, 9-11. Cf. with it too Dante, *Paradiso* XXXIII, 14-15.

1275-1309. C. The conversation is C.; but the kisses, vows, endearments, etc. are all due to *Fil.*

1310-23. *Fil.* III, 31, 33.

1324-37. C. Author's comment.

1338-65. *Fil.* III, 34-37.

1366-72. C. The lovers make the world-old pledge of constancy by exchanging their rings.

1373-86. *Fil.* III, 38-39.

1387-93. C. Midas and Crassus are cited as moral instances of "coveityse."

1394-1414. *Fil.* III, 40-41.

1415-28. *Fil.* III, 42-43. Cf. also 1420 with Dante, *Purgatorio*, XIX, 4. The classical allusions in these lines are additions by Chaucer. Analogues to Jove and Alcmena, 1427-8, may be found, according to Wise (pp. 11-12), as follows: Statius, *Theb.* VI, 266; XII, 300; Boccaccio, *Tes.* IV, 14.

1429-42. C. Criseyde's apostrophe to Night, as a sort of companion piece to the *aubade* sung presently by Troilus.

1443-49. *Fil.* III, 44.

1450-70. C. The suggestion for this *aubade*, an everyday convention in romances of courtly love, is traceable to *Fil.* III, 44,

> Il giorno che venía maledicendo
> Che lor così avaccio separava.

Cf. also "Tytan," 1464, with *Tes.* IV, 72.

1471-92. *Fil.* III, 44-48.

1493-1512. C. The amatory conceits in Criseyde's vows are similar to many of those in Petrarchan sonnets.

1513-55. *Fil.* III, 50-56.

1556-89. C. The visit of Pandarus to Criseyde on this occasion is not paralleled in *Fil.*

1590-1624. *Fil.* III, 56-60.

1625-28. Dante, *Inferno* V, 121-3. Cf. also Boethius, *Cons.* II, pr. 4, "But this is a thing that greetly smerteth me whan it remembreth me. For in alle adversitee of Fortune, the most unsely kind of contrarious fortune is to han ben weleful."

1629-38. C. A development of 1625-28.

1639-80. *Fil.* III, 61-65.

1681-94. C. Author's comment.

1695-1701. *Fil.* III, 70.

1702-8. C. Another brief *aubade*. Cf. the reference to the horses and the chariot of the sun with *Tes.* X, 88.

1709-43. *Fil.* III, 71, 72, 84, 72, 73.

1744-71. Boethius, *Cons.* II, met. 8. Lines 1744-64 are virtually a translation; 1765-71 are Chaucerian, largely summary of preceding Boethian passage.

1772-1806. *Fil.* III, 90-93. Lines 1794-9 are an enlargement by Chaucer.

1807-1813. *Tes.* I, st. 3 and st. 1.

1814-1820. C. Author's comment.

Book IV

1-10. *Fil.* III, 94.

11-21. Author's comment.

22-28. C. Cf. Chaucer's invocation to all the Furies and to Mars for aid in this book with *Theb.* XI, 57 ff., 344 ff.; V, 66; IV, 53; and with Ovid *H.* XI, 103; *M.* VIII, 481. See Wise, p. 11.

Cf. also Chaucer's association of the Furies with Mars with Boccaccio's *Teseide* III, 1.

29-119. *Fil.* IV, 1-11. Lines 36-42, it should be noted merely repeat the contents of 29-35, which spring from *Fil.* IV, 1.

120-26. C.

127-168. *Fil.* IV, 12-16.

169-210. C. Hector's intercession to save Criseyde, 176-182, is a striking illustration of Chaucer's ability to pick up the several threads of his narrative. The poet who improvised the episode of Criseyde at the house of Deiphebus, seeking aid of both him and Hector, perceives now that it is only natural that in this new crisis in the lady's fortunes Hector shall again champion her cause.

211-322. *Fil.* IV, 17, 22, 23, 26-36. Cf. also 225-8 with Dante, *Inferno* III, 112-18.

323-29. C. A Boethian attitude.

330-50. *Fil.* IV, 38-41, 43.

351-55. C. The knight in attendance at Troilus's door is a new touch tending toward a realistic expression of the rank of the prince.

356-57. *Fil.* IV, 43.

358-64. C. But this picture of Pandarus's distress is paralleled in *Fil.* Cf. II, 4; IV, 46, etc.

365-85. *Fil.* IV, 44-46.

386-92. C. Skeat assigns 391-92 to Boethius, *Cons.* II, pr. 2, 7-9; 61-2.

393-406. *Fil.* IV, 47-48.

407-13. C.

414-17. *Fil.* IV, 49.
418-31. C.
432-52. *Fil.* IV, 50.
453-624. *Fil.* IV, 52, 54, 56-58, 60-65, 67, 69, 68, 70-75. The translation in this passage is quite free and greatly enlarged over its original, but it adds nothing to the material contents of *Fil.*

Koeppel assigns to the *Rose.* 6406-7, the *alembic*, 519, employed in the description of Troilus weeping.

625-30. C.
631-37. *Fil.* IV, 76.
638-44. C. Resumptive however, of 533-34 and 582-88. Cf. also *Fil.* IV, 65 and 71.

645-787. *Fil.* 77-89, 92, 93, 88-90, 89, 90, 91. A few unimportant lines of this passage are Chaucerian in origin; 648-51, 654-58, 767-70, 771-73, which anticipate 774-77, and 780-84, which merely enlarge the thought of 778-79, lines coming from *Fil.*

788-98. C. A Chaucerian touch of altruism in Criseyde's nature hardly accounted for by *Fil.* IV, 88-94. In 788-91 another classical allusion is used by Chaucer.

799-821. *Fil.* IV, 95-96.
799-821. *Fil.* IV, 95-96.
822-826. *Fil.* IV, 95. Rossetti assigns this passage to Chaucer, but I attribute it to Boccaccio.

Cf. the two passages:

> For which this Pandare is so wo bi-goon,
> *That in the hous he mighte unnethe abyde,*
> As he that pitee felte on every syde.
> For if Criseyde hadde erst compleyned sore,
> Tho gan she pleyne a thousand tymes more.

> Chi potrebbe giammai narrare a pieno
> Ciò che Griseida nel pianto dicea?
> Certo non io, che al fallo il dir vien meno,
> Tant' era la sua noia cruda e rea.
> Ma mentre tai lamenti si facieno,
> Pandaro venne, *a cui non si tenea*
> *Uscio giammai, e'n camera sen gio,*
> Là dov' ella faceva il pianto pio.

Observe particularly Chaucer's peculiar translation in 823 of the enigmatic clause in lines 6 and 7 of the Italian stanza. From Boccaccio's apparent statement that no door was ever closed to Pandaro, "a cui non si tenea uscio giammai," Chaucer derives the idea that Pandarus was so affected with grief that he could hardly remain in the house of Criseyde.

827-840. C. A passage filled with Boethian influence. Skeat assigns 835-36 to *Cons.* II, pr. 4, 90.

841-47. *Fil.* IV, 96-97. Rossetti assigns this passage to Chaucer. The lines, however, render subjective, through Criseyde's speech, the contents of the two Italian stanzas, which are presented objectively by Boccaccio.

Cf.

Who-so me seeth, he seeth sorwe al at ones,
Peyne, torment, pleynte, wo, distresse,
Out of my woful body harm ther noon is,
As anguish, langour, cruel bitternesse,
A-noy, smert, drede, fury, and eek siknesse.
I trowe, y-wis, from hevene teres reyne,
For pitee of myn aspre and cruel peyne!

with

El vide lei in sul letto avviluppata
Ne' singhiozzi, nel pianto e ne' sospiri;
E'l petto tutto e la faccia bagnata
Di lacrime le vide, ed in disiri
Di pianger gli occhi suoi, e scapigliata
Dar vero segno degli aspri martiri;
La qual come lui vide, fra le braccia
Per vergogna nascose la sua faccia.

Crudele il punto, comminciò a dire
Pandar, fu quel nel quale i' mi levai;
Che dovunque oggi vo doglia sentire,
Tormenti, pianti, angoscie, ed altri guai,
Sospiri, noia, ed amaro languire
Mi par per tutto: o Giove, che faccia?
Io credo che dal ciel lacrime versi,
Tanto ti son li nostri fatti avversi.

Observe that Chaucer uses stanza 96 also in the earlier lines 813-21.

848-926. *Fil.* IV, 98-107, 106.

927-938. C.

939-45. *Fil.* IV, 108. Rossetti attributes only three lines of Chaucer's stanza to Boccaccio. But the suggestion for the whole of it is in *Fil.*

946-52. C. But for the figure of Troilus in the temple praying, 947-950, cf. *Fil.* III, 4,

Ch' egli trovò in un tempio pensando.

953-1085. Boethius. This long discourse of Troilus on predestination, which, it should be remembered, is not found in all the manuscripts of *Troil.*, is taken bodily by Chaucer from the *Cons.* V, pr. 3, 7-71.

1086-95. *Fil.* IV, 109-110.

1096-1106. C. Cf. 927-938.

1107-1171. *Fil.* IV, 110-119. Only the simile of 1135-41 is Chaucer's.

1172-76. *Fil.* IV, 121-122. Rossetti does not make this assignment, but Chaucer's lines certainly anticipate what follows in lines 1191-1204, which are derived from *Fil.*

1177-1253. *Fil.* IV, 119-127.

1254-1309. C. This passage contains an interesting development of lines 934-38,

So shapeth how distourbe your goinge,
Or come ayen, sone after ye be went.
Wommen ben wyse in short avysement;
And lat sen how your wit shal now avayle;
And what that I may helpe, it shal not fayle.

these lines are an adroit substitution for *Fil.* IV, 107,

Però levati su, *rifatti tale*,
Che tu alleggi e non cresca 'l suo male.

Pandaro merely advised Griseida to control her own grief and so be more able to alleviate Troilo's sorrow. Chaucer converts this counsel into Pandarus's advice to Criseyde to devise means—a thing which, as a woman, she will be perfectly competent to do—that will enable her to return to Troy and to be reunited with her lover. In this passage then Criseyde is putting Pandarus's advice into execution.

But it must not be forgotten that the gist of the comfort which Criseyde offers to Troilus, her insistence that she will return within a week or two, 1275-78, is present also in *Fil.* In the Italian poem Griseida is hardly less insistent. Cf. *Fil.* IV, 154-55, 159-61. The limit of her absence is there set for ten days, a period which Chaucer adopts later on in *Troil.* Cf.. IV, 1595-98, etc.

1310-48. *Fil.* IV, 131, 133, 131, 134, 131.

1349-58. C.

1359-65. *Fil.* IV, 134-35.

1366-1414. C. A consummately clever development of a situation, merely suggested by Boccaccio, *Fil.* IV, 166, and then dropped; viz;—Griseida's intention to find in her father's avarice a means to return to Troy. The passage will be discussed more fully in another section of this dissertation.

1415-21. C.; *Fil.*; *R. de T.*; Guido. In all four of these works there are indications that Troilus's lady fully believed that she would remain true to him. The statement of 1415-16 might very well look to *Fil.*; to the *R. de T.* 13469-77, a passage the sentiment of which is very similar to that of the *Troil.* just cited; or to the passage, "Que dum queritur de sua separatione . . . vita sue vite solacia dependebat," of Chapter 40 of Guido's *Historia Trojana.*[1]

1422-49. *Fil.* IV, 137-40.

1450-63. C.

1464-75. *Fil.* IV, 141-42.

1476-77. C.

1478-1537. *Fil.* IV, 142-46.

1538-40. C. Another classical allusion.

1541-42. *Fil.* IV, 146.

1543-54. C. Invocations.

1555-1659. *Fil.* IV, 147-152, 154-160, 158, 160, 160, 159, 161, 160-62, 161-63. The astrology of lines 1590-93 is Chaucer's addition. Lines 1615-17 are a repetition of 1605-1607.

1660-66. C. A conventional prayer to Venus.

1667-1701. *Fil.* IV, 164-67. Observe that lines 1695-1701, which are not assigned to *Fil.* by Rossetti, are but a repetition of 1689-94.

Book V.

1. *Teseide* IX, 1, line 1.

2-7. C. For the invocations cf. Statius, *Theb.* I, 212; III, 241; VI, 354; *et aliter.*

---

[1] Brief selections from the Latin text of Guido's history are available in H. Oskar Sommer's edition of: *The Recuyell of the Historyes of Troye, Written in French by Raoul Lefevre, Translated and Printed by Caxton, about A. D. 1474*, 2 vols., David Nutt, London, 1894.

For Chaucer's debt to Guido see G. L. Hamilton: *Chaucer's Indebtedness to Guido delle Colonne*, Macmillan, N. Y., 1903.

8-11. *Teseide* II, 1, lines 1-4.

12-14. **C.**

15-91. *Fil.* **V**, 1-6, 9-13. A few unimportant lines of this passage such as 35 and 91 are **Chaucer's.**

92-175. *R. de T.*; *Fil.*; **C.** This passage represents a fusion of material drawn from the *R. de T.* and *Fil.* together with some additions of Chaucer's own invention.

Chaucer like Benoit, and unlike Boccaccio, has Diomede address his suit to the mistress of Troilus immediately upon his first meeting with her. Cf. *Troil.* V, 92-175 with *R. de T.* 13529-13584. But for the contents of this first speech of Diomede the poet depends not only upon the *R. de T.* but also upon the contents of a soliloquy and the later speech of Diomede in the *Fil.* (VI, 10-12, 14-25).

I append below several parallels, hitherto not pointed out, to illustrate the derivation of a number of the lines of *Troil.*

Thoughte, 'al my labour shal not ben on ydel,	E seco disse nella prima vista;
If that I may, for somewhat shal I seye.'	Vana fatica credo sia la mia. *Fil.* VI, 1.
. . . .	
But nathcless this thoughte he wel ynough,	
'That certeynly I am aboute nought	
If that I speke of love.' V, 94-5, 99-101.	

. . . and gan hir eek biseche,	"Jos criasse mout *grant* merci,
That if that he encrese mighte or eche	Qu' a chevalier e a ami
With any thing hie ese, that she sholde	Me receüssiez tot demeine.
Comaunde it him, and seyde he doon it wolde. V, 109-112.	Ainz en voudrai sofrir grant peine
	Que, se vos plaist, a ço n'en vienge."
	R. de T., 13511-515.

For trewely he swoor hir, as a knight,	"Ja Deu ne place, s'a vos fail
That there nas thing with which he might hir plese,	Que mais por autre me travail:
That he nolde doon his peyne and al his might	Non ferai jo, co sai de veir,
To doon it, for to doon hir herte an ese.	E se vostre amor puis aveir,
And preyede hir, she wolde hir sorwe apese. V, 113-117.	Guarderai le senz rien mesfaire;
	N'orreiz de mei chose retraire
	Que vos desplace a nes un jor.
	Des granz sospirs e del grant plor
	Dont vos vei mout chargiee e pleine,
	Metrai mon cors en mout grant peine."
	R. de T. 13567-576.

He seyde eek thus, 'I woot, yow thinketh straunge,	Lei domandando quel che le ne pare,
	S'e 'lo. pensier credea frivoli o vani:

No wonder is, for it is to yow newe,
Thaqueintaunce of these Troianes to
chaunge,
For folk of Grece, that ye never knewe.'
V, 120-23.

Quinci discese poi a domandare
Se le parien de' Greci i modi strani.
Fil. VI, 12.

"But wolde never god but-if as trewe
A greek ye shulde among us alle finde
As any Troian is, and eek as kinde."
V. 124-26.

"E non crediate che ne' greci amore
Non sia, assai più alto e più perfetto
Che tra 'Troiani; e 'l vostro gran valore,
La gran beltà e l'angelico aspetto
Troverà qui assai degno amadore." *Fil.*
VI, 22.

"Comaundeth me, how sore that me
smerte." V, 132.

"Ne refusez le mien homage.
Tel cuer prenez e tel corage
Que mei prengiez a chevalier:
Leial ami e dreiturier
Vos serai mais d'ore en avant
A toz les jorz de mon vivant."
R. de T. 13555-56.

"And if I may your harmes not redresse,
I am right sory for your hevinesse." V.
138-39.

"Metrai mon cors en mout grant peine
. . . .
Si metrai tel confort en vos
Dont vostre cors sera joios."
R. de T. 13576, 13579-580.

"O god of love in sooth we serven bothe.
And, for the love of god, my lady free,
Whom so ye hate, as beth not wreth
with me.
For trewely, ther can no wight yow
serve,
That half so looth your wrath the wolde
deserve." V, 143-47.

"Come il destruient voz amis
E la terre dont estes nez,
E qui voz tres granz heritez,
Voz richeces, voz mananties.
E voz honors avez guerpies
Por estre povre e eissilliez.
Come iert ja mais vostre cuers liez,
Qui de tel uevre estes aidanz?
Vostre clers sens, li hauz, li granz,
Qu'est devenuz? Ou est alez?" *R.
de T.* 13690-99.

"Thus seyde I never er now to womman
born;
For god myn herte as wisly glade so,
I lovede never womman here-biforn
As paramours, ne never shal no mo.
And, for the love of god, beth not my fo;
Al can I not to yow, my lady dere,
Compleyne arighte, for I am yet to
lere." V, 155-61.

"Bele," fai seit Diomedès,
"Onques d' amer ne m' entremis,
N' amie n'oi ne fui amis;
Or sent qu' Amors vers vos me tire."
R. de T. 13526-29.

"Mainte pucele avrai veüe
E mainte dame coneüe:
Onc mais a rien ne fis priere

Vos en estes la premeraine,
Si seriez vos la dereraine."
  R. de T. 13561-566.

"For I have herd or this of many a
    wight,
Hath loved thing he never saugh his
    lyve." **V, 164-65.**

"Mais j' ai ol assez parler
Que gent qu' onc ne s' erent veü
Ne acointié ne coneü
  S' amoënt mout, c' avient adès."
  R. de T. 13522-25.

"Eek I am not of power for to stryve
Ayens the god of love, but him obeye
I wol alwey, and mercy I yow preye."
              V, 166-68.

"Amerai vos d' amor veraie,
Tant atendrai vostre manaie
Que vos avreiz de mei merci
E que me tendriez por ami."
  R. de T. 13655-658.

'But mighte me so fair a grace falle,
That ye me for your servaunt wolde
    calle."**V. 172-73.**

"Pregovi dunque . . . .
. . . .
E me . . . .
Qual si conviene a vostra signoria,
In servidor prendiate. *Fil.* VI, 25.

176-189.   C.   The poet's chief source in this passage is the *R. de T.*
13617-618, 13637-640, 13676-678, 13706-708, according to Professor
Young, whose belief would, of course, be supported further by the
additional parallels I have just pointed out.

190-231.   *Fil.* V, 14-21.

232-245.   *Fil.* V, 25, 21.   Rossetti attributes less than half of this
passage to *Fil.*, but the sources of other lines can also be found in the
Italian text.   Cf. especially 239 with *Fil.* IV, 154-55.

246-73.   *Fil.* V, 26-28.   Lines 267-73 repeat, in the comment of
the author, the theme of the preceding stanza.

274-79.   C.   This description of the dawn Skeat attributes to
Boethius, *Cons.* II, met. 3, 1, 2.

280-82.   *Fil.* V, 22.

283-87.   C.   Observe that, as ever, where Boccaccio merely states
a fact, Chaucer furnishes also the reason for the fact.   In the *Fil.*
V, 22, we read

"Pandar non era il dì potuto andare
A lui, ne alcun altro, onde il mattino
Venuto, tosto sel fece chiamare."

But Chaucer explains that Pandarus is unable to come because he is
obliged to be in conference all day with Priam.

288-297.   *Fil.* V, 22-23.   Only three lines are translated, but the
others are reminiscent of earlier scenes of Troilo's grief.

298-329. C. The instructions given by Troilus to Pandarus as to the disposal of his property after his death, the bequest of his horse and armour to Mars, etc., are probably touches derived from Boccaccio's *Teseide* rather than from Statius, as Dr. Wise would have us believe (pp. 21-22). Teseo pledges arms to Mars, *Tes.* II, 61, and Arcita does likewise, *Tes.* VII, 28. The funeral pyre of which Troilus discourses, 302-305, is, no doubt, suggested to Chaucer by the scenes attending Arcita's funeral, *Tes.* XI; and the gathering of his ashes and putting them in an urn of gold, requested by the Trojan prince, is a touch due very likely to the action of Egeo, who in the *Tes.* (XI, 58) reverently gathers the ashes of Arcita and puts them in "un' urna d'oro."

The origin of the owl, Ascaphilo, 316-322, is not easily determined.

330-64. *Fil.* V, 29-32. Lines 337-350 merely repeat the theme of 330-36.

365-85. C. Credit, however, for the suggestion of the futility of trying to interpret dreams must be assigned to *Fil.* V, 32. I can hardly agree with Koeppel that lines 365-68 come from the *Rose* 18709, ff., for the passage he quotes has no bearing upon the idea of interpretation by priests of revelations made in dreams.

386-693. *Fil.* V, 33-38, 40-62, 67, 69, 68, 70, 71; VI, 1, 6. Lines 547-53 repeat the contents of 539-46, and lines 624-30 those of 617-23. The astrology of 655-58 is Chaucer's, as well as the allusion to Phaeton, 662-65.

694-707. C. In this passage the poet very skillfully picks up the threads of *Troil.* IV, 1366-1414, and resumes the scheme of Criseyde to cajole her father through his covetousness. The able management of such details as this should raise Chaucer far above the suspicion of being merely a wearied translator in the Fifth Book of his poem, with much of his enthusiasm for the work gone.

708-743. *Fil.* VI, 1-6.

744-49. C. Dr. B. L. Jefferson, apparently correctly, attributes the origin of this passage to Boethius, *Cons.* V, pr. 6, 10-16.[1]

750-56. *Fil.* VI, 7.

757-63. C. Skeat attributes 763 to Boethius, *Cons.* III, pr. 2, 6-8.

764-798. *Fil.* VI, 8, 10, 11, 33. Rossetti does not assign the material of 778-84 to *Fil.* Much of it is, however, discoverable in *Fil.* V, 13, and VI, 10-11.

[1] Dr. Jefferson makes this assignment in a work now in preparation.

799-840. C. Recent discoveries of Professor R. K. Root demonstrate convincingly that the three descriptions of Diomede, Criseyde and Troilus, which Chaucer here inserts, are taken in large part from the *De Bello Trojano* of Joseph of Exeter.[1] Cf. lines 799-805, therefore, with Joseph's *History*, Bk. IV, 124-27; 806-26 with IV, 156-162; 827-40 with IV, 61-64.

841-847. *Fil.* VI, 9.

848-854. C. The hospitality furnished to Diomede by Criseyde is a Chaucerian touch.

855-945. *Fil.* VI, 12-25. The reference to Polimites, 938, however, is not found in the Italian poem.

946-52. C. Author's comment.

953-57. *Fil.* VI, 26-27.

958-966. C. Criseyde's sense of patriotism.

967-1001. *Fil.* VI, 28-31.

1002-1014. C. Professor Young assigns 1009-1014 to *R. de T.* 14983-85, 13673-75.

1015. *Fil.* VI, 32, line 8.

1016-22. C. Astrology.

1023-32. C. Cf. however 1023-4,

> *Retorning in hir soule* ay up and doun
> *The wordes* of this sodein Diomede.

with *Fil.* VI, 33,

> Le quai cose Griseida ne' suoi guai,
> Partito lui, *seco venne pensando,*
> D'accortarsi o fuggirsi dubitando.

1033-36. *Fil.* Not so assigned by Rossetti, but cf.

> *So wel he for him-selve spak and seyde,*
> *That alle hir sykes sore adoun he leyde.*
> And fynally, the sothe for to seyne,
> He refte hir of the grete of al hir peyne.

with *Fil.* VI, 34,

> Queste la fer raffreddar nel pensiero
> Caldo ch'avea di voler pur reddire:
> Queste piegaro il suo, animo intero
> Che in ver Troilo aveva, ed il disire
> Torsono indietro, e 'l tormento severo
> Nuova speranza alquanto fe' fuggire:

[1] Professor Root's article, *Chaucer's Dares*, will appear shortly in *Modern Philology*.

> E da queste cagion sommossa, avenne
> Che la promessa a Troilo non attenne.

1037-39. *R. de T.* 15046-47, 14238-276.

1040-41. *Fil.* VIII, 9-10. We have here the record of the gift of the brooch, which is recorded only once by Boccaccio, in a correspondingly later passage of *Fil.*

1042-43. *R. de T.* Professor Young assigns these lines correctly to 15102-4.

1044-85. *R. de T.* Professor Young shows us, pp. 125-136, that these lines contain many adaptations from the *R. de T.* Cf. the following lines of the French work: 20194-271, 20228-308.

1086-1110. C. Lines 1086-99 contain author's comment. Two lines, 1100-1101, come from *Fil.* VII, 1. In 1107-1110 Chaucer describes a sunrise with classical allusions.

1111-1365. *Fil.* VII, 1-16, 18-33, 37, 40, 43, 41, 43, 48, 49-52, 74, 53-59.

1359-72. C.

1373-86. *Fil.* VII, 60-72.

1387-93. C. The appeal of Troilus, however, that Criseyde shall write to him is present in the *Fil.* VII, 70-72.

1394-1439. *Fil.* VII, 73, 75, 73, 76, 105, 77.

1440-42. C.

1443-49. *Fil.* VII, 24-27. Rossetti does not make this assignment, but this resumption of the dream of Troilus, no less than the previous account of it in 1240-53, should be accredited to the Italian passage.

1450-1519. C. A very notable passage. Chaucer deftly substitutes the divination of Cassandra for the painful altercation which takes place between that lady and Troilo in *Fil.* VII, 86-102.

The material describing the Calydonian Hunt, 1464-84, was derived by Chaucer possibly from Ovid's *Metamorphoses*, Lib. VIII, 260-546; possibly from Boccaccio's *Genealogiis*,[1] Lib. IX, cap. 15, cap. 19.

Lines 1485-1519, which are omitted in two manuscripts of *Troil.* (viz.—*Rawl.* and *Harl. 2392*) present a summary of the *Thebaid* of Statius.

The interpretation of Troilus's dream, now transferred to Cassandra's mouth, 1513-19, is the same as that of *Fil.* VII, 27, which was previously employed in part by Chaucer in *Troil.* V, 1247-1253. Rossetti very properly attributes it to *Fil.*

---

[1] The best Latin edition of this work is as follows: Boccaccio, Giovanni: *Genealogiae cum demonstrationibus arborum designatis et cet.* Venice, 1511.

1520-33. C. Troilus's rebuke to Cassandra comes from *Fil*. VII, 89 ff.; but the excuse for the upbraiding is changed in Chaucer's poem. In *Fil*. the malign prophetess taunts Troilo for loving the low-born Griseida; in *Troil*. she angers her brother by her correct interpretation of the dream.

For the allusion to Alcestis, 1527-33, cf. Boccaccio's *Genealogiis*, Lib. XIII, cap. 1.

1534-40. C. But cf. *Fil*. VII, 102, 104, and particularly 80, where Troilo is described rising with sudden vigour.

1541-47. C. A passage influenced by Boethius, *Cons*. IV, pr. 6, 75-77. Skeat assigns 1541-44 to Boethius, *Cons*. IV, pr. 6, 75-77.

1548-61. C. Lines 1558-61, however, describing the death of Hector at the hand of Achilles, come from the *R. de T*. 16166-16177.

1562-89. *Fil*. VIII, 1-5.

1590-1631. C. The letter written at this time by Criseyde is found only in Chaucer's text. But we know that in some way, and Chaucer would suppose that that way consisted in letter-writing, Griseida communicated at this time with Troilo in Boccaccio's poem. See *Fil*. VIII, 5-6.

1632-1764. *Fil*. VIII, 6, 7, 5, 7-18, 21, 17, 19-26. A few unimportant lines are Chaucer's.

1765-99. C. But Chaucer's epilogue of warning and apology to ladies and his injunction to his little book must be compared with Boccaccio's injunctions to his "canzon . . . pietosa" to go and present itself to his lady, "Fiammetta," or Maria d'Acquino, in *Fil*. IX.

1800-1806. *Fil*. VIII, 8, 27-29.

1807-27. *Tes. IX*., 1-3.

1828-48. C.

1849-55. *R. de T*. 13771-3, 21679-683, 21698-706. See Young, pp. 120-21.

1856-62. C. The poet's address to the moral Gower.

1863-65. Dante, *Paradiso* XIV, 28-30.

1866-69. C.

N. B. It must of course be remembered that Rossetti's parallels between *Fil*. and *Troil*. were arranged with the *Harl. MS 3943*. The two stanzas of Book V, of *Troil*., wherein the soul of Troilus, freed from its habiliments of flesh, looks back from Heaven and holds for all vanity "this litel spot of earth," found in other MSS, originate, we recall, in the *Teseide*, IX, 1-3.

B. *Chaucer's Increase upon Situations in the Narrative of Filostrato*

From the foregoing notes on the sources of *Troil.* various facts become evident. In the first place, it is perceived that Chaucer's dependence upon Boccaccio's work is really far greater than one would suppose from an examination of Rossetti's work. There are indications at almost every turn of the advantage which Chaucer had and used in his development of both the plot and characterization of the romance. We discover him using elements of Boccaccio's poem, in passages of his own, in positions correspondingly much later or much earlier than their positions in *Fil.* He is able to characterize Troilus at any point, not merely by drawing upon the particular section of the Italian original in use there, but by drawing upon the conception of the whole character of the young knight, which he had obtained through a completed reading of *Fil.* In a word, we find in Chaucer's *Troilus* at any moment the fusion of the poet's general conception of Troilo with his particular concept of any one act or trait of the latter. Troilus is, at such a time, the complete, plus the particular, Troilo. The same remark holds true of Chaucer's Criseyde and of his Pandarus. With all three figures there are associated certain elements of character portrayal, certain fragments of dialogue or soliloquy, as the result of Chaucer's anticipation of future scenes or of his reflection over the totality of effect in Troilo, Griseida, or Pandaro. The poet has, then, the advantage over his precursor, Boccaccio, of being able to rationalize any given action of any one of his characters in accordance, not only with the few traits of them he has hitherto presented in *Troil.*, but with what he remembers to have been the *ensemble* of the characteristics of each in *Fil.*

As a concrete instance of Chaucer's tendency to use elements of *Fil.*, in correspondingly earlier passages of *Troil.*, the first approaches of Diomede to Criseyde may be cited (V, 106-175). As the wary Greek leads the lady to her father's tent, he makes advances to her in words, which, in the Italian poem, are employed on the occasion of his later visit to Griseida. Numerous other instances of such changes as this made by Chaucer might be pointed out.

A second fact of significance becomes evident on a closer observation of the notes I have submitted. Boccaccio is no longer to be credited with having furnished Chaucer with only one third of the materials for *Troil.* In various ways the greater indebtedness of Chaucer to him was detected. Not only did the latter use more lines of the

Italian poem than Rossetti paralleled, but he used many of the lines of the work two or three times. Frequently he translated a stanza rather literally by one stanza, and then appended another stanza, repeating the same thought in slightly changed language.

Rossetti's method of tabulation cannot, therefore, adequately set forth Chaucer's indebtedness to Boccaccio. Thorough as the scholar's work is, it is yet another example of the futility of mathematical tabulation. Such a method can never hope for any final success in determining the influence of one poet over another. Nor can such a method ever account for the many ideas of one author employed by another, though not involved in the mechanical process of translation.

However many lines of his poem Chaucer may have derived from Benoit or Boethius or from other sources, the truth yet remains that, for the body of *Troil.*, Chaucer is under obligations to Boccaccio and to Boccaccio only, or, as he himself supposed, to "myn auctor called Lollius." That cosmos cannot be reckoned by number. It contains an essence that can be interpreted only by spirit. We have, after all, in *Troil.* the problem of the reaction of the spirit of Chaucer, expressing itself largely in a philosophical manner, upon the spirit of Boccaccio, which reveals itself mainly in the vein of romantic idealization.

To study the reaction of these two forms of spirit is the prime duty of the critic who interests himself in *Troil.* Its effects upon the general technique of the poem, upon narrative, upon action, upon characterization, upon the poem's philosophical or moral ideals only are subjects worthy of consideration. Furthermore it should be the aim of the critic to discover how much of the atmosphere of *Fil.* Chaucer retains or discards, or what changes he creates in its atmosphere, in the English poem.

I shall first compare, in several very concrete instances, the more synthetic method of Boccaccio's workmanship with the more analytical method of Chaucer's. We have already seen in our notes the tendency of Chaucer to analyse and increase upon a situation, a thought, or a trait of character as suggested by Boccaccio.

This form of increase may be first observed in a few details presented in Chaucer's account of the vicissitudes of Criseyde.

We behold the lady on her knees, craving mercy of Hector, just after her father's desertion from Troy has become known, and we realize the insecurity of Criseyde among her father's indignant fellow citizens. Hector very courteously assures her that she may remain

unharmed in Troy, and otherwise comforts her. This scene occurs
in both *Fil*. I, 12-13, and the *Troil*. I, 106-123. The pleas of Criseyde
and the kindly responses of Hector present Chaucer with the idea of
making his Hector especially solicitous for the welfare of Criseyde.
Hence it is that, when she is, later, apparently endangered by the
reported machinations of Poliphete (*Troil*. II, 1465-67), Chaucer
informs his readers of the very high esteem in which the lady is held
by Hector (*Troil*. II, 1450-56). When much later on in the poem
the Greeks, prompted by Calcas, demand the exchange of Criseyde,
Hector again evinces his friendliness toward the lady in ardent
opposition to the overture.

> "Sires, she nis no prisoner," he seyde;
> "I noot on yow who that this charge leyde,
> But, on my part, ye may eft-sone him telle,
> We usen here no wommen for to selle." (IV, 179-82)

So it is that, in scenes entirely of his own invention, Chaucer makes
use of elements, such as the friendship of Ettore for Griseida, found
in *Fil*.

That Pandaro is himself in the throes of passionate love we learn
from Boccaccio. Troilo demands querulously of his friend,

> ". . . . . .come avuto
> Da te l'avrei, che sempre te doglioso
> Per amor vidi, e non ten sai atare?
> Me dunque come credi sodisfare?" (II, 9)

and Pandaro rejoins,

> "Io ho amato sventuratamente,
> Ed amo ancora per lo mio peccato;
> E ciò avvien, perchè celatamente
> Non ho, siccome tu, altrui amato.
> Sarà che Dio vorrà; ultimamente,
> L'amore ch' io t' ho sempre mai portato,
> Ti porto e porterò, nè giammai fia
> Chi sappia che da te detto mi sia." (II, 11)

At another time in Boccaccio's poem we find Pandaro again speaking
of his love.

> "Lasciagli a me e questi e gli altri guai,
> C'ho sempre amato, e mai un guatamento
> Non ebbi da colei che mi disface,
> E che potrebbe sola darmi pace." (IV, 47)

Upon these suggestions of Pandaro's own lingering passion **Chaucer** builds several passages. (*Troil.* I, 715-721; II, 50-63; II, 1096-99) In these a quite sentimental Pandarus is exhibited to us, who at one time is so affected by the malady of love, in the month of May, that he resorts to his bed in woe and spends the night in making "many a wente." It is really a charming picture, that of the Pandarus, who is so often characterized as an unscrupulous worldling, reduced himself by the sweetness of the May to romantic grief. At another time he is almost as charming. While he is on his way to Criseyde with one of Troilus's letters, we find him trying the efficacy of "japes" to quiet the smart of the emotions which beset him,

> ". . . . . .y-wis, myn herte,
> So fresh it is, al-though it sore smerte,
> I may not slepe never a Mayes morwe;
> I have a joly wo, a lusty sorwe."   (II, 1096-99)

Such are the scenes Chaucer devises from Pandaro's loving "sventuratamente."

The jealousy of Troilus is another striking example of Chaucer's development of suggestions. In *Fil.* Troilo several times manifests his jealousy, but always with a rather brief expression of it. Early in the Italian poem we find him possessed of an unspeakable grief in the fear

> "Che Griseida non fosse d'altro amore
> Presa, e per quello lui vilipendendo
> Ricever nol volesse a servidore."   (I, 49)

Later Pandaro appeals to Griseida to love and have compassion upon Troilo because the latter's sorrow, now combined with jealousy, is torturing him almost beyond endurance.

> ". . . . . .non sai tu quanto rea
> Vita si trae con esso amor languendo,
> Nella qual sempre convien che si stea
> In pianti, ed in sospiri, ed in dolendo?
> Avendo poi per giunta gelosia,
> Che peggio è assai che non è morte ria."   (II, 75)

In *Fil.* IV, 139-145 the prince indulges his grief over the future absence of Griseida between fits of protestations of his love and of jealous fears that Calcas will never permit his daughter to return to Troy, but will insist that she make a marriage among the Greeks. In *Fil.* VII, 18, Troilo's jealousy is in open flame,

". . . . . e 'l nemico
Spirto di gelosia gravoso affanno
Più ch' alcun altro e di posa mendico."

From these brief instances of jealousy in the Italian work Chaucer
takes warrant for the false statement of Pandarus to Criseyde that
Troilus is jealous of Horaste (III, 796-98), which results in the long
dialogue, filled with rebukes and apologies, between the lady and her
lover in the house of Pandarus (III, 796-1175). And, in addition,
the poet is enabled by the assistance of these details to produce the
scenes of *Troil.* Book V, wherein Troilus's jealousy is further and
genuinely manifested.

The shrewd insight of Chaucer into the potentiality of a brief
literary suggestion is nowhere better examplified than in his development of the avarice of Boccaccio's Calcas. Griseida informs Troilo
that her father is old and miserly, "vecchio ed avaro," and has left
in Troy property, which, she will assure him, can be better protected
if he allows her to return to the city, and she is confident that

". . . . . .el per avarizia
Della mia ritornata avrà letizia." (IV, 136)

Upon this assertion of Griseida that she will induce her father to let
her return to take care of his interests in Troy, Chaucer constructs a
passage six stanzas in length (IV, 1373-1414). His Criseyde is made
to enlarge very much upon the measures she will use to cajole Calcas
in order that she may obtain permission to come and secure for him
the "moeble" which she has been obliged to leave behind her in the
city. Trusting implicitly in the disposition of men to "spenden
part, the remenaunt for to save," and in the ability of humankind to
"grave . . . with gold . . . the herte . . . of him that set is upon coveityse" (1377-78), the subtle lady promises to persuade her
father that the property she brings with her is only an insignificant
part of the possessions to acquire which his friends would be glad to
help him. All that is necessary is that he permit her to return as an
intercessor for him (1380-86). Furthermore, she will insist to her
father that in the event of the establishment of peace, through the
influence of her friends at court, she can procure the restoration of
Calcas to the royal favor (1387-93). "Desyr of gold," she is sure,
"shal so his sowle blende" (1399), that, wearied at last by her constant
plucking at his sleeve and her insisting that "goddes speken in amphi-
bologyes . . . and tellen twenty lyes" (1406-7), he will begin to discount the value of Apollo's prophecies concerning the destruction of

the Trojan city (1410). Once the seer is converted to his daughter's views, Troilus may expect the speedy return of Criseyde. Such is the elaborate play of cajolery, devised for the canny Criseyde by Chaucer from two or three meagre expressions of *Fil.*, "avaro," "ciò che . . . s' egli l' ha caro," and "per avarizia."

It is interesting also to note the use of the "fermaglio" or "fibbi-aglio," which it is recorded in *Fil.* VIII, 9-10, Troilo had given to Griseida. Boccaccio presents no account of the occasion when the gift was made to the lady, but simply describes to us the scene when Troilo discovers that his favour has disloyally been handed over to Diomede. Chaucer, on the other hand, creates three scenes out of the gift. Just after her union with Troilus Criseyde presents him with a brooch set with a heart-shaped ruby (III, 1370-72); later Criseyde gives to Diomede a brooch which Troilus had presented to her (V, 1040-41); and subsequently it is recorded by Chaucer that Troilus had given her this brooch as a pledge of remembrance on the day of her departure from Troy (V, 1660-65).

Chaucer's use of the *cinghiar* in Troilo's dream, at the feet of which the youth seems to behold Griseida lying (*Fil.* VII, 23), is also notable. The Italian poet merely presents the dream (*Fil.* VII, 24), and Troilo's own interpretation of it as an omen, indicating not only that his lady is untrue to him, as Chaucer's Troilus interprets it (V, 1247-60), but also that she has actually transferred her love to Diomede,

"Questo *cinghiar* ch' io vidi è Diomede,
Perocchè l' avulo uccise il cinghiaro
Di Calidonia, se si può dar fede
A nostri antichi, e sempre poi portaro
Per soprasegna." (VII, 27)

The English poet postpones the interpretation of the dream of Troilus until the time of Cassandra's conversation with him (V, 1450-1519), and then has the prophetess, not Troilus himself, expound it. In her explanation of it the poet takes the opportunity to tell the whole story of the boar, or *cinghiar*, and the famous Calydonian Hunt, with a complete history of the family of Diomede. Again, from the terse suggestion of *Fil.*, Chaucer constructs a brilliant scene. In the epic manner a classic prophetess narrates a series of great events, much as Vergil's Aeneas reviews the history of the fall of Troy in the court of Dido; and then finally she consents to interpret the vision of her brother Troilus.

Such, then, are the illustrations of the ability of Chaucer to analyse and expand or change the material furnished him by Boccaccio. Others could be cited if there was any necessity for the enlarging of our evidences of Chaucer's manner of workmanship.

The analytical method of the English poet can be perceived, too, in other ways. Already it was pointed out in our notes that the number of words in a translated work always exceeds the number of words in the original. It is interesting to see this principle working itself out in *Troil.* Frequently two or three stanzas of Chaucer's *rhyme royal* grow out of one stanza of Boccaccio's *ottava rima*. Especially common is it for one stanza of *Fil.* to be translated by two stanzas in *Troil.* References to this phenomenon may be cited as follows:

Fil. I,	28	becomes	*Troil.* I,	288-301.
II,	13	"	I,	701-714.
II,	131	"	II,	1331-44.
III,	5	"	III,	239-52.
III,	50	"	III,	1506-19.
III,	70	"	III,	1695-1708.
IV,	44	"	IV,	358-371.
IV,	145	"	IV,	1506-1519.
IV,	167	"	IV,	1688-1701.
V,	32	"	V,	358-371.
V,	53	"	V,	540-53.
V,	60	"	V,	617-30.

Larger growths from the Italian lines should also be noted:

Fil. II,	69, line 1	becomes	*Troil.* II, 743-49.
II,	90, lines 3-6	"	II, 995-1001.
III,	16, " 1-4, 6-7	"	III, 386-99.
III,	44, " 1, 2, 5	"	III, 1443-49.
IV,	142, " 2, 3, 8, 4, 5		
	143, " 1, 8	"	IV, 1478-98.
	144, " 1		
V,	1, " 6-8		
	2, " 1-5	"	V, 22-35.
V,	25, " 1-4		
	21, " 3-5	"	V, 232-245.
V,	29, " 6-8		
	30, " 1-2, 5-6	"	V, 330-350.
	29, " 5,		

Such, then, are the methods of increase which Chaucer employs again and again in his work upon *Troil*. From a simple suggestion he builds an elaborate situation. If the more concise Boccaccio declares that the "pianti" or "sospiri" of any one of his characters were pitiful to hear, the analytical Chaucer makes their sighs or their grief vocable. Several stanzas of self-articulated sorrow in the *Troil*. make us, then, comprehend the piteous condition of Troilus or Criseyde or Pandarus. If Boccaccio tells us that Griseida went off into her room to peruse one of Troilo's letters, Chaucer more generously admits us to Criseyde's boudoir and we witness there her complete self-analysis. If Troilo exclaims "Oimè," Troilus is made to digress at length upon his sigh; if Pandaro shrewdly feels something "nel petto," Pandarus is permitted to inform both himself and us of the full contents of his feelings; if Diomede indulges in "argumenti seco," his Chaucerian counterpart is allowed to develop his arguments at length and to make us witness to them also.

On the whole, Boccaccio's presentation of dialogue or reverie in *Fil*. is more subjective than Chaucer's. In the Italian poem we are left often to read between the lines, for, strangely enough, Boccaccio is far from being as diffuse in *Fil*. as he is in numerous of his other works, such as the *Filocolo* or the *Teseide* or the *Ameto*. Chaucer's *Troil*. really grants us few such opportunities. The English poet is bent upon telling the whole story himself. There is indeed seldom a thought in his poem that is not made objective.

The forms of increase in Chaucer's work, upon which we have so far been making comment, are of course largely the result of unconscious or subconscious tendencies. They are immediate rather than predetermined. To avoid elaboration would have been an impossible feat for Chaucer. There are, however, forms of increase in *Troil*. which are of the most conscious and deliberate aim. These are included mainly in the improvisation by Chaucer of the scenes in the house of Deiphebus and the house of Pandarus, which lead to the final culmination of Troilus's and Criseyde's clandestine *amour*. To produce them Chaucer adds about 1450 lines to his poem (II, 1394-1757; III, 50-238, 288-329, 442-1309). But many, even of the minuter details of these lines, it will be remembered, were shown in our notes on the sources of *Troil*. to have had their inception in *Fil*.

So far our investigation has considered only Chaucer's additions or his changes in the Troilus story, as he derived it from its main source, *Fil*. It may now be well to consider in what respects

Chaucer's treatment of the narrative theme resembles Boccaccio's.

In the English version of the story of Troilus many new elements are introduced, to be sure, which tend to differentiate it from its Italian model. It is ornamented with classical allusions, invocations and astrology. It is filled with the philosophical ideas of Boethius in regard to Love, to mutability in fortune, and to predestination, and made still further sage by the introduction of proverbs and admonitions such as abound in the *Roman de la Rose*. Its historical details are, as it were, verified by references to the *Roman de Troie* and the works of Joseph of Exeter and Guido delle Colonne. One great scene in it, the Calydonian Hunt (V, 1464-1479) is probably borrowed from the classics. Yet the reader of *Troil.* and *Fil.* is aware of no really great difference in the two poems except that the one is in English, the other in Italian. Even the additions of such new episodes as Pandarus's fabrication of the measures which he claims Poliphete is about to take to injure Criseyde, the shrewd assignation at the house of Pandarus, and the prophecies of Cassandra do not postulate the existence of a materially different view-point in the English version. For the shorter one makes a statement of each of the two plots, the greater similarity, i. e., the nearer identity in essentials, one discovers in the two works. Still it must not be inferred that a resemblance in the two skeletons of the two narratives denotes an inherent resemblance in the general unity of effect in the two romances. To establish the theory of such a resemblance, other elements of technique, motivation in character and atmosphere, must be taken into consideration.

In the review of our notes on the sources of *Troil.* we perceived the tendency of Chaucer to analyse and increase upon a situation, a thought, or a trait of character, as suggested by Boccaccio. Let us examine this tendency more particularly in the last named respect of character.

C. *The Characterizations and Atmosphere of the Filostrato and of Troilus and Criseyde*

In interpreting the characters of *Troil.* and *Fil.* the critic must first of all be careful not to rationalize their inner psychological states by twentieth century standards. Nor must he judge their conduct by modern criteria of morality. He must remember rather that they are, in origin, creatures of the mediaeval realm of romance, retainers in the great Court of Love, related closely to the whole assemblage of characters in the romances of chivalry, akin to the knights and ladies of Arthur's court, to the chevaliers and *damoiseaux*, the *damoiselles* and the *amies* in the lays of Marie de France, to the blithe and languorous spirits that drift musically through the measures of the love poetry of Provence. Even in Chaucer the actions of Troilus or of Criseyde seldom belie their kinship. In the verses of a poet, whose tendency it was ever to convert romance into reality, they continue to linger on the borderland. Troilus with all his martial or even athletic prowess, remains the sentimental, plaintive devotee in Cupid's Court to the end; Criseyde with all her womanly *avysement*, her shrewdness, and sometimes practical trend in life, is not long other than the lissome damsel of the metrical romances.

Let us study, then, in order the four romantic figures which we find in the Italian and in the English poem, comparing Troilo with Troilus, Griseida with Criseyde, Pandaro with Pandarus, and Diomede with Diomede.

Troilo and Troilus

In his brief introduction to the recent edition of *Fil.* (*Bibliotheca Romanica*, 146, 147, 148, Heitz & Mündel, Strasburg) Paolo Savj-Lopez writes, "Troilo è il vero protagonista del poema. La stessa Griseida così profondamente descritta e seguíta nel breve periodo che precede la dedizione, è quasi abbandonata dal poeta quando in lei comincia il nuovo amore ad oscurare l'antico; perchè a dipingere la solitaria disperazione di Troilo basterà sapere che la sua diletta ha cessato d'amarlo. I suoi moti intimi sono ben altrimenti impetuosi e profondi che nel *Roman de Troie:* e qualche indizio ci fa ritenere che in ciò fosse presente al poeta il ricordo di Tristano. S' intrecciano inoltre più o meno precise le reminiscenze cavalleresche dell' amor cortese della Tavola Rotunda, e gli accenti derivati dai poeti del dolce stil nuovo o daile rime del Petrarca e di Cino. Così varia e complessa è adunque la passione di Troilo" (pp. 6-7). The commentator very correctly designates Troilo as the "protagonista" of Boccaccio's poem, and with no less discrimination assigns him his position in the romances of chivalry; but what is most significant about his comment is that, unlike the comment of many critics, especially of those whose temptation it is always to give Chaucer precedence over Boccaccio as a literary artist, it perceives the variety and complexity of Troilo's passion. And one other hint Signor Savj-Lopez gives us, as to the correct method of criticism to apply in a study of *Fil.* "Il descendere profondamente nell' intimo del cuore senz' aver riguardo al mondo esterno, la delicata analisi psicologica, l'assorbimento cieco nel solo pensiero amoroso ci appariscono dal *Filostrato* come novissimo esempio nella poesia narrativa d' Italia: ed in ciò sta l'essenza di un' originalità che mette il poema ben più in alto del suo modello francese" (p. 9). For *Fil.* not only presents romance; it presents a high order of psychology in the interpretation of southern character, the truth to life of which is indeed more than above that of the French romances, and certainly not on a lower plane than that of Chaucer's *Troil.*

Boccaccio's Troilo is a graceful figure. When first we behold him, the sweet irony of youth is luminous in his eye and revelling on his lips. He stands scornfully in the temple of Pallas, twitting his boon companions about the folly of their several passions, proudly posing himself as the sage and experienced bachelor now grown impervious to love, a veritable oracle.

> Che è a porre in donna alcuno amore?
> Che come al vento si volge la foglia,
> Così in un dì ben mille volte il core
> Di lor si volge, nè curan di doglia
> Che per lor senta alcun loro amadore,
> Nè sa alcuna quel ch'elle si voglia.
> O felice colui che del piacere
> Lor non è presso, e sassene astenere!   (I, 22)

But his show of high disdain is of brief duration. The vision of Griseida makes him a moment later the most adulatory lover in the court of Cupid. His pride, however, serves him in some good stead, and enables him to dissemble "in lieta vita—per lungo spazio" (I, 32) with his companions, before he is compelled to take refuge in his chamber, and kneel an abject before the throne of Love:

> E in verso Amore tal fiata dicea
> Con pietoso parlar: signore, omai
> L' anima è tua che mia esser solea,
> Il che mi piace, perciocchè tu m' hai.   (I, 38)

The more facetious his raillery has been, the more extravagant are now his sighs. Never a moment of respite can he enjoy, in the hours of his solitude, from the torment of his passion. His condition is all tears, lamenting, and apprehension. Only in the thick of battle can he assuage his grief, and dissembling can no longer keep the pallor from his face (See I, 47).

Henceforth his destiny is a sort of romantic clay to be molded by the hand of Pandaro, who is ready to manage his *amour* with all the finesse of an expert in the art of match-making. With such instruments as Troilo's reputation for valor (II, 42), his gallantry in jousts, his generous distribution of gifts, his delight in rich apparel (II, 84), his ability to write love letters, incomparable in their erotic beauty and expression of devotion (II, 96-106), it is really no hard task for his witty friend to bend the will of his cousin Griseida to favour the young knight's suit. And news of it affects Troilo as it always affects youth.

> E sì come la nuova primavera,
> Di frondi e di fioretti gli arboscelli,
> Ignudi stati in la stagion severa,
> Di subito riveste e fagli belli;
> I prati, e' colli, e ciascuna riviera
> Riveste d'erbe e di be' fior novelli,
> Così di nuova gioia tosto pieno,
> · Sì rise Troilo nel viso sereno.   (III, 12)

The two lovers are soon happy in one another's arms; and days of romantic exaltation follow for Troilo.

> Era contento Troilo, ed in canti
> Menava la sua vita e in allegrezza;
> L'alte bellezze e i vaghi sembianti
> Di qualunque altra donna nulla prezza,
> Fuor che la sua Griseida, e tutti quanti
> Gli altri uomin vivere in trista gramezza,
> A rispetto di sè, seco credeva;
> Tanto il suo ben gli aggradiva e piaceva.   (III, 72)

But with all his exuberant fancy Troilo is never at a loss, as he practices his discreet art of simulation in the presence of all who are not privy to his *innamoramento*. So trained a dissembler is he that, when in his father's council the ill news comes to him that Griseida must be exchanged for Antenor, he completely conceals his anguish by an equable exercise of his reason, and quietly withdraws (IV, 14-16). Wild and inconsolable as is his grief, he will indulge it only in the seclusion of his room or in the presence of his intimate, Pandaro. Before the inevitable he must needs bow, but it is only because he has the sacred, altruistic duty of shielding Griseida from reproach that he consents to do so.

> Poi temo di turbar con violenta
> Rapina, il suo onore e la sua fama.   (IV, 68)

He comports himself with dignity and resignation until the last
hour for his bliss with Griseida has come, but is no longer able to
control himself when the lady's unhappy swoon induces him to believe
that she lies cold in death before him.

> Ell' era fredda e senza sentimento
> Alcun, per quel che Troilo conscesse,
> E questo gli parea vero argomento
> Che ella i giorni suoi finiti avesse.   (IV, 119)

Then comes upon him the full flood of romantic emotion, conventional
but intense, and "con animo forte" his sword is drawn and he is ready

> . . . . di prender la morte,
> Acciocchè il suo spirto seguitasse
> Quel della donna si trista sorte,
> E nell' inferno con lei abitasse.   (IV, 120)

But Griseida recovers from her faint, and the hour of Troilo's complete dejection is postponed. The lady departs from Troy, and he is
left to weary days of impatient languishment, unable to find relief
in the song of birds or the beauty of

> Li fior dipinti. . . . .
> Ch' e' prati fan di ben mille colori (VII, 62-63),

and envying the mountains, the waves descending to the sea, near
which his mistress now dwells, without their ever comprehending how
sweet a privilege it is to have her presence there (VII, 64-56), and the
sun that every day can look upon her (VII, 66). With lofty pride
and loyalty he preserves his secret from all, until the prying and
censorious prophetess, his sister Cassandra, finally suspects the truth
and, with her contemptuous railing, forces him into a betrayal of it
(VII, 89-101).   In a burst of romantic fury he rejects the insinuations
of the vituperative scold, and leaps to the defence of Griseida.

> "Io non vo' ragionar della bellezza
> Di lei, ...
> . . . .
> Ma vegnam pure alla sua gentilezza.
> . . . .
> È gentilezza dovunque è virtute,
> Questo non negherà niuno che 'l senta,
> Ed elle sono in lei tutte vedute,
> Se dall' opra l' effetto s' argomenta."   (VII, 93-94)

And such is the high esteem he retains for her, until his unreasoning
faith must yield before the shameful truth revealed to him by the

golden brooch upon the captured garment of Diomede (VIII, 8-9). In the succeeding days his lot is but fatalistic apathy, to be dispelled only by relentless battle and ruthless slaughter, till the weapon of Achilles lays him low.   It is a dread picture, heavy with the weight of doom, that of the once chivalric, buoyant lover converted into the desperate warrior.

> L' ira di Troilo in tempi diversi
> A' greci nocque molto senza fallo,
> Tanto che pochi ne gli uscieno avversi
> Che non cacciasse morti da cavallo,
> Solo che l' attendesser, sì perversi
> Colpi donava; e dopo lungo stallo,
> Avendone già morti più di mille,
> Miseramente un dì l' uccise Achille.   (VIII, 27)

Turning from the figure of Troilo to Chaucer's Troilus, we find in him too a son of the south, temperamental, emotional, without a single phlegmatic trait in his nature, hardly less Italian than Boccaccio himself, and more Italian—if that is possible—than Shakespeare's Romeo, demonstrative in every ounce of his being, able only to keep one great secret, but able to dissimulate that with every inch of his supple young manhood.   He moves in a circle of demonstrative people.   Criseyde as well as Pandarus is more than possessed of that characteristic.   Diomede himself is quite susceptible to emotion. The sensibilities of all, despite their several individual characteristics of self-control, or subtlety, or cunning, or guile are as outwardly active as were the sensibilities of Elizabethan Englishmen—not modern Englishmen or Americans—as are the sensibilities of many a continental European of to-day.   It is the exception rather than the rule for Chaucer to satirize their emotions.   One must be on his guard not to read satire into situations—similar presentment of which to-day would create only the effect of burlesque—wherein the poet with his mediaeval view-point is really only permitting his characters to indulge their feelings as he must sometimes have indulged his own.

It is very early in the poem that Troilus is discovered in almost luxurious indulgence of his emotions.   We forget the disdain of the scorner who went to the temple "Palladiones feste for to holde" (*Troil.* I, 161), the valour, second only to Hector's, of the warrior wreaking slaughter upon the Greeks, the goodly manner of the figure on horse-back, passing Criseyde's window, even the fair courtesy of the chevalier, hawk in hand, escorting his lady out of Troy, as we behold, all mockery fled, the solitary youth sighing, groaning, dreaming, picturing in his mind the beauty of Criseyde, purposing ever to remain secret in his passion, seeking to allay his instinctive sorrow with a song, fully assenting "with good hope"

"Criseyde for to love, and nought repente";

for although we know that many of his sighs, his groans and his fancies (*Troil.* I, 365-623, etc.) were those too of Boccaccio and Boccaccio's creatures, Florio, Panfilo in the *Fiammetta*, and Troilo, and his song one that Petrarch had sung, we recognize in him the perennial spirit of all youth, buoyant in hope, abundant in fancy, and cruelly responsive to pain. Pity surges within us at the spectacle, not the pity we feel in the presence of a great and noble soul tragically defeated, but the pity urged upon us by the knowledge that beautiful things like this, beautiful youth, beautiful imagination must perish in their conflict with the callous universe. Subdued by the glamour of romance, we pardon Troilus for all the extravagant scenes which, we surmise, we are still to witness. For the nonce he tempts us to forget that Troilus is a hero whom "alle the Grekes as the deeth him dredde" (I, 483).

Nor is the reader disaffected when next he catches sight of the young Trojan, able by pretexts of fever to conceal his infatuation from others, yet in the solitude of his room well nigh mad for fear that Criseyde

. . . . .som wight had loved so,

That never of him she wolde have taken hede (I, 499-500),

and violently tearing his passion to tatters. Here after all is but a temperament, marked by an ability, which is almost universal with men, to sink as low in dejection as erstwhile it can soar on flights of joyous fancy.

Of such a character as Troilus passivity is inevitably a quality to be expected. No surprise will be occasioned by one's witnessing the decay of his resolution on absolute secrecy at all costs, when the cajolery of Pandarus comes to play upon it. Petulant retorts, the refusal to be consoled will soon yield, is the instinctive prophecy; the secret will not long remain undivulged, and Troilus will deliver himself passively into Pandarus's guidance. Such indeed the case proves to be.

But Troilus's passivity is not immediately evinced. For a time he resists the wheedling of Pandarus, giving him quip for quip, detecting and exposing the subtleties of his friend's arguments. When, in the end, he confesses his love for Criseyde, he does submit passively to

Pandarus, to be sure, but he submits with the abandon of a youth, who, fired with a great desire, hopes he may attain realization of it through the agency of his colleague. His passivity is that of the man who yields a point only in order to gain a benefit, however complete his dependence upon the initiative of Pandarus may subsequently appear.

There is little development in the character of this alternate reveller and timorous doubter during the progress of three books of *Troil*. He desponds, dissembles, and rejoices all in a moment. Success in the achievement of his *amour* by dint of some feigning of his own, more or less adroitly managed, and with the constant and loyal diligence of the scheming Pandarus, works no perceptible change within him. His cheer never assumes permanency. He continues to be the type of the romantic lover, proud, sensitive, somewhat self-centered, determined only upon the enjoyment of his own pleasure, and occasionally apprehensive as to its continuance.

In the Fourth Book, however, we become aware of qualities within him, consistent with the valour of the knight which we know him to possess. Present at the council, when the plans for the exchange of Criseyde and Antenor are made, despite the fervent objections of Hector, he contains a manly sorrow. The tragedy of having allowed his love to remain a clandestine one is brought full home upon him. He controls his grief, exercises his will-power and reason, moves with caution.

> But natheless, he no word to it seyde,
> Lest men sholde his affeccioun espye;
> With mannes herte he gan his sorwes drye.
>
> And ful of anguish and of grisly drede
> Abood what lordes wolde un-to it seye;
> And if they wolde graunte, as god forbede,
> Theschaunge of hir, than thoughte he thinges tweye,
> First, how to save hir honour, and what weye
> He mighte best theschaunge of hir withstonde;
> Ful faste he caste how al this mighte stonde.
>
> (IV, 152-61)

Although Love urged him to immediate action, reason urged quiet measures and deliberation, and reason won. There follows inevitably that revulsion of feeling which always occurs, when reason prevails over an impulse to indulge the will in its pleasure or to preserve to one's enjoyment a supreme treasure. Never so profound and so absolute had been the grief of Troilus, as it is now, when behind closed doors and windows he delivers himself over to it. Fortune, Cupid, his own "wery goost," obstinate in its refusal to flee forth from his heart, he arraigns in turn. His very eyes fall under his objurgations.

> O wofulle eyen two, sin your disport
> Was al to seen Criseydes eyen brighte,
> What shal ye doon but, for my discomfort,
> Stonden for nought, and wepen out your sighte?
> Sin she is queynt, that wont was yow to lighte,
> In veyn fro-this-forth have I eyen tweye
> Y-formed, sin your vertue is a-weye. (IV, 309-15)

To comfort such a man is an impossible task. Even the resilient, effervescent Pandarus, in the presence of such a sorrow, perceives all his efforts must dissolve into impotency. Once he has hasted on his errand to encourage his hapless friend, who quietly retired from the council, and has obtained entrance to the room of Troilus, he melts into genuine "tendreliche" tears. Pale of hue, he speaks his unavailing counsel, knowing that his advice to the prince not to repine at the caprice of Fortune, not to forget that, unlike himself, he had known the full enjoyment of his love, to remember that the town is full of ladies and, above all, the proverb,

> The newe love out chaceth ofte the olde (IV, 415)

—that none of these measures can ever hope to be adopted by such a despondent but loyal lover as Troilus.

> Thise wordes seyde he for the nones alle,
> To helpe his friend, lest he for sorwe deyde.
> For doutelees, to doon his wo to falle,
> He roughte not what unthrift that he seyde.
>   (IV, 428-31)

Troilus at last answers, argument for argument, expounding his love. With consummate judgment he rejects the last futile suggestion of Pandarus to "ravisshe" Criseyde from the city, or to request her of his father. Parliament, in its high place of authority, "hath hir eschaunge enseled" and Priam "nil for me his lettre be repeled" (IV, 559-60), and the lover is conscious he must needs abide content. There can be no kicking against the pricks, no changing of the laws of the Medes and Persians.

With resignation there creeps into the character of Troilus a new note of altruism. He thinks no longer entirely of his own comfort. He knows that to save the honour of Criseyde he must remain inactive, and gradually he perceives that Criseyde's sorrow may prove as infinite as his own. The swoon, and apparent death of his despairing mistress, prompts him to self-slaughter—as all truly romantic lovers are prompted under similar circumstances—but after the bitterness of that experience he becomes more considerate.   Fearful though he is that Criseyde shall "seen so many a lusty knight among the Grekes" (IV, 1485-6), he yet realizes, after her departure, the comfortlessness of her position in the Greek camp.

> "Who can conforten now your hertes werre?
> Now I am gon, whom yeve ye audience?
> Who speketh for me right now in myn absence?
> Allas, no wight, and that is al my care;
> For wel wot I, *as yvel as I ye fare.*"   (V, 234-8)

In the anxious days of romantic yearning, of southern-tempered apostrophes to gates and palaces, once hallowed by Criseyde's presence, and of sad premonitory dreams, his thought is ever of the lady's constancy.   Of guileless, unsuspecting temperament, he deceives himself to the end with false hopes.   Criseyde's wisdom is to be commended; she will not arouse the curiosity of idlers by riding into the city by day, but softly in the night she will come (V, 1151-54).   Even his vision of the boar, and Cassandra's interpretation of it, fail to shatter his belief in Criseyde's loyalty.   Furiously he retorts to the "sorceresse,"

> "Thou wenest been a greet devyneresse;
> Now seestow not this fool of fantasye
> Peyneth hir on ladyes for to lye?"   (V, 1522-4)

The loyalty and love of Criseyde he knows are as finely tempered as were those of Alcestis,

> ". . . . . .of creatures, but men lye
> That ever weren, kindest and the beste."   (V, 1528-9)

And even, when at last the fatal truth is revealed to him by the brooch upon the coat, reft by Deiphebus from Diomede, he cannot long upbraid the faithless woman.   His sorrow, unspeakable though it is, is not wholly for himself.   "Allas," he cries,

> ". . . . . . .your name of trouthe,
> Is now for-doon, and that is al my routhe."   (V, 1686-7)

Although she is now proved disloyal, he cannot cease to love her.

> "Ye han me cast, and I ne can nor may,
> For al this world, with-in myn herte finde
> To unloven yow a quarter of a day."   (V, 1696-8)

And the very last time he moves his lips in the presence of Chaucer's readers he sighs,

". . . . . .Criseyde, swete may,
Whom I have ay with al my might y-served,
That ye thus doon, I have it nought deserved." (V, 1720-2)

To pose this sensitive, buoyant figure as a hero would of course be folly; but to pose him as an imaginative, a great and a loyal lover is a more than justifiable endeavour. In him, as in Boccaccio's Troilo, is all the sweet plaintiveness of love, all the devotion of a faithful servant in the Court of Love, all the dignity of romance, no more, no less!

Griseida and Criseyde

Boccaccio's Griseida is a figure hardly less graceful than his Troilo, neither less conventional nor less romantic. So fair is her carriage, as she enters upon our view, that we immediately suspect that her outward charms will be accompanied by inner spiritual graces.

Sì bella e sì angelica a vedere
Era, che non parea cosa mortale,
Griseida nomata, al mio parere
Accorta, savia, onesta e costumata
Quanta altra che in Troia fosse nata. (I, 11)

And so winsome is her modesty (VI, 26), so unaffected her expression of patriotism (VI, 27), and so simple her admission to Diomede that, after victory has decided one way or another the fate of Troy, she will know better "che farmi" (VI, 31), when last we see her in *Fil.*, that we can in little measure realize how frail and inconstant a creature she is soon to prove herself. Instinctively we are grateful to Boccaccio for not having exhibited her to us in her shame and disloyalty.

She is a rare combination of modesty and abandon, at one moment blushing like a morning rose (II, 38), and at another wantonly giving herself over to the most erotic of passion with a jest upon her lips (III, 31). She is as gracious in her courtesy (III, 28) as she is merry in her laughter (II, 35-36). In Troy she is universally loved,

. . . .e da ciascuno amata
Che la conobbe fu ed onorata. (I, 15)

With discretion and caution she receives through Pandaro the advances of Troilo (II, 50, 51, 65, 66, 82, 84, 140, etc.), but at the same time with a quite precipitate welcome (II, 78). Her wavering is but brief. Adept at feigning though she is, she cannot control the instant palpitation of her heart as she reads the letter of Troilo, but delivers herself over to her infatuation with a wild admixture of yearning and joy (II, 115-117). The clever woman, who with a pertinent, penetrating query, "Che vuol dir codesto?" (II, 37), a "Now what does he mean by that?"—can bring an immediate halt to the flattery on Pandaro's lips, and bring him to confess the purpose of his errand, is no match at all for the attack made by Amor upon her heart. She has early surrendered herself to Troilo's arms, and become a devotee in Cupid's court.

> Griseida seco facea il simigliante,
> Di Troilo parlando nel suo core;
> E seco lieta di sì fatto amante,
> Grazie infinite ne rendea ad Amore:
> E parle ben mille anni che davante
> A lei ritorni il suo vago amatore,
> E ch' ella il tenga in braccio e baci spesso,
> Come la notte avea fatto d' appresso. (III, 55)

But Griseida is not merely a character who makes a show of feminine reserve, and then passively submits. Her nature is not sheer fragility. When unhappiness approaches, she is prepared to play her part with dignity. Overcome with sorrow though she is at the ill news that she must part from Troy and leave her Troilo there, so cruelly affected by her agony that, her system collapsing before it, she swoons away (IV, 117), it is yet she who henceforth takes the master hand in the affairs of herself and Troilo. She is confident that she can so skillfully manipulate her father's avarice as to obtain for herself a speedy reunion with Troilo in Troy (IV, 133-6). And momentarily she can allay the grief of Troilo (IV, 137-8).

The day for parting comes, and she passes quietly to the possession of her father,

> Pure a Troilo avendo fermo il core (V, 14)

There, in the Greek camp, follows a season of loneliness; her nights are consumed in tears which she dare not reveal in the day, and the colour fades from her cheeks (VI, 1). In fervent apostrophes she turns to the unresponding towers and palaces of Troy (VI, 4-7), and she watches with apathy the advances of her new lover, Diomede (VI, 8-13), all unsuspecting of his cunning.

> Dell' astuzia di lui non s' accorgea. (VI, 13)

Gently, all too gently, she refuses his approaches for a time (VI, 26-31); and then we see her no more.

The problem of the temperament of Chaucer's Criseyde is not so readily solved. Yet, notwithstanding, it presents really no Gordian knot for solution. She is not so simple nor so direct as are generally the heroines of mediaeval romance, but it is a mistake to regard her as complex.

As the name of Troilus spells romantic emotion, so hers spells the weakness and loveliness of woman. The lissomeness of the ladies of the Breton lays of Marie de France clings to her, the perfume of chivalric courts breathes about her. In her person are vested all the conventional mediaeval ideals of feminine beauty.

> Nas noon so fair, for passing every wight
> So aungellyk was hir natyf beautee,
> That lyk a thing inmortal semed she,
> As doth an hevenish parfit creature,
> That doun were sent in scorning of nature.   (I, 101-5)

And her beauty seldom varies from this ideal mould, as we catch glimpses of her fleeting through the pages of the poet. Within her soul, Chaucer seldom lets us forget, dwell

> Honour, estat, and wommanly noblesse.   (I, 287)

Through the "pure wyse of here meninge" (I, 285) we are given every opportunity to "gesse" her inward beauty. The sincerity of Pandarus's encomiums in her favour needs no questioning,

> For of good name and wysdom and manere
> She hath y-nough, and eek of gentilesse.   (I, 880-1)

Bounteous she is, of gracious and friendly speech, possessed of a heart, in comparison with which

> A kinges herte semeth . . . a wrecche.   (I, 889)

To read into such a temperament too much subtlety is precarious. Some of it is there. No one should question that fact, but, after all, it is the subtlety of the lady brilliant in repartee rather than that of the designing woman. We discover as soon as we enter her "paved parlour" and observe her rise from amidst her maids to greet her uncle, Pandarus, that she is fond of persiflage. To his facetious query concerning the book of the *Sege of Thebes*,

> "Is it of love? O, som good ye me lere!"   (II, 98),

she makes an immediate teasing rejoinder.

> " 'Uncle,' quod she, 'your maistresse is not here.' "   (II, 99)

From the laugh in which both join at once we know that there has been earlier rallying between these two. So intimate are they that it has become a delight to them to talk in innuendo. They can have

their little jokes at one another's expense, and no outsider be the wiser
for it.   For such a past-master of repartee to dissemble is an instinct.
Simulation is bound to affect almost her every mood.   It penetrates
her sentimental desire to spend her "widewes lyf" reading "on holy
seyntes lyves" (II, 118), it cloaks her curiosity with a down-cast eye,
it makes possible for her the interchange of "freendly tales" and
"mery chere" (II, 149).   Pandarus, clever sophist as he is, knows
how to meet it with his own adroit dissembling, and how, through
it, to whet her curiosity until she even believes that she is wheedling
a secret out of him.

But once the secret of Troilus's passion is known to her, the sentimentalist in her nature becomes uppermost again.   She is fain to cry
out upon the uncle who advises her to love again, the nearest of her
relatives and the best of her friends, who ought to curb in her all
amorous desires! .

>"When he, that for my beste freend I wende,
>Ret me to iove, and sholde it me defende?"   (II, 412-3)

It is only the tenderness of the mediaeval lady of romance that
finally dissipates her reserve.   No woman of such a realm could resist
the plea of tears.   But, with the realization that she will yield to the
love of Troilus, her faculty for simulation urges again within,

>"It nedeth me ful sleyly for to pleye."   (II, 462)

Thereafter she proves her capacity for playing the game.   And
she plays it, not as the simple love-struck virgin, but as the experienced
widow, not hasty to put again into thrall her treasured liberty (II,
750-6), ever chary of her favours, but irresistibly drawn to Troilus.
Such is the attitude she maintains in her first actual interview with
Troilus feigning illness in the house of Deiphebus.

>With that she gan hir eyen on him caste
>Ful esily, and ful debonairly,
>Avysing hir, and hyed not to faste
>With never a word, but seyde him softely,
>"Myn honour sauf, I wol wel trewely,
>And in swich forme as he can now devyse,
>Receyven him fully to my servyse."   (III, 155-61)

Her every act is characterized thus by *avysement*.   Undue haste has
no part in her nature, until the evil throw of circumstance has brought
her outside the walls of Troy.   It is with full consciousness of the
meaning of her promise that she assures Troilus,

". . . . .I shal trewely, with al my might,
Your bittre tornen al in-to swetnesse;
If I be she that may yow do gladnesse,
For every wo ye shal recovere a blisse."   (III, 178-81)
Nor do the embraces and kisses with which she accompanies her
promise signify any other form of comprehension.   She hears Pan-
darus exclaim,

"But I coniure thee, Criseyde, and oon,
And two, thou Troilus, whan thow mayst goon,
That at myn hous ye been at my warninge,
For I ful wel shal shape your cominge;

And eseth ther your hertes right y-nough;
And lat see which of yow shal bere the belle
To speke of Love a-right" (III, 193-9);
and later she should not be excused on the plea, that she is ignorant of
the fact that Pandarus was making easy for her an assignation with
Troilus, when he invites her to come and sup at his house.   Critics,
who to-day like to think of the sweet and guileless Criseyde as having
been betrayed through her uncle's wiles, forget the young widow's
avysement, and furthermore forget that the conventional heroine in
mediaeval romance never for a moment would look upon such an
amour with such a Troilus as a seduction!

Not unlike the enigmas of their first conversation are the subtleties
of the later colloquy at Criseyde's house between the lady and Pandarus, which result in her accepting the latter's invitation to supper.
Again there are the playful insistence of Pandarus that she shall not
escape him, the same sardonic laughter and excuses of his niece,
followed by inquiries about the absence of Troilus.   Again comes the
insinuating retort,

"For rather than men mighte him ther aspye,
Me were lever a thousand-fold to dye."   (III, 573-4)
Criseyde's final consent to come is, as ever, attended by the cautious
injunction,

"For to be war of goosish peples speche."   (III, 584)
If an analysis of Criseyde's fears and qualms, after she has learned
of the actual presence of Troilus in the house of Pandarus and realizes
that, without revealing her whole intrigue with Troilus, she can make
no appeal to her sleeping women, be made, it will be found, in the end,
that they are, in essence, only the psychological trepidations of a heart

in the presence of intense erotic emotion. She is fearful, she would fain summon assistance only because she finds herself "at dulcarnon" (III, 931), at her wits' ends. At such a moment fear is the inevitable concomitant of feminine tenderness. With Criseyde it is not the simple dread that she may in some way lose her honour. With her, not less than with the Wyf of Bath, honour is no mere synonym of negative chastity. It stands for loss of reputation, it is the great foil with which one must resist the attacks of calumny. In her conception there can be no dishonour in the surrender of her whole affections to Troilus, in becoming the *amie* of a *chevalier*. From the moment that she learns of Troilus's love for her until she has finally surrendered herself to his arms, we have ever the feeling that she will be the willing victim of any conspiracy Pandarus may devise, whether or no she be a party to the secrecy of it. No careful reader will experience a shock to his sensibilities, when he hears the lovely, simulating woman of Chaucer's romance answering the entreaty of Troilus to yield herself with

> "Ne hadde I er now, my swete herte dere,
> Ben yolde, y-wis I were now not here!"   (III, 1210-1)

Just as in the case of Troilus we see little development in character, before the hard news of his necessary separation from his mistress comes, so we behold in Criseyde little change until that occasion. She alternates between laughter and tears. Like her lover she indulges moods of apprehension or bursts into ecstasies of delight. Once she even reveals to us the charming femininity of the female scold. But surely no one ever more deserved rebuke than the tremulous Troilus from her. She is never less sentimental, less sweet, or less romantic than she is, when, the evening after she has received the great news of Pandarus, she lies abed listening to the nightingale.

> A nightingale, upon a cedre grene,
> Under the chambre-wal ther as she lay,
> Ful loude sang ayein the mone shene,
> Paraunter, in his briddes wyse, a lay
> Of love, that made hir herte fresh and gay.
> That herkned she so longe in good entente,
> Til at the laste the dede sleep hir hente.   (II, 918-24)

Sentiment and romance are perennial with her.

Even after the ill news comes we do not find great changes occurring in Criseyde's character. Her wild grief, her fatalism, her swoon do not at all surprise us. Of her sensitive range in temperament we can expect nothing else.

Those of us who are skeptical about the lady's crafty disposition, may be astonished to find her unselfish in her expressed love for Troilus, but that discovery is hardly to be termed marvelous. Having known her for a woman of *avysement*, we do not wonder to see her becoming the aggressor in plans to procure happiness for Troilus and herself, even in their evil hour. Hardly has she recovered from her faint to behold the piteous figure of Troilus, sword drawn, at her side, before she is in the midst of her shrewd schemes to cajole her father through his covetousness. Accustomed ever to success in her previous simulations, she is certain that she can manage one more final great one.

Our surprise comes later, when we discover the inability of Criseyde to deceive her father by the exercise of her cunning and to secure his permission to return to Troy.

There are, however, one or two noteworthy features in Criseyde's character revealed to us in Book IV of *Troil.*, such as bear out her reputation for "honour, estat, and wommanly noblesse." She is wholly unselfish in her love for Troilus. It is because her lover is in such heaviness, she tells Pandarus that she feels all her own grief made intenser.

"Can he for me so pitously compleyne?
Y-wis, this sorwe doubleth al my peyne." (IV, 902-3)
For his sake she promises she will "don al my might" (IV, 940) to keep from weeping in his sight. To make him glad shall be the purpose of her every endeavour (IV, 939-945). And there is one further revelation in her. She is in love with Troilus, not for his royal estate, not for his prowess in war, not for his noble array and pomp and martial tourneying, but for the inward nobility of his soul.

"Moral vertue, grounded upon trouthe,
That was the cause I first hadde on yow routhe." (IV, 1672-3)

It is for this reason that Criseyde gives us the real surprise, the real shock in the Fifth Book of *Troil.* We have first discovered in her a woman, whose conception of love vested in it the beauty of the inner and the ideal life, and now we find in her a woman untrue to the man whom she had found endowed with that very beauty of inwardness, recreant to the faith she had professed. Criseyde does not play false to Troilus, because his relations with her have made her lax in her conceptions of the holiness of chastity. She plays false in spite of her belief, that those relations themselves partook of a sanctity to be enjoyed in the recesses of her soul.

The critic may not condone her fall,—Chaucer himself had to resist the temptation to do so—nor may the critic look upon her fall as tragedy. There is change, not decay in her soul. She left Troy and Troilus in genuine grief, and purposed to return. She believed, herself, that she should return. As Diomede escorted her to her father's tent, she received his courtesy with apathetic courtesy, with the graciousness of a well-bred woman, hearing only here or there a word or two (V, 176-89).

Days of rueful waiting ensued. Calcas was obdurate in his refusals; Diomede, persistent in his approaches. Relying upon her skill in repartee, retaining her old fondness for simulation, and confident of the strength of her love for Troilus, she hazarded conversation with the new admirer. Diomede urged that Troy and the Trojans, all must inevitably perish. And the lonely woman, torn between the despair she felt for Troy and the vanity she felt at having the attentions of another gallant man, fell. She had toyed all innocently with her own tendency to guile, without realizing that it was of too frail a texture to make a competent weapon against the cunning of a Diomede. And of course her trifling proved her undoing. If we may not condemn, neither may we commend her. Little can be said for her in apology. Criseyde was impressionable as all women are impressionable, weak as only lovely woman can be weak, succumbing to the stress of circumstance (V, 1025-9), to her own lack of faith in the ultimate happy issue of events. And being lovely, sensitive woman, she is doomed to some bitterness of remorse.

> "For now is clene ago
> My name of trouthe in love, for ever-mo!
> For I have falsed oon, the gentileste
> That ever was, and oon the worthieste!"   (V, 1054-7)

To pursue her farther in her shame would be unwarrantable. The blithe lady of romance has become a branded woman, a creature of a drear reality.

Pandaro and Pandarus

Boccaccio's Pandaro has been so passed over in criticism, that we instinctively infer that he must have been, in literary parlance, an undeveloped character; and we conceive of him merely as a young figure, dashing and brilliant, but unfortunately profligate. We conclude that he must be only shadowily portrayed by Boccaccio, and then turn to Chaucer's Pandarus, and observe knowingly to ourselves that, in his treatment of the latter, the English poet has created a character psychologically far superior to his unpromising Italian proto-type. From a very negligible *donnée* Chaucer, we are prone to believe, has produced one of the most unique characters in English literature, Pandarus.

But these conclusions are by no means justified. Boccaccio's Pandaro is no inconsiderable character. He is a dashing youth, but he is not an ingenuous one. There is no less subtlety than there is brilliance in his make-up. Designed as he is to play the part of a go-between in a romance of courtly love, he must have combined within him the graces of a gentleman and the shrewdness of an intriguer. And with these prime requisites Boccaccio has fitly endowed him. In interpretation of his character over-emphasis should not be given to one or to the other of these necessary phases.

Pandaro enters upon our stage very quietly, but at the same time very coolly. Seeing the prostrate Troilo on his bed, he interrogates abruptly,

"Hatti già così vinto il tempo amaro?"   (II, 1)

But as Troilo responds to his penetrating query, he is struck with pity and becomes all solicitude (II, 4-5). Something of the sentimental type is at once revealed in him. He fairly inundates his comrade with demands that he immediately communicate his sorrows, that he remember the sacred right of a friend to share in every pain that besets his intimate, that he enable him to offer more intelligently his comforting.

A few dexterous questions and a few generous assurances of assist-ance on the part of Pandaro suffice to elicit from Troilo the secret of his woes; he is in love with Griseida, the cousin of his friend. In a moment the man who was all solicitude has become all enthusiasm. If only Troilo will deliver the business into his hands, Pandaro will find the way for him "con mie parolette" into the lady's heart (II, 23). He is ready to undertake any service to Troilo so long as his *amour* be kept a secret from the vulgar throng.

> "Non creder, Troilo, ch' io non vegga bene
> Non convenirsi a donna valorosa
> Si fatti amori, e quel ch' a me ne viene,
> Ed a lei ed a' suoi, se cotal cosa
> Alla bocca del volgo mai perviene,
> Che, per follia di noi, vituperosa
> È divenuta, dove esser solea
> Onor, dappoi per amor si facea."   (II, 25)

A firm believer in the tenets of the devotees in the court of Love, Pandaro enters with a clear conscience into the intrigue. If the *innamoramento* remain a clandestine one, it must needs be above all reproach, thoroughly honourable in the romantic world "dappoi per amor si facea." In the manifestation of such beliefs Pandaro is, then, a stock figure.

But such a figure he is not for any long interval. He rises into the world of reality as he enters the house of Griseida, bound on his new errand for Troilo, and demonstrates his truth to life at every turn. A very clever dialogue ensues there between the lady and her cousin. Confident though he is that "ogni donna in voglia viva amorosa" and certain that Griseida must give her love in the end to Troilo (II, 27), Pandaro is yet fully aware that, to play his game well, he must not play it too abruptly. It is, after all, a woman with whom he has to deal. He begins therefore

> . . . . . .con risa e con dolci parole,
> Con lieti motti e con ragionamenti
> Parentevoli assai. . . .   (II, 35),

then assumes the important air of one who has come on some weighty business, "con nuovi argomenti," fastens next his eyes fixedly upon his fair relative, and, when his stare has drawn the desired question to Griseida's lips,

> " . . . . . .Cugin, non mi vedesti mai,
> Che tu mi vai così mente tenendo?"

—he thoroughly arouses her curiosity by his commonplace rejoin-"You look prettier than ever to-day,"

> "Ma tu mi par più che l' usato assai
> Bella"   (II, 36).

His apparent distraction works to perfection. Griseida is ready to know the purpose of his errand; henceforth he can play upon her eagerness. But, now that flattery and gracious conversation have served their ends, he knows the policy, most adequate to excite the lady's interest keenly, is delay. To tell all he knows, he is in no hurry. Hers is the most fortunate face in the world, he assures Griseida coolly (II, 37). It has especially pleased a certain man. After that only a few seconds can elapse before the query comes from her,

> "Chi è dunque colui che si diletta
> Sì di vedermi?"   (II, 41).

and the game is on in earnest. A young widow wants to know something, and Pandaro has something to tell.

He eulogizes the spirit of the mysterious lover, he dilates upon the beauty of the woman who is listening, upon the high appropriateness of the union of such a pair as they (II, 42-43). And then, being a sentimentalist, he interposes just enough of an allusion to his own pathetic condition of lonely lovelessness (II, 44) to soften a woman's heart, before he confesses that it is the brave prince Troilo that loves Griseida, that for her Troilo

vive in pianto misero e meschino (II, 46).

Tears and questions come at once, in quick succession, from Griseida. Protests of devotion to the memory of a deceased husband follow (II, 49). But Pandaro knows that these are fleeting emotional reminiscences, and waits. Finally he arises as if to go (II, 52), apparently satisfied that his mission has proved a futile one. It is an adroit manoeuvre. As he takes his farewell, he can murmur a few words of his own great love for Troilo as a sort of justification for the errand, which has appeared to be unwelcome to his cousin (II, 52-53), without seeming to trespass upon her leisure. Without offence to her he can sigh,

"Non perder tempo, pensa che vechiezza,
O morte, torrà via la tua bellezza." (II, 54)

Another time the ruse works. Griseida is moved to compassion, and Pandaro knows that he is welcome to dally longer. Her pity induced at last, he realizes that other efforts are yet to be made. There is a woman's fancy to be played upon.

The wily relative has only a pretty, sentimental tale of the romantic Troilo, disconsolately apostrophizing Love in the shady woods, to improvise for Griseida's now interested hearing, before the citadel is taken (II, 56-61). The appeal of the pathetic story is irresistible. In another moment, "dopo un gran sospiro," Griseida has pledged her favour to the suit of Troilo (II, 66).

Pandaro is, then, a player of shrewd histrionic ability. When a point is to be gained, he manifests an ingenuity and a faculty for simulation, which comport only with the most perfect of literary psychologizing. He has the skill of a master hand.

But there are other qualities in Pandaro. We know that he is romantic, sentimental, and adroit. He is, in addition, assiduous and aggressive. With supreme diligence he manages the *amour* of Troilo and Griseida. Almost every one of their several acts is initiated by him; their occasional meetings (II, 84), their letter-writing, the consummation of their intrigue.

Pandaro is moreover a royal-hearted friend to Troilo, ready to share in his every happiness or his every grief. He rejoices with Troilo in the final attainment of his love; he weeps with him in the moments of his agonizing knowledge (III, 56, 73) that Griseida is to be taken from him (IV, 46). He clings to him as he wanders wearily about the city, waiting for the return of his mistress (V, 71 and VII). His loyalty to the Trojan prince sometimes prompts him to effusion, in kisses (II, 81) or in tears (IV, 101), sometimes to reckless advice or to impotent dissembling. At one time he counsels Troilo to ravish Griseida from Troy (IV, 64); at another he seeks to divert the prince by accompanying him to visit other ladies at festivities in the house of Sarpedone (V, 38-42); and, again, confesses the utter impotence of his own shrewd counsel (IV, 46). In the later books of *Fil.* he is sadly at a loss. His genius for initiative no longer avails him. He is as completely balked as is Troilo himself. When the convincing evidence of Griseida's infidelity is at last discovered by the unhappy lover and he turns in desperation to the comrade of his happier days, Pandaro has no word of comfort to offer him. He can only protest that he is unable properly to reproach Griseida, that in furthering Troilo's *amour* with her he had acted only in love for him, that only God can adequately punish his delinquent cousin (VIII, 23-24). The complete subjection of Pandaro's resilient, romantic spirit, hardly less than the utter apathy of Troilo in the closing scenes of *Fil.*, deepens our sense of tragic doom. In the presence of inevitable odds he has lost his old capacity for easy cynicism. His faculty for clever acting has left him.

Such, then, is the Pandaro from whom Chaucer is to develop Pandarus, a character not altogether profound, not altogether complex in his psychology, but yet a character of considerable range in temperament and of genuine human traits, a character, in no sense of the word, undeveloped.

Let us turn to the more voluble Pandarus. It has been believed by many critics that Chaucer virtually created this, the subtlest of his characters in *Troil.*, that in developing him the poet depended far less upon *Fil.* than he did for his treatment of either Troilus or Criseyde. His conversion of the youthful Pandaro into an uncle, instead of a cousin to Criseyde, gave the students of Chaucer just enough of a cue to make of him a character, obsessed with the phenomena of callous middle age. Ten Brink,[1] Morley,[2] Jusserand,[3] and Professor R. K. Root[4] concur rather closely in their estimates of the unscrupulous middle-aged worldling, cynical, humorous, lachrymose, tricky, worldly wise according to the wisdom of the base, parasitical, garrulous, indecent, coarse, abhorrent to our moral sense. All are

[1] Bernhard ten Brink: *History of English Literature*, translated by W C. Robinson, Volume II, Part I, pp. 93-94. Henry Holt & Co., New York, 1893. "In this character the creative power of the poet is most strongly expressed. It is a work of such intellectual boldness and assurance as can only be found equalled in the productions of the greatest masters. The more innocent Criseyde is, the more inexperienced and helpless Troilus is, the greater grows the rôle of him who brings them together. Pandarus is here properly adapted for a pimp, and his name has remained in language as a synonym for this word. He is an elderly gentleman with great experience of life, uncle to Criseyde, not—as in Boccaccio— her cousin. It is the poet's intention to excuse, or at least to explain, the part he plays, by the intimate friendship between him and Troilus. . . . To the insipid and somewhat cynical views of an old worldling, Pandarus unites a good dose of naïveté. And Chaucer makes him push his trade as pimp as naïvely as possible."

[2] Henry Morley: *Chaucer, English Writers*, Volume V, pp. 208-9. Cassell & Company, London, 1893.
"From this stanza (i. e., Fil. II, 1) Chaucer has struck out the description of Pandarus as a brave young Trojan of high lineage. He brings him to Troilus as simply 'a friend of his.' His question to which Boccaccio gives two lines, Chaucer expands into ten, with seven more of comments. He is to be Criseyde's garrulous uncle, humorous, lachrymose, tricky, worldly wise according to the wisdom of the base; the sentimental comradeship with Troilus being an oddity which we may refer, if we please, to the fact that Troilus was a king's son, who might have any form of parasite. . . . In Boccaccio, Griseida is represented as the cousin of Pandarus; Chaucer makes her his niece, and ascribes to him craft of age instead of the fresh valour of youth."

[3] J. J. Jusserand: *Histoire Littéraire Anglaise*. Volume I, pp. 304-5. Paris, 1896.
"un homme mûr, depourvu de scrupules, bavard, impudent, rusé, dont la sagesse consiste en proverbes choisis parmi les plus aisés à suivre; il fait songer aux héros comiques de Molière ou de Shakespeare. . . . Il est indécent et grossier, sans le vouloir et par nature comme la nourrice de Juliette. . . . Chacune de ses idées, de ses paroles, de ses attitudes est la contre-partie de celles de Cressida et de son amant et leur donne du relief par un contraste d'ombres."

[4] Robert Kilburn Root; *Poetry of Chaucer*, p. 121, Houghton-Mifflin, New York 1906. "It seems at first sight a curious friendship—that of the middle aged cynic, whose ideals, if they ever existed at all, have faded into the monotone of common sense, for the extravagant idealist and enthusiast of twenty-odd," p. 120. "By adding some twenty years to his age, and making him Criseyde's uncle instead of her cousin, still more by causing him to use the more intimate relationship as an occasion for an act of down-right treachery, Chaucer has made the character of Pandarus infinitely more abhorrent to our moral sense."

satisfied that he is a new creation, and all commend Chaucer for his
ability to produce so shrewd a character. M. Émile Hyacinthe
Legouis[1] is the first of the critics to examine, really critically, the
characterization of Pandarus, the first to perceive flaws in its artistic
effect. He objects that the garrulity of Pandarus "tends to render
the action much slower,"[2] but finds in his verbosity "not his chief
defect, from a literary point of view."[3]   It is "in his remodelling"
that "Chaucer included such diverse and incompatible traits that
the character does not stand out clearly."[4]   The clever Trojan is a
rather unfortunate compromise, in his opinion, "between the young
knight of friendship as drawn by Boccaccio and the Shakespearean
Pandar, the obscene and dotard uncle."[5]   The criticism is not altogether unjustified. It is fair rather than magnanimous. But M.
Legouis should at least exercise caution in his insistence that, owing
to the complexity of Pandarus, "It is impossible to judge him, to
realize the character as a whole, for we see two figures, one a young
man with a gift of humour as in Boccaccio, and the other a grinning
old man as in Shakespeare." "Chaucer's Pandar," he concludes,
"in fact makes us see double."[6]

M. Legouis should remember that complexity in character is
admissible, psychologically speaking, and that there is such a thing
as dualism in personality. It is possible for middle age, nay even
for old age, to retain something of the facile spontaneity of youth. It
is possible for a man to be a sentimentalist, and, at the same, time be
capable of depraved tastes. And, crafty though he is, Chaucer's

---

[1] Émile Hyacinthe Legouis: *Geoffroy Chaucer*, Bloud e Cie. Paris, 1910.
The passages quoted are from the translation into English by L. Lailavoix,
J. M. Dent & Sons, London, 1913, pp. 128 ff.   In subsequent notes I append the
original French of the quotations.

[2] "Ce bavardage, s'il est un trait curieux de caractère, produit un ralentisse-
ment énorme de l'action." p. 120.

[3] "Mais les longueurs de Pandarus ne sont pas son plus grand défaut—
littérairement parlant," p. 120.

[4] "En meme temps qu'il l'a fait parler avec intempérance, Chaucer a rassemblé
sur lui des traits si divers et si disparates qu'on ne le voit pas avec netteté," p. 120.

[5] "Son Pandarus est intermédiaire entre le jeune chevalier de l'amitié présenté
par Boccace, parfait de zèle et de sagacité dans un rôle spécial, et le Pandare shakes-
pearien, oncle dévoyé . . . vieillard radoteur et obscène . . .," p. 120.

[6] "On n'arrive pas à le juger, ni à le voir. Ou plûtot on voit double: une
silhouette de jeune homme caustique comme dans Boccace, une figure âgée et
grimaçante, comme dans Shakespeare. Le Pandare de Chaucer fait loucher,"
p. 121.

Pandarus is seldom other than a sentimentalist. He luxuriates in emotion. He suffers because he believes he is suffering. His is one of those temperaments, which never rationalize their moods or their grounds for emotion, to detect their sincerity or their insincerity, which are prone to indulge the intensity rather than to consider the motives of their feelings. He never distinguishes between the simulated and the genuine qualities of his tears; and of both kinds he is lavish.

Like Troilus and Criseyde he too belongs to southern climes. His sensibilities are ever near to outward interpretation. Subtle as we know him to be, we are yet aware that hidden behind his irony there is a sympathetic and responsive geniality, a disinterested devotion to Troilus. Like Pandaro he is a firm believer that nothing is nobler in life than romantic passion. Of Criseyde he early declares,

> "But trewely, it sete hir wel right nouthe
> A worthy knight to loven and cheryce,
> And but she do, I holde it for a vyce." (I, 985-7),

and until Criseyde has begun to cherish her knight as Pandarus thinks suitable, he is incessant in his diligence. Every moment he is agog, bustling from interview to interview.

If he were not so able and so complacent a scholastic philosopher, so cunning in his arguments, so shrewd in his use of proverbs, one might suspect that in him Chaucer was satirizing some mediaeval exponent of scholastic dialectic. It is this aptness for proverbiality, for the employment of philosophy in the preparations for an *amour*, that inclines critics to see in Pandarus a sort of premature senility, an approximate dotage. But both youth and middle age, it must not be forgotten, are not unadroit in the conversion of reason into sophistry. The genius for repartee belongs largely to the youthful spirit.

Already we have discussed Chaucer's literary use of the unfortunate love affair of Pandaro. The whole of it is taken over into English, as is only proper in a work devoted to the treatment of worshippers at the Court of Love, where no age that yet remains robust is ever denied admittance. Chaucer's inclusion of it in *Troil.* is not primarily for purposes of satire. Tormented himself by the *grande passion*, the unselfish Pandarus will be more pressed to bring about the happiness of the lovers, to whose wishes he is devoting all his time and energy. So he goes on, assuming the initiative, devising pretexts to interest Deiphebus in the supposititious wrongs of Criseyde, encouraging Troilus, supplicating his niece, employing mendacity that

does not deceive, wiles that do not conceal, until at last he has brought
Criseyde to Troilus's embraces.

But it is not without misgivings that Pandarus works toward that
culmination. Chaucer in his treatment of the merry bachelor adapts
into his poem one of the genuine laments of Pandaro (cf. *Fil.* III, 6).
And on the lips of Pandarus it is no less sincere. Out of his love
for Troilus he perceives he has become

> Bitwixen game and ernest, swich a mene
> As maken wommen unto men to comen (III, 254-5),

has done that which he would never do for another,

> "Al-though he were a thousand fold my brother." (III, 252)

At the deed he does not, however, repine so much as at the fearful
consequences of gossip, the ruin of the fair name of Crisyede, if
Troilus be indiscreet. He does not so much condemn himself as
criminal, as, knowing the inconstancy of human nature, he fears the
tendency of men to be disloyal to women who have given them their
love in secret. So it is that he counsels Troilus to remember that the
"firste vertu is to kepe tonge" (III, 294). His mingled laments and
instructions he closes with the enigmatical utterance so common to
him, an ever recurrent surcharge of sentimentality,

> "And bid for me, sin thou art now in blisse,
> That god me sende deeth or sone lisse." (III, 342-3)

Just as, being a genuine fatalist, he feared the consequences of
Troilus's *amour*, so, after the lovers have known the culmination of
their joy, being a fatalist, he feels constrained to advise Troilus to be
measured in his happiness, remembering

> ". . . of fortunes sharp adversitee
> The worste kinde of infortune is this,
> A man to have ben in prosperitee,
> And it remembren, whan it passed is." (III, 1625-8)

It is for this reason that he enjoins,

> "Thou art wys y-nough, for-thy do nought amis;
> Be not to rakel, though thou sitte warme,
> For if thou be, certeyn, it wol thee harme." (III, 1629-31)

But neither the cunning nor the counsel of Pandarus was long to
avail. Calcas outside the walls of Troy began to long for his daughter. The Trojan parliament "enseled" its decree; and the result was
the picture of Pandarus we find in the late Fourth, and in the Fifth
Book of the poem—completely balked. Beyond the arrangement of
one more assignation he can do nothing further for the lovers. He

is reduced, as Pandaro was, to the folly of trying to comfort Troilus
by plaintive references to his own grief (IV, 393-9), of holding epi-
curean visions of other delights, other ladies (IV, 400-427) before the
eyes of the youth, and asserting the truth of the time-worn dictum,

The newe love chaceth ofte the olde (IV, 415),

although he is painfully conscious all the while that he is talking the
sheerest twaddle.   Not so unscrupulous is he, as he is feeble, in this
consolation, which Chaucer tells us was spoken *"for the nones alle,*

To helpe his freend, lest he for sorwe deyde
For doutelees, to doon his wo to falle,
He roughte not what unthrift that he seyde."   (IV, 428-31)

Upon the inefficacy of his advice to Troilus to abduct Criseyde comment already has been made.

In the Fifth Book, himself better counseled, Pandarus again recom-
mends nepenthes to Troilus, but not such apparently unscrupulous
but really *fainéant* ones as those which we have just observed.   Instead of proposing to Troilus to seek favours among other ladies, he
offers simply, for the sake of diversion, such "lusty lyf in Troye that
we han had" (V, 393-4).   Beyond transient pleasures to wile away
the tedious ten days of expectancy, he has nothing to suggest.

Our last glance at Pandarus further reveals his impotency.   Like
all worldlings he is powerless to help a friend when real distress is
upon him.   Troilus has discovered and deplored Criseyde's treachery,
and all that Pandarus can say, in reply to the youth's lament, when
finally he acquires command of his voice, are words of apology, simple
pleas that he had meant well, a puerile protest,

". . . . . . I hate, y-wis, Criseyde!
And god wot, I wol hate hir evermore!   (V, 1732-3),

and a fruitless sigh,

"Right fayn wolde I amende it, wiste I how."   (V, 1741)

It is a mistake to think of Chaucer's Pandarus as an absolute moral
pervert.   We may not sanction his conduct, but on the other hand
we need not brand him as a member of the most revolting profession
conceivable among men.   We have no warrant in Chaucer's text for
believing that Pandarus advocated that men ever be "wanderingly
lewd."

Nor, on the other hand, have we any real cause to view him as a
dotard.   He is, after all, a man in the prime vigour of life, still agile
in conversation with youth, alternately sage and ironical with Troilus,
playful with Criseyde, and, despite his vigour, a sentimentalist mooning

over a languishing passion. A clever actor, a shrewd inventor, a cunning counselor, a trusted adviser of Priam himself, and withal a merry comrade, he should not impress us with his dotage. We ought not to be influenced in our interpretation of him by the unfortunate degeneration of his name through seven centuries into a mere synonym of reproach for a revolting trade.[1]

No better summary of the character of either Chaucer's Pandarus or Boccaccio's Pandaro can be made than one which is contained in one stanza of *Fil.*

> A cui ridendo Pandaro rispose:
> "Niente nuoce ciò che tu ragioni,
> Lascia far me, che le fiamme amorose
> Ho per le mani, e sì fatti sermoni,
> E seppi già recar più alte cose
> Al fine suo con nuove condizione;
> Questa fatica tutta sarà mia,
> E 'l dolce fine tuo voglio che sia."   (II, 32)

For both were firm believers that the enjoyment of love was all innocuous in effect; and Pandarus, who knew the "olde daunce" so well, was no less a master of the "fiamme amorose" than Pandaro. To devise "sermoni" was second nature with each of them; and each knew consummately well how to bring "alte cose" to a fitting conclusion "con nuove condizione."

Diomede

Of neither Boccaccio's nor Chaucer's Diomede do we see a great deal. In both poems the character is primarily interesting, because

---

[1] It is interesting to note that only in the English language has the name of Pandarus deteriorated into a common noun. To-day the term, "pander," is in as common use as "go-between," "procurer," or "pimp," and equally distasteful in significance. Even in Italy, the country which first read the story of Pandaro, the proper name has not fallen into disesteem. The mild term, "ruffiano" is there employed to designate a person of the pander's profession. In France the pander is agreeably termed a "complaisant" or a "ministre des amours"; in Germany a "Kuppler" or "Gelegenheitsmacher," and in Spain an "alcahuete." Chaucer, it would seem, is responsible for the odious meaning the word has assumed in English. The earliest use of it, cited in the New English Dictionary, in a work of Lyndesay, is dated 1530. North uses it in his "Plutarch," 1579-80, Spenser in his *Mother Hubberd* in 1591, and Shakespeare himself, in the *Merry Wives of Windsor* in 1598, eight years before the appearance of his *Troilus and Cressida*, from which the evil connotation of the name to-day might, one would think, more justifiably spring.

in him lies the power to captivate the mistress of another lover. In
Fil. Diomede, not unlike Troilo, falls in love with Griseida at first
sight, but he knows that he is falling in love with a lady who is already
enamoured of another man. Troilo has gallantly accompanied
Griseida as far out of the walls of Troy as discretion will permit,
before he must surrender her to her new Greek escort, in whose
presence he maintains a sullen silence "tutto tinto nel viso"; and the
acute Diomede perceives in his and Griseida's behaviour

> L'amor de' due, e dentro al suo pensiero
> Con diversi argomenti ne fa fede,
> E di ciò mentre seco ne pispiglia,
> Nascosamente di colei si piglia.   (V, 13)

We comprehend at once from this immediate infatuation of the Greek
knight, who is not deterred by the realization that Troilo and Griseida
are already lovers, that he will soon be urging his suit to the lady.   In
Boccaccio's poem, however, Diomede, not so impetuous as his Chaucerian counterpart, does not make any approaches of love to Griseida
on the occasion of this first meeting.

But it is not long before he begins to ply his craft, once Griseida is
safely ensconced in the Greek camp. His first belief,

> "Vana fatica credo sia la mia;
> Questa donna è per altrui amor trista,"

soon yields to the pressure of his pride,

> "Troppo esser converria sovrano artista
> S' io ne volessi il primo cacciar via
> Per entrarv' io"   (VI, 10).

Matters come to such a pass that even though he should die for it,
"dovesse per certo morire," he must reveal to Griseida,

> . . . . .l' aspre offese
> Ch' amore gli facea per lei sentire (VI, 11).

With ingratiating sympathy he begins his conversations with the
lady at her father's tent. What does she think of the asperities of
the war between the Trojans and the Greeks? Does she regard the
thoughts of both parties as vain and frivolous? Do the manners of
the Greeks seem a bit strange to her? (VI, 12) He follows his
queries with flattery, then with comparisons between the prowess of
the Trojans and the Greeks, then with dire prophecies as to
the ultimate doom of Troy, and last of all with the assurance that
there is love to be had among the Greeks even "più alto e più perfetto" than among the Trojans (VI, 14-22). And at the end of his

declarations the gay deceiver becomes "vermiglio Come fuoco nel viso," and modestly lowers "in terra . . . il ciglio"! (VI, 23) The favour of a new lover such as this soon penetrates the reserve of Troilo's mistress.

Boccaccio's Diomede is in fact not an unattractive figure. His person is very pleasing,

> Egli era grande e bel della persona,
> Giovane fresco e piacevole assai,
> E forte e fier siccome si ragiona,

and this knight too, the Italian poet assures us,

> . . . ad amore la natura aveva prona.   (VI, 33)

Chaucer's Diomede differs little from Boccaccio's. He is, like Pandaro and Pandarus, possessed of cunning; like Troilo and Troilus, of a certain gracefulness. He knows more than the creed in the craft of love-making. Like his prototype in the Italian romance, he perceives the pallor of Troilus and its cause, as the young Trojan relinquishes the lady Criseyde to his escort. But his is a world of give and take, with each man for himself, and the devil entitled to the hindmost. Without qualms and without hesitation, therefore, he begins his game the moment he is alone with Criseyde, realizing like every true gallant,

> For at the worste it may yet shorte our weye.   (V, 96)

He commences with dalliance and winds up with cajolery. The zest of winning out over another man keeps him in the game, until his flatteries, together with his courtesies and the knightliness of his person, avail. But like the Diomede of *Fil.* he also feels no scruples about playing with veiled intimidation upon the fears of Criseyde that Troy and her Trojan friends must inevitably perish (V, 887-89). And his conquest of the lady, although presented by Chaucer in fuller detail (V, 848-1015, 1030-43), is achieved as easily.

Just as we found that we cannot help telling the story of *Troil.* and the story of *Fil.* in much the same words, so now we discover, as we write the character sketches of the four figures in the two poems, we instinctively employ the same vocabulary. There are really no preponderant differences in the characterizations of the two groups. What differences exist, are due chiefly to Chaucer's analytic method. His characters express themselves more in words, without expressing themselves very differently in manner. Troilus is more frequently in tears than Troilo, but sheds them at such times no more profusely than his prototype. The emotional qualities of the two are not unlike; in grief equally violent, in romance equally compelling. Criseyde, like Griseida, is fond of raillery, disposed to lachrymose effusions, apprehensive about her honour, secret in her concessions, endowed with the proper amount for a mediaeval lady of romance, of "gentilezza," "virtute," "onestade," "discrezione," "costumi palesi," and worthier far than those who sit "in real trono" or boast of "sangue reale." Pandarus is more mature than Pandaro, at times more languorous, in his tears more extravagant, in his speech more garrulous, in his cunning more inventive; but withal the same sentimentalist, the same railer, the same sophist. Diomede, we have seen, is more impetuous in Chaucer's poem than in Boccaccio's, but is otherwise unchanged.

It is in fact unwise to over-emphasize, as is the tendency among critics, Chaucer's deviations from his models in characterizing the *dramatis personae* of *Troil.*

Troilus and Criseyde and Pandarus and Diomede are the fruits of many imaginations, not entirely the products of the minds of Boccaccio's predecessors, nor of the mind of Boccaccio, nor of Chaucer. They are the literary heirs of all the *faerie*, all the charm of mediaeval chivalry growing out of monastery and church, out of royal court and feudal system, out of the blending of Christian ideals with the old pagan worship of beauty, out of ancient classic epics and the love-lore of Ovid's poetry. Troilus and Criseyde are not conventionally wedded husband and wife, bound to one another by ring and bell and book, by the ritual and sanction of the church,—mediaeval romance would never admit the beauty of such a relation, whatever adherence the writers of it might and did yield to ecclesiastical authority,—but they are lovers, *chevalier* and *amie*, indissolubly bound to one another by all the sanctity of their secret vows in the presence of Love, majestic in deity and in beauty incomparable. Troilus is Criseyde's champion and servant; she is his *friend* and mistress. In the domains of the cycle of the Court of Love no bond more sacred could exist. One must not think of Troilus as lewd or of Criseyde as wanton. Their *amour*, for all its being clandestine, was in their own view a relationship quite holy.

The atmosphere of *Troilus and Criseyde* then, like that of the *Filostrato*, is permeated with the breath of romance. The defining cosmos of the two poems remains much the same. The devices of love-lore in Boccaccio's work, its spirit of southern romance, its erotic exuberance, all are brought into the English poem. And there they remain very largely in their own pure essence. It is only Chaucer's maturer spirit, half in conflict with itself, as it broods with divided feelings over the folly and beauty of youth, that creates some change in them. But even the introduction of Boethian philosophy and Chaucer's instinct for the analysis and enlargement of character psychologically, do not far succeed in changing the totality of effect of the *Filostrato*, as its materials and spirit are fused into *Troilus and Criseyde*.[1]

[1] After the foregoing study of the *Filostrato* and *Troilus and Criseyde*, as poems belonging essentially to the *genre* of the Court of Love cycle of mediaeval romances, had been completed, the writer's attention was called to a recent book by Mr. William George Dodd, in which one chapter is devoted to a somewhat similar treatment of Chaucer's poem. The views expressed therein contain the most adequate interpretation of the characters in Chaucer's poem which has yet been published. But Mr. Dodd's study is confined chiefly to Chaucer's poem, with no extensive consideration of the relations of it to the *Filostrato*. I make reference to the book here, because its general conclusions more than support my own contentions that *Troilus and Criseyde* can be correctly interpreted only when considered as a mediaeval romance.

In Mr. Dodd's work, which is entitled *Courtly Love in Chaucer and Gower* (*Harvard Studies in English*, Volume I, Ginn and Company, Boston, 1913), the first chapter, on the "System of Courtly Love," is especially significant (pp. 1-20). Particularly interesting are the summaries which he makes of "the abstract principles and the laws underlying the courtly system," as he finds them defined in the *De Reprobatione Amoris* of Andreas Capellanus, an adherent to the codes of love established by Marie of Champagne. I append the topic sentences of his fourfold classification of these principles.

1. Courtly love is sensual.

2. Courtly love is illicit and, for the most part, adulterous. "Indeed, in the courtly love system marriage has no place."

3. A love, sensual and illicit, must needs be secret.

4. Love, to meet the requirements of the courtly system, must not be too easily obtained (pp. 5-8).

CHAPTER VI.

CHAUCER'S USE OF THE *Teseide*.

For many years scholars have felt the almost inestimable indebtedness of Chaucer to Boccaccio's romantic epic, the *Teseide*, (*Opere Volgari*, Vol. IX) and various ones among them have, from time to time, submitted, as the results of their inquiries, very significant appraisals of its magnitude. We know to-day that the Italian poem made certain contributions to *Troil.*, that it exerted a general influence over the *Anelida and Arcite*, that it provided the *Parliament of Fowls* with a beautiful description of the Temple of Venus,[1] and that it supplied the basic material for the *Knight's Tale*. Professor J. L. Lowes has proposed to us, too, very interesting and conclusive grounds for believing that it was the origin of several passages in the *Legend of Ariadne*.[2]

Admittedly the influence of the *Teseide* over Chaucer's works was most dominant and valuable in the *Kn. T.*; and about the nature of it in that poem discussion has generally centered. Until recent years all problems that arose pursuant to the study of it, became early entangled with a supposition of Tyrwhitt[3] that the story of *Palamon and Arcite*, mentioned in the *Prologue of the Legend of Good Women* (A. 408-9, B, 420 -21), had been "a mere translation" of Boccaccio's work, and with a theory of ten Brink[4] that Chaucer originally wrote a *Palamon and Arcite* story, which was practically a translation of the Italian poem, in the same seven-line stanza as is used in *Troil.*, and later altered the narrative to its present form in the *Kn. T.*

The prominence of ten Brink as a scholar secured to his theory almost universal acceptance for nearly four decades. As a preliminary to his own critical examination and refutation of it in 1907,

---

[1] Cf. *Tes.* Lib. VII, 51-66 with *P. F.* 183-291.

[2] See J. L. Lowes: *The Prologue of the Legend of Good Women Considered in Its Chronological Relations*, Publ. Mod. Lang. Assoc., 20 pp., 802-10. Especially significant is Professor Lowes' footnote on the "maister-strete" of Athens (*Leg. G. W.* 1965).

[3] Thomas Tyrwhitt: *The Canterbury Tales of Chaucer*, 2nd Edition, Oxford, 1798. See Intr. Dis. section ix, p. 81.

[4] Berhard ten Brink: *Chaucer Studien*, Münster, 1870, pp. 39-69.

Professor J. S. P. Tatlock[1] wrote of ten Brink's theory, "Dr. John Koch[2] defended and developed it in an article in the first volume of the *Englische Studien*; he regarded the *Teseide* passages in all three of the stanzaic poems as a part of the *débris* of a *Palamon and Arcite* deliberately broken up before the *Knight's Tale* was conceived. Ten Brink's theory, and usually Koch's modification of it, was accepted by Dr. Eugen Kölbing,[3] by Mr. A. W. Pollard,[4] by Professor Skeat,[5] and by many others, and to this day may be called the orthodox view."

Within the last fifteen years, however, as the result of the expression of a change in view by Mr. Pollard[6] and of the new views expressed by Professor F. J. Mather[7] and Professor J. L. Lowes,[8] and particularly of the painstaking and profoundly scholarly work of Mr. Tatlock, a new and unmistakably saner position of orthodoxy has been established for us. The deductions of the latter (*Development and Chronology of Chaucer's Works*, pp. 51-66), offered in support of the self-evident *à priori* arguments against the presumption that the seven-line stanzaic version of the *Palamon and Arcite* story ever existed, more than obviate any consideration whatever, in the future, of the validity of ten Brink's theory. Chaucerian scholars do well to discard it completely, and to believe no longer that Chaucer once made a stanzaic translation of the *Teseide* and afterwards wantonly destroyed it, or from its fragments made selections to insert as passages in other of his works.

If, then, we are no longer to believe that the *Palamon and Arcite* story was ever written in English in stanzaic form by Chaucer, we can henceforth more justly make an appraisal of the poet's use of the *Teseide* in the second of his great romances, the *Kn. T.*

It is not possible for us, as it was in the case of the *Troil.*, to point out in the *Kn. T.* a greater indebtedness to Boccaccio's poetry than

---

[1] J. S. P. Tatlock: *Development and Chronology of Chaucer's Works. Chaucer Society*, 1907, p. 46.

[2] John Koch: *Englische Studien*, 1877, pp. 249-93.

[3] Eugen Kölbing: *Englische Studien*, 2, 528-32.

[4] A. W. Pollard: *Chaucer Primer*, London, 1893, pp. 76-77.

[5] W. W. Skeat: *Prioress' Tale*. Oxford, 1893, pp. xvi-xvii.

[6] A. W. Pollard: *Chaucer Primer*, London, 1903.

[7] F. J. Mather: *The Date of the Knight's Tale* in the *Furnival Miscellany*, 1901.

[8] J. L. Lowes: *The Legend of Good Women, Publ. Mod. Lang. Assoc.*, 20, 809, note 1.

has previously been suspected. We can do nothing except define more clearly the influence of the Italian poem on the English.

In *Troil.* Chaucer employed much the same scheme of versification and division as he had found in *Fil.* In the *Kn. T.* he abandons entirely such effects as he finds them in the *Teseide*. Boccaccio's long romantic epic of more than 10,000 lines he converts into a tale of 2,250 lines. This reduction in scale is bound very much to affect the nature of the Boccaccian influence in Chaucer's poem. It enjoins upon the poet certain responsibilities and it throws open to him certain opportunities. If he is to be successful in the conversion of Boccaccio's beautiful pseudo-epic into an artistic English poem, he must be very careful in the selection of the details he wishes to take over from the Italian into his own production; and on the other hand, now that the reduction frees him from the necessity of following a literary model, he can find an easy escape from every temptation toward imitation, and create a poem that will be more entirely his own. He can work with a greater sense of emancipation, but he must work with a faculty for selection.

The transformation of the mediaeval pseudo-epic, characterized, as the *Tes.* is, by great stateliness of movement and a profusion of wealth and colour, into a mediaeval romance such as the *Kn. T.*, wherein stateliness must yield to a greater rapidity of action and profusion to a simpler beauty, is not an altogether inconsiderable task. Both the stately dignity of the Italian work and the occasionally more rapid narrative quality of Chaucer's poem are elements good in their kind. The transformation of the one into the other denotes for the English poet neither retrogression nor advance in poetic merits, when his art is compared with Boccaccio's.

If the main elements of the Italian poet's work were to be gracefully incorporated into the series of the stories told by the pilgrims in the frame-work of the *Canterbury Tales*, they had to be very much compressed. And compression meant inevitably a change in the manner of treatment, if the story of Palamon and Arcita was to be rendered with anything of artistic beauty. Chaucer could no longer indulge the analytical tendency he pursued in his handling of *Fil.* It was denied him now to take a suggestion from a word or phrase of Boccaccio and out of it develop a situation, or enlarge a particular aspect of character. The objective method of *Troil.* had to be discarded. Long soliloquies had perforce to disappear.

To determine just how far Chaucer solved this problem of compression will be one of the aims of the present chapter. The Italian version of the *Palamon and Arcite* story was a good one. A material change of the manner in which it was originally produced involved a very considerable risk, for, containing in itself an abundance of material, excellent and admirably adaptable to narrative treatment of considerable scope, such as the episodes of Teseo's invasion of the land of the Amazons, the happy marriage consummated between him and Ippolita, his triumphal entry into Athens, the suppliant ladies of Thebes whom he found awaiting him upon his return, his war with Creon, the discovery among the dead of the two friends Palamon and Arcita, their subsequent imprisonment and consequent infatuation for Duke Teseo's sister-in-law, Emilia, the varying fortunes of the lovers, the great tournament, the defeat of Palamon, the joy of the ill-starred Arcita and his all too unfortunate accident, and the final marriage of Palamon and Emilia,—there is no imperative reason why the plot should be confined to the limits of a short story, or even to the limits of a poetic romance of two thousand and odd verses. If further episodes of importance and intrinsic worth in the *Tes.* were to be enumerated, it would be discovered that they more than equal in number the significant episodes in a modern novel. In a word, then, there is no *à priori* reason for reducing the scale of Boccaccio's epic.

In no work written previous to the *Canterbury Tales* had Chaucer so clearly revealed his power of invention as in *Troil.* But, as he adapted the material of *Fil.* to the needs of that poem, he was never really constrained to produce any changes in it, and, despite the additions which he made to Boccaccio's narrative, resulting in a greater intricacy of plot and a more concrete reality of characterization, Chaucer interfered but little with the internal structure of the Italian poem. After all, the differences which we detect between *Troil.* and *Fil.* are largely the effect of superadditions externally, no matter how intimately Chaucer connected them with the main body of his work. In the *Kn. T.*, however, the poet makes more frequent internal transformations.

Not only does he change the characterization of Palamon and Arcite and Emilye and Ippolyta and Theseus, but he changes the order of episodes, and even the inner constitution of episodes, with the utmost hardihood. With the plot of the *Tes.* he takes whatever liberties he pleases. He disregards many an element of pseudo-classicism to be found in the epic, and inserts at will many elements of what one might term a feudal realism, for which no ultimate suggestion can be traced

to Boccaccio's poem. At one point of his poem he would compress
passages of significant beauty or intrinsic value in the plot, and at
another he would expand an excerpt of slight worth into many verses.
Valuable descriptions or episodes he rejects, and valueless ones he
too often retains. For the romantic sentiment of the lovers or the
chivalric sentiment of Teseo, he is sometimes so capable of bad art
as to substitute the philosophy of Boethius. From the *Kn. T.* he
banishes all the knightly companions-at-arms of Palamon and Arcita
except

> Ligurge him-self, the grete king of Trace (2129),

and him he shifts to the side of Palamon, only to introduce a new
knight,

> The grete Emetreus, the king of Inde (2156),

of whose valiant person no vestige can be found in the *Tes.*, and then
to enroll him in the party of Arcite! He retains to some extent the
gorgeous colouring and trappings of the Italian poem, but discards
almost wholly its stately progress and pageantry. And with the
pageantry there disappears from Chaucer's poem much of the solem-
nity of Boccaccio's romantic epic. The long succession of dignified,
but vindictive, single combats of which we read in the eighth book of
the *Tes.*, Chaucer converts into a wild and simultaneous onslaught of
the whole two bands of knights, feeling, as mayhap he does, a keen
desire to describe the mad rush of a tournament as he had himself
some time seen it, rather than to try, like Boccaccio, to project his
vision of it into the far-off atmosphere of pagan antiquity. Yet it
must not be inferred that Boccaccio's pseudo-classicism is inartistic.
It is, in fact, admirably sustained by the Italian poet through constant
devices, allusions, invocations and the most perfect of Homeric
similes. But the *Tes.* is deficient in real action, and Chaucer displays
a sagacity that is almost modern when he omits the most tedious
part of all Boccaccio's narrative, the long series of minor combats.

Yet the English poet's work loses, as it omits from time to time
various elements of pseudo-classicism such as these. For in Boccaccio's epic there is just enough of the serenity and high-seriousness of a
classic atmosphere to preserve for the poem a distinct and admirable
unity of conception. The *Kn. T.* Chaucer fails to endow with a
similar unity. But what the English work loses in the way of a
unified setting by the partial discarding or retaining of pseudo-classic
touches, it more than makes up for by the more patent unity of
action it acquires in Chaucer's hands.

The changes, introduced by the poet into the *Kn. T.*, are then greater than those introduced into *Troil.*; and they mark an independence of spirit, not so easily detected in his earlier employment of sources, a more positive emancipation from the thraldom of literary influence. It is well that he has acquired this new attitude of mind as he begins to work upon the *Canterbury Tales.*

Let us first of all examine the effects of this spirit of emancipation in Chaucer's methods of reduction. Various forms of statistics are available for our use in studying with the aim designated. We shall depend chiefly, however, upon those which have been prepared by Mr. Henry Ward, Professor Skeat, and Mr. J. S. P. Tatlock.

The earliest of these consist in the marginal references to the *Tes.* presented by Mr. Ward in the Chaucer Society's *Six-Text* edition of the *Canterbury Tales*, in two of the manuscripts, the *Lansdowne* and the *Cambridge.* From the marginal references given with the *Lansdowne* manuscript (see *Chaucer Society, 1st. ser.* 7, 13, 20, 36, 43, 55. *Lansdowne MS, Edited by F. J. Furnivall*, 1868-1879) the following simple little table can be readily constructed:

Lines in the *Kn. T.* showing a slight likeness to lines in the *Tes.*	131
Lines showing a general likeness to the *Tes.*	379
Lines actually translated from the *Tes.*	272
Total	782

From this table it would appear, at first view, that only 782 lines of the *Kn. T.*, i. e., slightly more than one third of the poem's total of 2,250 lines, were due to the *Tes.* The inadequacy of that testimony is eloquent. For we remember that a great number of other lines in Chaucer's poem, although marked by no verbal resemblance to Boccaccio's lines, are yet performing the same office as the Italian verses. They are telling the story of Palamon and Arcita, and, in doing so, are simply unrolling the fabric, warp and woof, of Boccaccio's poem. Just as we perceived the indirect influence of the narrative elements of *Fil.* upon *Troil.*, so here in the *Kn. T.* we see the same sort of influence at work.

From Mr. Ward's marginal references Professor Skeat, with the desire to reveal more clearly the distribution of parts of the *Tes.* in parts of the *Kn. T.*, prepared the following table.

Kn. T.	Tes.
Lines	Bks. and sts.
865-83	I and II.
893-1027	II, 2-5, 25-95.
1030-1274	III, 1-11, 14-20, 47, 51-54, 75.
1361-1478	IV, 26-29, 59.
1451-1479	V, 1-3, 24-27, 33.
1545-65	IV, 13, 14, 31, 85, 84, 17, 82.
1638-41	VII, 106, 119.
1668-1739	V, 77-91.
1812-1860	V, 92-98.
1887-2022	VII, 108-110, 50-64, 29-37.
2102-2206	VI, 71; 14-22, 65-70, 8.
2222-2593	VII, 43-49, 68-93, 23-41, 67, 95-99, 7-13, 131, 132, 14, 100-102, 113-118, 19.
2600-2683	VIII, 2-131.
2684-2734	IX, 4-61.
2735-39	XII, 80, 83.
2743-2808	X, 1-67.
2809-2962	XI, 1-67.
2967-3102	XII, 3-19, 69-83.

(See *Skeat's Chaucer*, V, p. 60.)

This table serves a two-fold purpose. It exhibits the varying degrees of compression used by Chaucer in his reduction of the *Tes.* into one of the *Canterbury Tales*, and it indicates the free hand the poet wields in his distribution of parts. At a glance we perceive that he compresses the first book, numbering 1,104 lines, together with 192 lines of the second book, within the scope of 19 English verses; or again we perceive that he works over the material of 56 lines of the fifth book (sts. 92-98) into 49 lines of the *Kn. T.* (1812-60). He reduces large sections of the Italian poem to infinitesmal parts of the *Kn. T.* at one time, and at another takes over a short passage with the hardly appreciable reduction of seven lines. At another point he takes the material of seven widely distributed stanzas (IV, 13, 14, 31, 85, 84, 17, 82) and condenses it into 21 lines (1545-65).

The table, it would seem, presents an erratic method of reduction, but in its real nature it is not so. Chaucer is selecting the details of the plot or the characterization of the *Tes.*, and inevitably, if he wishes to avoid monotony, he must guard himself lest he reproduce those details in proportions relative to their volume rather than to their importance in the Italian source. It is impossible to make mathematical generalizations about Chaucer's reductions in the *Kn. T.* They defy every law of the equations of lines or curves. Yet by an examination of the contents of the lines tabulated by Professor Skeat, we can discover the manner in which Chaucer distributes the several parts of the *Tes.*, and what faculty for selection the poet possesses.

Chaucer has very much altered the order of the verses which he takes over from Boccaccio. Material of Book V is in the *Kn. T.*, wedged in between material of Book IV. Following IV comes material from VII, which is succeeded by material from V again, and then by further material from VII. The latter is followed by material from VI, and once more by another passage from VII. The same shifting of parts continues in Chaucer's introduction of the other five books of the *Tes.* Books VIII and IX come in normal order after VII. Then a passage from XII is inserted, before Chaucer goes on with his use of Books X, XI, and XII in correct relative order.

Skeat's table, then, gives us some hints as to Chaucer's method of reduction and distribution, and in so far it is both suggestive and tisasfactory. But it does not provide us with altogether adequate means for any particular inferences as to the value of the poet's method.

Professor Tatlock, in his *Development and Chronology of Chaucer's Works* (pp. 227-30), presents another table of very great interest, but the very particular purpose, for which it was prepared, viz.— to assist him in his refutation of the old stanzaic theory of ten Brink and Koch, somewhat detracts from its general usefulness. Yet it reveals to us several very significant possibilities. Through it we can trace to their source, line for line in the *Tes.*, 498 lines of the *Kn. T.*; and from it we derive the further definite knowledge that from the great bulk of the Italian poem only 504 lines in all are translated by Chaucer, and of these only 96 translated closely. The 498 translated English lines, however, coincide in the great majority of cases with the lines cited in Mr. Ward's marginal references, and designated there either as "translated" or as containing a "general likeness."

In so far Professor Tatlock contributes to our knowledge only by providing us with more specific references. And, in addition, he points out here and there a number of lines containing a general likeness (*Kn. T.* 1078, 1120-22, 1292, 1391, etc.), which Mr. Ward missed, and here and there a line actually translated and previously not cited (*Kn. T.* 2204, 2205, etc.).

The inadequacy of the testimony, offered by the brief table we
derived from the marginal references of Mr. Ward, is, however, not
wholly obviated by the additional testimony afforded by the tables of
Professor Skeat and Professor Tatlock. It still remains true that
numerous lines in the *Kn. T.* are performing the same function for
the story of Palamon and Arcite as that already performed by lines
in the *Tes.* It is too often forgotten by scholars, that episodes as
well as verses, can be transferred from a poem in one language to
a poem in another. And those episodes, too, denote an influence.
In the realization of that latter fact, I wish to add to the work of
Mr. Ward, Professor Skeat, and Mr. Tatlock a short table. It will
consist of lines in the *Kn. T.*, which, although not translated from
the *Tes.*, embody nevertheless certain contents of the Italian story,
which will be indicated in some detail.

Lines in *Kn. T.*	Origin in *Tes.*	Contents
1060-74	III, 10-26	Palamon and Arcite discover Emilye, become infatu-
1077-78		ated, and converse with one another in regard to
1080-95		their love.
1098-1128		
1133-68		
1177-90		
1216-1223	III, 53-59	Arcite is released by Theseus and goes reluctantly
	69	into exile.
	74-79	
	82	
	85	
1380 1436	IV, 1-60	Arcite returns in disguise to Athens and is taken into
1441-50		favour by Theseus.
1480-1544	V, 33-76	The returned Arcite and the escaped Palamon fight
1556-1661		their duel in the woods. According to Ward a few
		lines in the group, 1556-1661, are translated from
		or are similar to lines in the *Tes.*, viz.—1557-65,
		1573-74, 1604-1605, 1638-42.
1664-67	V, 77-82	The royal hunting party of Theseus comes riding into
1670-72		the woods.
1674-77		
1680-85		
1687-96		
1697-1703	V, 82-91	Theseus interrupts and begins to harangue the com
1705-09		batants.

1711-24
1727-34
1736-38
1740-84

1818-25   V, 92-93   Theseus pardons the lovers conditionally.

1832-34   V, 96-98   Theseus dismisses Palamon and Arcite to seek com-
1836-47   100-101   panions-at-arms for the great tournament.
1860-80   VI, 11

1881-86   V, 97   The theatre.
           VII, 108-110

1903-12   VII, 23, line 1,   The shrines of Venus, Mars, and Diana. These are
           42, 5-8   in the *Kn. T.* "oratories," and in the *Tes.* "tempii."
           72

1914-21   VII, 36-38   The temple of Venus. According to Ward, of the
1922-38   50   group, 1922-38, a number of lines bear a general
1955-66   54   likeness to the *Tes.*, 1922, 1925, 1926-28, 1931,
           55-66   1936-37. But there are no lines actually trans-
                   lated in the description of the temple of Venus.
                   Chaucer had already used, we remember, the *Tes.*
                   VII, 51-60, 63-66, 61-62 in the *Parliament of Fowls*,
                   183-259, 260-280, 281-287, translating the Italian
                   passage almost word for word.

2001   VII, 34, lines 1-2   The temple of Mars. Lines 2018-23 reveal only a
2008   general likeness to the *Tes.* VII, 34-36. Chaucer
2011   35, lines 3, 1, 4-8   here, just as in *Troil.*, takes the abstract suggestive-
2013-17   ness of Boccaccio and makes it concrete. But the
2018-23   36, lines 4-5   earlier part of Chaucer's description of the temple of
                   Mars (1967-2004) is almost purely a translation, as
                   Ward shows us, of the *Tes.* VII, 31-36, the order of
                   parts only being changed. (N. B. The materials
                   for his description of the interior of the temple of
                   Diana (2051-2088), it should of course be remem-
                   bered, Chaucer does not derive from the *Tes.* In
                   that poem, when Boccaccio ushers Emilia into the
                   shrine of the goddess, he gives us no description of it
                   whatever, although he has described minutely the
                   temples and their interior decorations of Venus and
                   Mars. Chaucer, who is at this time more methodi-
                   cal in his manner than Boccaccio, devises a de-
                   scription for Diana's temple, paralleling it with the
                   descriptions of the shrines of the other two deities.
                   An investigation of Boccaccio's *Ninfale Fiesolano*,

Caccia di Diana, and Amorosa Visione, the two first
of which poems develop in a very great detail the
myths of Diana, reveals to us no material that
Chaucer could have used in this particular description. It appears to be a Chaucerian invention, and
one that resumes, in several instances, myths that
Chaucer had previously employed in such other
works as Troil. and the Parliament of Fowls. Cf.
Troil. V, 1457-84, P. F. 281-294.)

2089-92	VII, 108-110	The lists and theatre complete and ready.
2093-2188	VI, 13-65	The arrival of the two hundred knights in Athens. Descriptions of their persons, armour, etc. The more concrete details are Chaucer's. Of these lines, according to Ward, the foll)wing are directly trans- lated: 2129, 2130, 2135, 2140-42, 2158, 2175. A number of others bear a general likeness to the Tes.: 2102-2103, 2105, 2138-39, 2162-64, 2182-83.
2483-90	VI, 69-70 VII, 1	The knights are received with festivities.
2491-2512	VII, 14, 95 97-99 101	The knights and people assemble to go to the thea- tre. Of these lines, according to Ward, 2491-98 are a general imitation of the Tes. VII, 95-99 and 2506-2507 are directly translated.
2517-2522	VII, 98, lines 3-8	Predictions are made as to the outcome of the tournament in Arcite's or in Palamon's favour.
2526-2532	VII, 96	The conference in Theseus's palace to learn the order of the day.
2533-2536	VII, 2-13 130-132	The orders of Theseus are publicly announced; in the Kn. T. by a herald (2533), in the Tes. by Teseo himself, (VII 130-132).
2593-2600	VII, 131	The qualifications of the knights are examined before they are admitted to the tournament.
2601-2675	VIII, 10-131	The tournament. In the Kn. T. it is one great melée; in the Tes. it is a succession of many combats, many of them little more than duels. Much is made, in the Italian poem, of Arcita's and Palamon's indi- vidual prowess. VIII, 85-92. Lines 2610-2620, Mr. Ward very properly suggests are similar to the Tes. VIII, 14, 29, 33, 40, 69, 81, etc. In the other

lines only the general situation is similar. Chaucer, who himself had witnessed tournaments, had no need here to depend closely upon an Italian description of such a spectacle.

2707-2717	IX, 23 61	Remedies are applied to save the life of Arcite and to heal the other wounded champions.
2718-2734	IX, 51-62	Theseus's courteous entertainment of the stranger knights.
2815-2821	XI, 4, lines 5-9	The grief of Emilye and Palamon at Arcite's death.
3003-3016	IX, 52-56 XI, 10-11	Theseus discourses of fore-ordination. The passage in the *Kn. T.* is of course Boethian, but its occasion is certainly to be found in the specified passages of the *Tes.* It should be noted that the continuation of this speech, lines 3017-3056, is properly accredited by Mr. Ward to the *Tes.* XII, 6-13.
3069-3108	Book XII	The espousal of Palamon and Emilye, and the worthiness of the lover. Of these lines Mr. Ward points out the fact that 3094-98, 3101-3102 are generally like the *Tes.* XII, 69, 72, 83.

The above table reveals several facts of importance. Although it establishes no additional parallels, line for line, it suffices to show that Chaucer used the materials of Boccaccio's *Tes.* in between 700 or 800 more lines of the *Kn. T.* It serves also to make the marginal references of Mr. Ward, and the tables of Professor Skeat and Mr. Tatlock, more adequate for our use. It reveals the greater preponderance of Boccaccian descriptive and narrative elements in the English poem. And furthermore it enables us to estimate more exactly what are some of the phenomena of Chaucer's independent treatment of the Italian poem, and what are the purely Chaucerian elements in the *Kn. T.*

Not all of the latter elements can be detected, but such of them as I find more striking I desire to submit in another table.

NEW ELEMENTS IN THE PALAMON AND ARCITE STORY

975-980   The description of the warrior Theseus, his "baner" and "penoun."
1042-1047   The potency of the month of May over lovers.
1250-1350   The two lovers, with many a Boethian note, bewail their misfortunes; Arcite that he must leave Athens, Palamon that he must remain in prison. Much of the querulousness and jealousy of this scene probably

grows out of various passages of the *Tes.* IV, 59-61, 74-81, V, 2, 37-60 or perhaps out of the later passages in the *Tes.* V, 37-83, which describe the duel of the lovers in the wood.

1380-1398 Arcite is counseled by Mercury in a dream to return to Athens.

1413-1447 The particular offices to which the disguised Arcite rises in the royal court of Theseus.

1785-1811 Theseus's discourse of the might of the god of Love, perhaps occasioned by the *Tes.* V, 88-92, VII, 3-8.

2443-2483 Saturn, after the controversy in Heaven between Venus and Mars, (*Kn. T.* 2438-2441 and *Tes.* VII, 67), occasioned by the prayers of the lovers, assures the weeping goddess of Love that he will fulfil her wishes in regard to Palamon's success. The dispensations of Saturn are altogether new in Chaucer's work. In the *Tes.* we are told merely that a way was found among the gods to satisfy the prayers of all parties.

> . . . . .ma trovata
> Da lor fu via con maestrevol arte
> Di far contenti i preghi d'ogni parte.
>
> (VII, 67)

2745-2760 The inefficacy of every mediaeval measure of leechcraft to save the life of Arcite.

2819 The swoon of Emilye at the death of Arcite.

2970 2975 A parliament is held at Athens to determine fully upon points of Theban "obeisaunce" and upon "alliaunce" with certain countries.

It is not so difficult a problem in mathematics to sum up the lines in the *Kn. T.* resulting from the introduction into the story of the new elements just cited in our table. The total of them is about 259 lines. That is to say despite the necessity for condensation in his version of the Palamon and Arcite story, Chaucer allowed himself to add lines, absolutely new, which represent somewhat more than a tenth part of the volume of the *Kn. T.* The poet's independence is manifested, then, not only in his condensation of the material of the *Tes.*, but in his daring improvisations in action, setting, and philosophy.

So far we have studied only those details in the *Kn. T.*, which Chaucer either himself devised or derived from the Italian poem. Let us now turn our attention to some features of the technique of the *Tes.*, which the English poet omitted. There are certain beauties in the context of the pseudo-epic, which unfortunately had to be suppressed or discarded in Chaucer's work. Among these are the following features of technique:

III, 11. The attraction of Arcita to the window of his prison by the sound of the voice of Emilia singing in the garden below.

III, 82.   The unspoken prayer of Arcita that he might see the delicate face of Emilia "solo un poco" before he parted from Athens.

III, 83, 84.   The vision of Emilia on a balcony looking compassionately after the figure of Arcita, as he departs into exile, and the last sweet glimpse which he has of her before he begins his journey.

IV, 1-32.   The disconsolate figure of Arcita wandering during his banishment from city to city in Greece.

IV, 33-37.   The news of Emilia, which Arcita learns of sailors, and which determines him at all hazards to return to Athens.

IV, 89.   Panfilo's discovery of the identity of Arcita, who under the name of Penteo has returned to Athens in disguise and succeeded in procuring royal favour as a servant of Teseo, and is now descanting among the trees upon the ills of fortune, followed by Panfilo's revelation of the exile's secret to his rival Palamon (IV, 90, V, 5).

IV, 6-15.   Palamon's astonishment at the revelation and determination to break prison and win Emilia "per arme."

V, 25-27.   The fidelity of the servitor, Panfilo, who exchanges his clothes with Palamon and so enables the latter to escape.

V, 27-28.   Palamon is provided with armour "all' ostiere" and aided out of the city by Alimeto.

V, 35-37.   Palamon's discovery of Arcita asleep in the woods outside of Athens, and his waiting for his rival to awake.

V, 38-80.   Details in the subsequent discussion and duel of the youths.

V, 81.   The discovery of the combat of Arcita and Palamon by the astonished damsel Emilia, who forthwith calls to Teseo and the other members of the hunting party to come and witness it.

VI.   The festivities which follow Teseo's pardon of his two prisoners, and the assembling of the hundred knights of each of the two latter, not as the result of their travels through Greece in search of champions, but as a consequence of the brilliant opportunities afforded to knights of prowess by the proposed tournament.

VII, 1-21.   The entertainments and processions preliminary to the final opening of the tournament.

VII, 133-143.   The solemn exhortation of the chivalric and magnanimous Teseo to the knights as they address themselves to battle.

VIII, 94-110.   The prayers of Emilia as she sits among the spectators, viewing the combat of the two lovers, not knowing which of the two she prefers, or whether she even loves at all; and the blushes that flit intermittently over the damsel's cheeks (III, 18, VIII, 94).

VIII.   The vicissitudes of the tournament.

VIII, 112-113. The apparition of Mars, disguised as Teseo, to Arcita, enjoining him to redouble his efforts in the combat.

VIII, 120-122. The sad mischance of Palamon, who is bitten through the arm by the vicious horse of Cromis and dragged from his saddle by the animal's firmly implanted teeth, only to be disarmed "senza alcuno indugio" by Arcita, to whom then the winning of the tournament is immediately adjudged.

Very few of these details from the *Tes.* are inartistic; some of them possess a particular beauty. And the retention of a number of them might very much have aided Chaucer in perfecting his technique.

If we turn to the *Kn. T.*, we find certain of Chaucer's substitutions for these details much less satisfactory. Compared with those which introduce the corresponding scene in the *Tes.*, the lines in the English poet's work which picture to us the first view that Palamon has of Emilye are almost crude. He was pacing up and down in his chamber, complaining of his woe, until it

> . . . . . . so bifel, by aventure or cas,
> That thurgh a window, thikke of many a barre
> Of yren greet, and square as any sparre,
> He caste his eye upon Emelye. (1074-77)

Much prettier is the picture in the *Tes.*, when Emilia comes straying into the garden, making garlands and

> Sempre cantando be' versi d'amore
> Con angelica voce a lieto core (III, 10),

and Arcita, attracted

> Al suon di quella voce grazioso (III, 11),

rises and forces his head through the bars of his prison window in order to catch a glimpse of the lady. And very winsome, too, is the picture of Emilia a few moments later, with her hand on her breast, turning her eyes in the direction of the sigh that has involuntarily escaped the lips of Palamon, and then blushing because she knew not "Chi si fosson color" (III, 17-18). In the delineation of Emilye Chaucer's story undoubtedly loses. On the other hand, although in Boccaccio's poem the damsel is never prominently presented until the two lovers are discovered duelling in the forest, she is frequently enough presented for one to comprehend her coy femininity and her consciousness of the admiring glances of Palamon and Arcita (III, 18, 83). She is not altogether unprepared for her discovery of the two men fighting in the woods, and they too have, before that occasion, met the glances of her eyes. The discarding of such details in the *Kn. T.* cannot but be regretted.

Chaucer's condensation of the experiences of the exiled Arcite is more commendable; but the poet makes his story suffer a second time, when he suppresses the details of Palamon's escape from prison. In the *Kn. T.* we learn merely that with the help of a friend Palamon broke his prison (l. 1468), without our ever having had the slightest hint from the poet that the prisoner ever as much as possessed a friend. In the *Tes.*, a poem, drawn as it is on a more royal scale, the two princes were granted during their imprisonment the attendance of numerous servitors, and accorded the most courteous treatment as prisoners of state. Consequently the Italian poet could very easily and very reasonably account for the escape of Palamon. The *Kn. T.* would have lost no beauty, if in it the prisoners had been royally treated, and the awkwardness of the sudden introduction of an unnamed friend to Palamon might have been in that way avoided. The *Kn. T.* loses nothing by its rearrangement of the several details of the rivals' meeting and duel in the woods, but it suffers a distinct loss in artistic effect, when it assigns to Theseus, and not, as in the Italian work, to the lily-like Emilia, the discovery of the combatants (*Kn. T.* 1698, *Tes.* V, 81). Nothing in the English poem surpasses the exquisite spectacle of the damsel gazing in mute and innocent wonderment.

> Ella sì stava quasi che stordita,
> Nè giva avanti nè indietro tornava;
> E sì per maraviglia era invilita,
> Ch' ella non si muova e non parlava (V, 81).

The omission of many brilliant features in the preparation for the tournament marks for the *Kn. T.* a loss in colour rather than one in perfectness of technique; but the abundance of other colour, other atmosphere, which the poem acquires from the hand of Chaucer, does much to compensate for that loss. To indemnify us for the omission of Teseo's chivalric exhortation to the knights (VII, 133-143), Chaucer substitutes the proclamation of the herald (2533-2560).

The suppression of the blushes and prayers of Emilia during the progress of the tournament, as well as that of the apparition of Mars to Arcita, is an unfortunate, but necessary procedure. Some features of the *Tes.* had to be discarded. For one must grant that Chaucer in a greatly reduced poem could not retain all the essential beauties of his source. And it is better for him to have discarded a few blushes and some of the accessories of pseudo-classicism rather than the more essential elements of Boccaccio's plot structure.

The last detail of Chaucer's omissions noted above was the biting of Palamon by the steed of Cromis. This accident seems to bring about a more unsatisfactorily fortuitous conclusion to the contest than Chaucer's Palamon's being drawn to the stake by the force of twenty knights (2641-42); but it has yet one point of value. For in the *Tes.* the knight is defeated only by a chance accident, and therefore deserves the hand of Emilia no less than Arcite, whereas in the *Kn. T.* he is more fairly defeated and is therefore less deserving of his later good fortune in securing the prize, the hand of Emilye. Boccaccio, it would seem in this matter, has a keener sense of poetic justice than Chaucer.

But the English poet's sense of poetic justice is by no means negligible. There are points of decided merit in the *Kn. T.* If it is not throughout an improvement upon the *Tes.*, it has yet many points of superiority. Let us, then, investigate some of the new episodes or changes in his story which make for a presence therein of artistic beauty.

The first striking innovation is one which we discover in lines 1069-78. Mr. F. J. Mather has already made note of it in his introduction to an edition of the poem. (See F. J. Mather: *The Prologue, Knight's Tale, and Nun's Priest's Tale.* Part I, lxiii. *Riverside Literature Series*, Houghton, Mifflin & Company, New York, 1899.) It is Palamon, and not Arcite, as in the Italian work, who first catches sight of Emilye (1077). The poet appears to be conscious of the principle of first come first serve, and so makes the knight who is eventually to win the fair Emilye sure of his title by causing him first to see her in the garden. The solution is thus made more satisfactory to us than the one in the *Tes.* can be.

The second episodic change, which admits an increase of beauty into Chaucer's Tale, is the rearrangement of the meeting in the grove (1502-1622). The fugitive and unarmed Palamon is hiding in a bush, all unwitting of Arcite's return to Athens disguised as Philostrate, a name that the poet derives from the *Filostrato*, and fearful of his own possible re-capture, when suddenly the second knight comes straying into the woods, singing of May, of his woes, and of Emilye. As he is presenting a character who has not, like the Palamon of Boccaccio, escaped from prison for the deliberate purpose of seeking out and slaying his rival, Chaucer takes advantage of a rare oppor-

tunity. He has Palamon, dismayed at the unexpected vision of
Arcite and dazed by the avowals of love to Emilye, which he hears
the latter make, rush defenceless from his retreat and cry with a
desperate but undaunted chivalric valor,

> . . . I am Palemoun, thy mortal fo.
> And though that I no wepne have in this place
> But out of prison am astert by grace,
> I drede noght that outher thou shalt dye,
> Or thou ne shalt nat loven Emilye.
> Chees which thou wilt, for thou shalt nat asterte.
>   (1590-95)

It is a scene worthy of Shakespeare that follows. Furious though
he is at the spectacle of his escaped rival, Arcite refuses to fight with
an unarmed foe. With knightly generosity he offers to bring "mete
and drinke this night" to the famished Palamon, and on the morrow
"harneys right y-nough for him"; and "chees the beste, and leve the
worste for me." On the next day Arcite keeps his promise, and we
have the charming picture of him riding to the forest, and carrying
the extra suit of harness for Palamon before him on his saddle. Then
the quintessence of the chivalric ideal is realized before us, as the
two knights

> . . . streight, withouten word or rehersing,
> Everich of hem halp for to armen other,
> As freendly as he were his owne brother.   (1650-52)

A third addition to the perfecting of Chaucer's technique is observ-
able when Theseus, moved by the tearful intercession of Ippolyta,
Emilye, and "alle the ladies in the companye," pardons the lovers,
whom he has just discovered in combat, and appoints for them the
great tournament (1748-65). A fourth and even greater addition is
to be found in the arrangement of Theseus's theatre. Above its gates
to the east, the west, and the north are erected "altars" and "orator-
ies" in honour of the divinities, Venus, Mars, and Diana, which take
the place of the three distantly located temples of the Italian poem,
and, by reason of their proximity to one another in the Chaucerian
story, serve admirably to concentrate the action. In the Kn. T. it
is not necessary, as it was in the Tes., for the prayers of Palamon and
Arcite to be first personified and then to travel to the distant abodes
of Venus at Mt. Citheron and of Mars in far off Thrace, and there
make intercession for the lovers (Tes. VII, 29-30, 50). The prayers
instead receive immediate answers from the images of the deities

before which the suppliants kneel, everything occurring with far less range of time and space.

Chaucer's suppression of the backgrounds of the three temples in the *Tes.*, and his substitution of the mural paintings within for them, accomplish much the same purpose of concentration.

Only one further comment in regard to episodic changes occurring in the *Kn. T.* and tending to improve its technique in certain details over that of the *Tes.*, need be made. A fifth great change appears in the reversal of the order, in which Palamon, Emilye, and Arcite make their prayers to their several guardian deities, Venus, Diana, and Mars. They approach the shrines in the order in which they have just been named, although in Boccaccio's pseudo-epic Arcita was the first suppliant to present himself before the altars, Palamon the second, and Emilia the last. The new position of Palamon's supplication adds prominence to his position in the Tale, and satisfies more keenly the sense of poetic justice in Chaucer's reader, as he beholds Palamon, the loyal servitor of Venus, who, like every proper suitor in her court, prayed only for success in love, at last awarded his just deserts and the hand of Emilye.

It would seem, then, that Chaucer in his transformation of episodes, in his introduction of new ones, and in his rearrangement of old ones did add materially to the technique of the Palamon and Arcite story. With a very delicate sense of selection the poet, in fact, joined a high order of inventive genius.

A few more notes on this sense of selection will not be inappropriate. It is especially perceptible in his use of the three prayers of Arcita, Palamon, and Emilia as found in the *Tes.* (VII, 24-28; 39-41; 43-49; 85-93). These Chaucer, for the most part, translates directly (*Kn. T.* 2373-2434; 2221-2260; 2297-2366). It is a rather delicate problem that the poet faces, if he is to obtain an efficient solution for his plot. Two young men of apparently equal merit and similar virtue are deeply enamoured of the same winsome damsel, who inclines no more to the passion of the one than to that of the other, but the loss of whom as a bride is destined to bring to him who loses an irretrievable sorrow and perhaps even death. According to the tenets of poetic justice a similar issue of pain or happiness is required for each. The story of the *Tes.* contained the only happy solution for this situation. Two men prayed, and for different boons. The gods responded to their supplications with equity. Each suppliant received the answer, as was proper according to the canons of the Court of Love,

to the letter of his prayer. Arcite prayed for victory in the tournament and received the boon he had asked, only to realize that he had
not requested the boon he had really craved, the love of Emilye.
Palamon prayed to Venus for success and joy in his love for the
princess and lost the tournament, but gained the consummate privilege he had desired. The indifferent Emilye, without excessive mental reservation, became the portion of him who desired most from the
favour of the goddess of Love. And through the wording of prayer
the Gordian knot of Boccaccio's complication was solved. Chaucer's
good judgment prompted him to perceive the delicacy and effectiveness of the Boccaccian solution and to make use of the same device.
Accordingly we find, in the three supplications, the closest translations discoverable in the *Kn. T.* Where the perfectness of his technique can be maintained by the assistance of the Italian poet, Chaucer is not loth to borrow.

But once he has employed the essential elements of Boccaccio's
plot, the English poet begins again to discard others. He omits the
lingering illness of Arcita and the formal betrothal of the latter to
Emilia, as well as the greater part of the funeral games and other
scenes at the pyre of the ill-fated prince. He minimizes the conversation of Palamon, Emilia, and Arcita at the bedside of the in-
jured man (IX, X, XI), and introduces new details of his own.

Very new is the scene of the controversy in heaven as it is presented
in the *Kn. T.* (2438-2482). In the *Tes.* we are merely told

E sì ne nacque in ciel novella lite
In tra Venere e Marte: ma trovata
Da lor fu via con maestrevol arte
Di far contenti i preghi d'ogni parte.   (VII, 67)

For this simple scene Chaucer substitutes Venus's long colloquy with
Saturn, and the innovation serves for some time to create an atmosphere of pseudo-classicism in the *Kn. T.*, but one that proves very
ephemeral. Chaucer sees the present in too clear a reality to desire, for
long to restore the vision of an earlier civilization, as Boccaccio strives
consciously to restore it in the Italian epic. Moreover, the English
poet proceeds immediately to weave the innovation into the woof of
his narrative fabric. Saturn is given a part to play in the new Palamon
and Arcite story, for it is he, remembering his promise to fulfill the
wish of Venus (2478), and not Venus herself, as in the *Tes.* (IX, 4),
who importunes Pluto (2685) to send the infernal fury that starts
out from the ground before the horse of Arcite. In brief, Chaucer

had another purpose for the figure of Saturn than the maintenance of a pseudo-classic atmosphere. The ancient deity was in his poem to relieve the goddess of Love from the guilty complicity, which she shared in Boccaccio's work, in the death of Arcita!

References have already been made several times in this dissertation to the two different atmospheres of the Italian and the English poem. The former is consistently pseudo-classic, the latter only intermittently so.

Boccaccio reveals ever a conscious effort at classicism. We perceive it in the wars of Teseo with the Amazons in Scythia, in the prayers of the grieving ladies from Thebes, who realize that their dead relatives and friends may not cross into the Elysian Fields before their bodies have received honourable burial; in the sack of Thebes and the punishment of Creon (II); in the wanderings of Arcita about Greece; in the travels of the prayers of the three persons to the distant abodes of Mars and Venus; in the great catalogue and in the figures of the knights, many of them clad like Hercules in the skins of lions or other animals, and carrying staffs of heavy iron (VI, 27 ff., 33, etc.); in the immediate and intimate relations existing between Teseo and his people; in the succession of minor combats and duels in the great tourney, scenes apparently adapted by Boccaccio from the *Roman de Troie*; in the apparition of Mars exhorting his favorite, Arcita, to mightier efforts (VIII, 112-114); in the processions to the temples and most of all in the long protracted funeral games (XI).

Besides these more scenic effects, many other elements in imitation of classical literature appear in the *Tes*. The Italian poem abounds in classical allusions, and in its use of Homeric similes it is hardly inferior to the *Divina Commedia* itself. Again and again they are found in the text. (I, 38-39, 67; VI, 27-28, 56-57; VII, 119; VIII, 3, 4-7, 63-64, 121; XI, 7, 12.)

Chaucer, of course, retains a number of Boccaccio's classical imitations. He even adds the one item of the controversy we discussed recently. The Homeric simile he drops in his briefer metrical romance. But more significant than these details, which are abandoned or retained, is the new atmosphere which the poet creates in the *Kn. T.*, a work which does not for a moment receive its colour from the pseudo-classicism that survives partially in its material.

Even in his earlier work in *Troil.* the English poet had introduced some realistic elements of fourteenth century life. Through Pandarus as an emissary Deiphebus was ready to offer to be Criseyde's

champion in a trial by combat, if Poliphete continued his reported
hostile machinations against her. (*Troil.* II, 1425-28). And Troilus,
like an English prince, had a household all his own with knights on
duty at his bedroom door (*Troil.* IV, 351-52).

In the *Kn. T.* Chaucer introduces, in comparison with the number in
Troil., a great many more such realistic elements, enough in fact to
substitute for the unity of conception, so admirably maintained in the
Tes. by the poem's pseudo-classic devices, a very palpable atmosphere
of feudal realism. A number of the predominant aspects of this atmosphere are discussed in an article by Mr. Gilbert Stuart Robertson,
Elements of Realism in the Knight's Tale (*Journal of English and
Germanic Philology*, XIV, 226-255). As the result of his investigation Mr. Robertson has detected a great many elements of what he
by terms a sort of mediaeval realism, which are either introduced purely
by Chaucer or are adapted, with very great modifications by the poet,
from Boccaccio's work. These realistic touches of Chaucer, he shows us,
are present in Theseus's battle with Creon and, in the sack of Thebes,
events of which the poet writes just as the chronicler Froissart writes
of the French and English wars; in the several references to ransoms
in the *Kn. T.* (1022-24, 1030-32, 1205-1206, 1175-76); in the fetters put upon the "shines grete" of Palamon (1279-80) in Chaucer's story, whereas Boccaccio's hero is treated as a royal prisoner;
in the disguise of Arcite, which enables him to become first a "page"
(1427) and later a "squyer" (1440) in the court of the royal family;
in the armed conflict of Palamon and Arcite in the woods; in the
descriptions of the several knights arriving for the tourney; in the
preparations about the town of Athens for the tournament; and in
many of the details of the tournament itself. The above list, borrowed from Mr. Robertson's work, is comprehensive enough to
demonstrate how thoroughly Chaucer's poem is permeated with this
atmosphere of feudal realism. It seems, therefore, at first thought,
irrelevant to adduce further testimony in corroboration of it. But
there are too many other interesting touches of this realism of arms
and the feudal system to admit of our passing them by without any
consideration. Especially should they be observed as further illustrations of Chaucer's perennial tendency to make Boccaccio's suggest-
iveness crystallize concretely.

They crop up at every point. The poet's old fondness for a May
morning, which led him to introduce in *Troil.* the picture of Pandarus
feeling "eek his part of loves shottes kene," induces him now to

present Emilye (1034-47) and Arcite (1500, 1509-1511) doing the proper English "observaunce" to the merry month. With reminiscences of his own earlier experiences, first as a page in the household of the Lady Elizabeth de Burgh, the first wife of Lionel, Duke of Clarence, the son of Edward III, of England, and with recollections of his subsequent promotion to be a squire in the court of that monarch, Chaucer first makes his Arcite a page in the household of Emilye and later has him promoted into service and favour in the establishment of Theseus (1417-1449).

Further realism is perceptible in certain mediaeval phenomena of rapine, pictured by the poet upon the walls of the temple of Mars, in carrion "with throte y-corve" lying in the bush, thousands slain, towns destroyed, ships burnt, children devoured by ravenous swine, the carter lying dead beneath the wheel of his over-turned cart, and the smith that forged upon his "stith" the weapons of death (2013-26). Again we see it in the choice of armour made by the knights who followed Palamon. Some were apparelled in one style of harness and others in other styles.

> Armed were they, as I have you told,
> Everich after his own opinion.   (2126-2127)

Chaucer's reader thinks instinctively of the profound discussions he hears about nose-guards or baseball gloves or golf clubs among athletes of his own day and generation. In the same way no doubt Chaucer had listened to the conversation of the athlete's prototype about his favourite style of armour.

Even more striking is Chaucer's realistic description of the assembling of the populace at the tournament,

> Yemen on fote, and communes many oon,
> With shorte staves, thikke as they may goon,

and of the

> . . . . .armurers also
> With fyle and hamer prikinge to and fro,

as well as of the spectators, who stand about the lists, exchanging their wagers as to who shall be the victor (2507-21).

Again we note his realism in his introduction of heralds to proclaim to the people the will of Theseus (2533-36, 2672); in the mortal symptoms of Arcite, and in the particular measures taken to save his life (2743-60); and finally in the parliament summoned to Athens to determine upon the just prerogatives of Athens and Thebes (2970-75).

The atmosphere of the *Kn. T.* is then, demonstrably, one of realism. It depends for its effect not merely upon either the devices of pseudo-classicism or those of the mediaeval metrical romances, but it depends upon life, and upon it no less than does the whole spirit of the *Canterbury Tales.* It abounds in characteristic modes of genuine mediaeval battle, tournament, court ceremonial, every-day speech and clamour, thought and philosophy. Before our gaze it humanizes the day of feudalism. We comprehend it alike with yeoman and knight, as convention recedes before reality in the poem.

Chaucer's greatest contribution to the story of Palamon and Arcite is this new atmosphere. The true superiority of his version over that of the Italian poet consists in its tendency to make all suggestions concrete. The process of analysis perceptible in Chaucer's development of *Troil.* is applied with more control, but to as good effect, in the second and last of his great poems from the Italian. In that process lies the real secret of Chaucer's continued emancipation and freedom from the domination of source influences.

The *Kn. T.* becomes, in the poet's hands, a thoroughly English poem. It has little or nothing of the southern atmosphere of *Troil.* It contains, moreover, just the sort of narrative, which one would expect of a knight. At every juncture it is filled with dramatic utterance. The constant talk of concrete phenomena in the system of feudal war and tournament,—ransoms, fetters, massacres, heralds, armourers,—makes it *par excellence* the one tale of all others that Chaucer's Knight should tell. Everything in it conduces, it seems, to the belief that Chaucer must, unquestionably, have written it with a view to having it narrated by the

> . . . . .worthy man,
> That fro the tyme that he first bigan
> To ryden out, he loved chivalrye,
> Trouthe and honour, fredom and courteisye. (Pro. 43-46)

a fact that should go far in the way of evidence that the story of *Palamon and Arcite* was not written by Chaucer before the poet's imagination was already busied with conceptions of the *Canterbury Tales.*

CHAPTER VII

CHAUCER AND OTHER LESS FAMOUS ITALIAN WORKS OF BOCCACCIO

Fiametta; Commento sopra Dante; Vita di Dante; La Caccia di Diana;
L'Urbano; Ninfale Fiesolano.

No student of Chaucer has at any time suggested that the English poet may have been acquainted with, or can have made use of, Boccaccio's other Italian works, the *Fiammetta*, *Commento sopra Dante*, *Vita di Dante*, the *Caccia di Diana*, the *Rime*, the *Urbano*, and the *Ninfale Fiesolano*. From my own careful examination of these works I have discovered nothing which points to the influence of any one of them over any one of Chaucer's works. It is my intention, however, for the convenience of other investigators of Chaucer-Boccaccio relations, to add here summaries of the few of these works which are narrative in form, excepting, of course, the *Vita di Dante*.

Fiammetta

The name Fiammetta is usually identified with Maria d'Acquino, the natural daughter of Robert, the Angevin King of Naples in the fourteenth century, a lady married to a gentleman of her father's court, but believed to-day to have been, for a time, the mistress of Boccaccio, during those early days when he lingered amid the corrupt Neapolitans. It is a number of times assigned by Boccaccio to heroines of his various works.

The *Fiammetta* (*Opere Volgari*, Vol. VI) is a work of very considerable charm, and among the most frequently read of Boccaccio's. In it he makes a rather psychological study of a beautiful young, but deserted, mistress, conceiving possibly that in the interpretation of her he is presenting the dreary longings and attitude of Maria d'Acquino after his own parting from her. The narrative is exceedingly simple,—devoid of all mythological, erotic, and allegorical features.

Fiammetta, although warned in a dream of future unhappiness, becomes acquainted with a young Florentine by the name of Panfilo, and falls impetuously in love with him, the young man responding to her passion. For a while a perilous and secret *amour* is carried on by the young wife and her lover, in spite of the good injunctions and friendly warnings of Fiammetta's shrewd old nurse. Ere long Panfilo, at the summons of his father, is obliged to leave Naples. Fiammetta attempts to dissuade him from this purpose, but receives from him only the assurance that his absence shall not exceed four months ("il quarto mese non uscirà che . . . tu mi vedrai qui tornato").

Left alone, she passes her days and nights in lamentation. Four months pass and Panfilo does not return. One day she is informed by a merchant that the young man has taken a wife. This news aggravates her torments, and sends her weeping to demand aid of Venus. Meantime her husband takes cognizance of her suffering, and, suspecting nothing, takes her to the baths at Baiae. Here, despite her attempts to forget, no distraction can remove the beloved Panfilo from her mind; the flames of love augment. Presently a new bit of news, not less unexpected than the other, reaches her through a servitor of her own house, returning from Florence. It was not Panfilo, but the father of Panfilo, who had married; the son is merely enamoured of another young woman. New jealousy and despair seize upon Fiammetta, who refuses to be comforted by her nurse. She contemplates death by suicide, and tries to throw herself from a window, but is saved from this attempt by her nurse and some other ladies. Finally the return of Panfilo is announced. Fiammetta thanks Venus for it, and resumes her ornaments in expectation of him. But it is only an indifferent Panfilo who returns, and one who no longer seeks Fiammetta. Whereupon the lady resigns herself to her unhappiness, and takes comfort in the thought of all those who suffer from love.

The romance ends with a farewell to the book, in which it is instructed by Fiammetta as to what sort of readers it should approach and what sort avoid.

Caccia di Diana

The *Caccia di Diana* (*Opere Volgari*, Vol. XIV) had been several times, in early catalogues of Florentine writers, attributed to Boccaccio before the editor of the *Moutier* edition, for stylistic reasons, assigned it in 1833 without hesitation to the poet. The matter of its authorship is still open to question, but as a supposititious work of Boccaccio, a brief summary of it may be offered here with entire relevancy. It is, like the poet's *Amorosa Visone*, a poem in *terza rima*, and is of considerable dimensions, consisting of eighteen cantos, which are, with one exception, fifty-eight verses in length.

The narrator stands, in the spring-time, sadly pondering the problems of love, when of a sudden he seems to hear a gentle spirit calling in a high voice: "Come, ye fair ladies, whom she has chosen to be her companions in Parthenope, come to the great court of the lofty goddess Diana." As he listens, he hears the spirit naming one by one the thirty or more ladies whom Diana has invited, except one of them, of whom the narrator will only speak as she whom "amore onora Più ch' altra per la somma virtute" (Canto I). The several ladies answer the summons, and the narrator stands by to observe their gathering. In the midst of a valley bound by four mountains, north, south, east, and west, Diana holds her court. Here the goddess divides the ladies into four groups to be sent on separate hunting expeditions, assuming command herself of the first party, and assigning the other three to the "bella Donna," i. e., the lady of whom the narrator is enamoured, to Isabella, and to Fiore (Canto II). She then leads her own train of ladies to the mountain in the east, where they have various adventures with various animals as they hunt (II-III). The other three ladies manage similar expeditions in the other three mountains, where they and their followers, with the utmost of courage encounter, and slay every variety of ferocious beast (IV-XV). At length they are recalled by Diana, at sultry mid-day, to rest in the fresh meadows, and all come in laden with their weapons and prey. Here Diana enjoins them to make sacrifices of their booty to Jove and to the honour of herself, under whose providence they have made their captures. At this injunction, without any apparent motivation, the "bella Donna" rises, her countenance disturbed, and declares unexpectedly that they will do nothing of the sort, that they have achieved the commands of Diana for the morning, and that now they no longer wish to follow her divinity, because they have hearts and minds inflamed with another fire. Thereupon the goddess hurries away angrily and returns to heaven (XVI). The ladies wait until they can no longer see her retreating figure, and then offer sacrifice and prayers to Venus, desiring her favour and contentment in love. Presently a naked maiden appears in a cloud to them, assuring them that the goddess will grant each one's request. At this point, by a sudden miracle, many of the slain beasts are transformed into beautiful youths, who bathe first in the brook, and then, after making themselves mantles of vermilion, approach the ladies, to whom they are instructed by Venus to yield themselves as subjects and lovers. Venus retires to heaven, and the erstwhile followers of Diana seek various delights with their lovers amid the flowers (XVII).

The narrator, who has stood observing all these events, suddenly finds himself seemingly transformed from a deer into a man, and, covered with a vermilion mantle, offered to the "bella Donna." In praise of her, and of her patron-goddess Venus, the poem ends (XVIII).

Urbano

The narrative of the *Urbano* (*Opere Volgari*, Vol. XVI), which is a comparatively brief, and rather uninteresting prose romance, can be summarized very simply. The Emperor Frederick Barbarossa, becoming separated one day from the other members of his hunting party, is obliged to seek shelter at nightfall in a peasant's hut. Here he finds a young girl, Silvestra, who has been left alone by her mother, and with whose beauty he becomes so violently enamoured that, taking advantage of her helplessness, he seizes and forces her. He seeks then to comfort the terrified and disconsolate maiden with the gift of a boar's head, the trophy of his hunt, and a rich and beautiful ring; and beseeching her for love of him to preserve the latter and show it to no one, he rides off presently to rejoin his companions. The girl's mother returns, detects after some time her daughter's pregnancy, and elicits from her the story of her betrayal. She thereupon takes Silvestra to the city, and, after leaving her there in the care of a friendly inn-keeper and his mother, dies of grief for the injury done her child. Not long afterwards the girl gives birth to a beautiful boy, whom she names Urbano. About the same time the royal wife of Frederick Barbarossa gives birth to a son, Speculo, and dies immediately after.

The two children are nurtured tenderly in their different environments until, in their fifteenth year, by some chance they become acquainted and are drawn very much to one another in friendship. About this time Urbano's mother reveals her poverty (and age!) to him, and he consents to take service in the inn to aid her, "sforzando sua natura" (*Urbano*, 14). Not long afterwards three Florentine merchants, observing Urbano's remarkable resemblance to Speculo, inveigle the young man into a plot by which they succeed in marrying him to Lucrezia, the daughter of the Sultan of Babylonia, whose parents as well as she herself suppose she is marrying Speculo, the son of the Emperor at Rome. Festivities follow at the Babylonian court until Urbano and his bride set out,—apparently for Rome,— in the vessel of the merchants. With them goes a great treasure,

with which the three Florentines make off one day, while Urbano and
Lucrezia are ashore in a strange port. The perfidy of the merchants
being thus discovered to him, Urbano is reduced to tears and lamentation, while his bride similarly bemoans her fate. After various
adventures the two succeed in getting to Rome and to the inn of
Urbano's old master and friend, where they find Silvestra still alive.
About this time Speculo dies, and the Emperor, learning of the youth
who resembled his son, and of his bride, receives them subsequently
into favour. It is presently discovered that Urbano is the son of
Silvestra, whom the Emperor finds at the inn and recognizes as the
girl he had wronged years before in the wood. In reparation he
marries Silvestra with the ring he had given her as a parting gift,
and acknowledges Urbano as his son and heir. All live happy ever
afterwards.

Ninfale Fiesolano

The *Ninfale Fiesolano* (*Opere Volgari*, Vol. XVII) is a pastoral
romance in *ottava rima*. The youth Affrico, wandering one day in the
woods, discovers Diana and a band of nymphs, the beauty of one of
whom, Mensola, so fascinates him that he thinks only of her during
the restless days and nights that follow. Presently Venus with her
little naked son, armed with his bow and other paraphernalia, appears
and instructs Affrico to pursue his love. Seeking for Mensola, he in-
quires about her of three nymphs who turn and flee. On his return home
he informs his father, anxious because of his unwonted absence, that
he had seen a doe and later three deer that had fled at his approach.
His father concludes that these must have been the deer of Diana, and,
illustrating his admonitions with reference to his own father, Mugnone,
who had been slain by Diana in punishment for having forced a nymph,
who also suffered death as a penalty, he warns Affrico of the danger
of pursuing such deer. The youth, however, refuses to be advised;
and, after days of various ruses, of feigned illness, and of parental
anxiety, he succeeds in finding Mensola and wilfully forces her —
Boccaccio describing the scene in the nudest of fashions. Mensola is enraged, but later consents to grant Affrico voluntarily the
favour he has stolen; and the two continue in amorous delight till
dawn, when they sing an *aubade* and separate, Affrico returning
home. Mensola becomes disconsolate, as she discovers she has
broken her vows of chastity, fears punishment from Diana, and
conceals herself successfully from Affrico, who again ranges the woods

in search of her. A month passes; and Affrico, unable to find Mensola, desponds, upbraids the absent nymph for her failure to keep her oath to him, rails upon the god of love, and slays himself. His father finds his dead body by the fountain's side. Later the two parents burn the corpse and cast Affrico's dust into the stream, which subsequently acquires his name.

Mensola, ignorant of Affrico's death, becomes pregnant and is sheltered for a time by an older nymph, Sinedecchia, until her child, Pruneo, is born. Presently Diana discovers Mensola, who flees her presence and is converted by the goddess into a stream. Diana finds Pruneo hidden in some shrubbery and carries him to Sinedecchia, who tells her the story of Mensola's betrayal. Diana is moved to pity, and permits Sinedecchia to do with the child what seems best; whereupon the nymph carries it to the parents of Affrico, who recognize it as their grandchild and rear it.

Pruneo grows up, carefully watched by his grandparents. At maturity his story is told by his grandfather, Giraffone (named by Boccaccio only very late in the poem), as well as the story of his father Affrico and that of his great-grandfather Mugnone, to Atalante, a stranger who comes into the region to found a city (Fiesole). Atalante receives both Giraffone and Pruneo with favour, and soon marries the young man to a lady, Tironea, who subsequently bears him ten sons. All these Pruneo lives to marry off.

The rest of the *Ninfale Fiesolano* is devoted to a mythical history of Fiesole and Florence; and at the end Boccaccio addresses a few stanzas to Love.

CHAPTER VIII

CHAUCER AND "*Myn Auctor Called Lollius.*"

Scholars who have worked upon Chaucer-Boccaccio problems have long looked upon it as one of the first of their duties to explain why Chaucer, who drew so liberally upon the literary product of the Italian poet, should never have acknowledged by name his indebtedness to him. And the necessity of an explanation has ever appeared the more urgent because, borrowing comparatively much less from the literary work of Boccaccio's contemporary, Petrarch, and his predecessor, Dante, Chaucer very frankly and very laudably acknowledged his indebtedness to them. Various opinions have prevailed in the matter. Some men have believed that Chaucer did not know the name of the author of the two Italian poems, from which he borrowed most, the *Filostrato* and the *Teseide*; others that, knowing the name of Boccaccio, he deliberately ignored his indebtedness to him and feigned to have drawn his material from other sources. The "auctor called Lollius," to whom the English poet acknowledges a certain indebtedness in *Troil.* has been an especially tantalizing puzzle. In view of the many attempts to solve it, which have ended either in failure or in what is worse, idle and precarious suggestions, one should hesitate before one proposes a new solution.

It is my purpose, therefore, not so much to propose a solution of the name as it is to combat the tendency of those previous solutions, which perceive in the name "Lollius" a desire on the part of Chaucer either to obtain a cordial reception for *Troil.* by virtue of its being of apparently ancient Latin origin, or to repudiate his debt to the real author of the *Filostrato*. I feel that one should not be dogmatic in regard to Chaucer's use of Boccaccio's work without apparent comment or acknowledgment. Upon those who would claim that the English poet deliberately repudiated the assistance he derived from Boccaccio, disguising the latter's name intentionally, must rest the burden of proof. On the other hand, I believe it will be possible to show that Chaucer's failure ever to refer to the name of Boccaccio was neither calculated nor insidious, was in fact hardly to be termed an omission, conscious or unconscious.

It is, too, a more important task to discover what was the attitude of Chaucer toward the author "Lollius," whose *Filostrato* he used, than to identify the name "Lollius" with any writer who may at one time have flourished in literature. Much will be accomplished if it be shown that Chaucer accepted "Lollius" as his master and the work of "Lollius" as his model. In a word, if it can be demonstrated from his citations of authorities in *Troil.* with how much seriousness Chaucer regarded authorities in general, and his one great authority "Lollius" in particular, we shall have a more secure basis for a correct interpretation of Chaucer's great poem in its relations to its sources. We can determine whether the poet regarded his sources with an earnest or a flippant temper of mind. We can conclude whether Chaucer looked upon *Fil.* as a joke and in *Troil.* wrote mere satire; or whether Chaucer looked upon the Italian poem and its author with reverent eyes, and, in imitation of both, wrote rather pure romance.

In the realization that, to obtain conclusions pointing either way, a careful examination of Chaucer's attributions to authority in *Troil.* was necessary as a first step, I prepared for the sake of convenience a table of all discoverable references of that nature in the poem, and after its compilation found myself very much impressed with the fact that the English poet was unvarying in his respect for his sources in the first place, and, in the second, eminently just in his attributions to them. The task, in brief, assured me that, when Chaucer made a reference to an "auctor," to a "story" or "olde bokes," he did it in a spirit of neither levity nor charlatanry. On the other hand, with only the most negligible of exceptions, which will be discussed later, all of the references revealed almost immediately the fact of their genuineness. Chaucer used them not as mere literary parentheses. Each one of them had in its own particular position in the poem a bearing upon the context.

In order to present an adequate discussion of the purely relevant nature of these attributions, it seems advisable to affix here the table of them. They appear in the following passages, which I have numbered here, for the sake of convenience, in their order in *Troil.*

1st.	I, 393-9.	7th.	III, 575-78.
2nd.	II, 8-28.	8th.	III, 1191-97.
3rd.	II, 47-49.	9th.	III, 1324-27.
4th.	III, 90-91.	10th.	III, 1772-74.
5th.	III, 449-51.	11th.	III, 1814-17.
6th.	III, 491-504.	12th.	IV, 15-18.

13th.	IV, 1415-16.	19th.	V, 1058-60.
14th.	V, 799-800.	20th.	V, 1086-88.
15th.	V, 834-37.	21st.	V, 1093-94.
16th.	V, 1037-43.	22nd.	V, 1474-81.
17th.	V, 1044-46.	23rd.	V, 1562-64.
18th.	V, 1051-53.	24th.	V, 1646-59.
		25th.	V, 1752-54,

Before we undertake a detailed examination of this list of Chaucer's acknowledgments to the several works from which he derived many of the materials of *Troil.*, we should pause for a momentary glance at two passages in which the poet informs us, where, if we are further interested, we can learn other particulars of the deeds of Troilus or of the Trojan War.

> But how this toun com to destruccioun,
> Ne falleth nought to purpos me to telle;
> For it were here a long disgressioun
> Fro my matere, and yow to longe dwelle.
> But the Troyane gestes, as they felle,
> In Omer, or in Dares, or in Dyte,
> Whoso that can, may rede hem as they wryte.
>   (I, 141-7.)

> And if I hadde y-taken for to wryte
> The armes of this ilke worthy man,
> Than wolde I of his batailles endyte.
> But for that I to wryte first bigan
> Of his love, I have seyd as that I can.
> His worthy dedes, who-so list hem here,
> Reed Dares, he can telle hem alle y-fere.
>   (V, 1765-71.)

It is readily perceived how thoroughly non-committal is the spirit of these two quotations. They do not even so much as declare that Chaucer himself was a reader of the writers, whom he urges others to consult, and some of whom he must himself have known. Nothing within them can be construed as a reference to an authority. Consequently they can in no way affect the deductions we shall make from the references cited in the above table. I have quoted them here only in order that nothing resembling in any way a reference to Chaucer's sources should appear to have been neglected.

Let us now turn to a study of our more definite references. **It** should at first be observed that the table presents them in their order of position in *Troil.* rather than in the order of their importance.

One fact is at once preëminently revealed by the most cursory examination of the twenty-five passages. Chaucer is following persistently—he would have us at times believe, doggedly—an authority or authorities! At one time it is "myn auctor called Lollius," at another an unnamed "auctor," at a third a "story," and at a fourth "olde bokes." He never claims either the conception or the narrative of *Troil.* as his own.

For the sake of convenience we may classify the twenty-five attributions of our table as follows:

Attributions referring the sources of *Troil.* to

"Lollius".....................1st. (I, 393-9); 24th. (V, 1646-59);

an author.....................2nd. (II, 8-28); 3rd. (II, 47-49); 6th. (III, 491-504); 7th. (III, 575-78); 8th. (III, 1191-97); 9th. (III, 1324-27); 11th (III, 1814-17);

a story..........................15th. (V, 834-37); 16th. (V, 1037-43); 18th. (V, 1051-53); 21st. (V, 1093-94); 24th. (V, 1646-59);

stories...........................17th. (V, 1044-46);

old books.....................4th. (III, 90-91); 22nd. (V, 1474-81); 23rd. (V, 1562-64); 25th. (V, 1752-54);

"folk"...........................12th. (IV, 15-18);

"bokes".......................10th. (III, 1772-4); 14th. (V, 799-800);

"thise bokes"..............19th. (V, 1058-60);

"non auctor"................20th (V, 1086-88);

miscellaneous authority. 5th. (III, 449-51); 13th. (IV, 1415-16).

Let us now observe these attributions more minutely. The 5th, 12th, 13th, 19th, and 20th, are hardly to be classified. We shall dispose of them first.

> 5th. But certeyn is, to purpos for to go
>   That in this whyle, *as writen is in geste*
>   He say his lady som-tyme.   (III, 449-51)

> 12th. For how Criseyde Troilus forsook,
>   Or at the leste, how that she was unkinde,
>   Mot hennes-forth ben matere of my book,
>   *As wryten folk thorugh which it is in minde.*   (IV, 15-18)

13th.   And treweliche, *as writen wel I finde*,
        That al this thing was seyd of good entente.   (IV, 1415-16)

19th.   Allas, of me, un-to the worldes ende,
        Shal neither been y-writen nor y-songe
        No good word, *for thise bokes wol me shende*.   (V, 1058-60)

20th.   But trewely, how long it was bi-twene,
        That she forsook him for this Diomede,
        There is non auctor telleth it, I wene.   (V, 1086-88)

The 5th, "as writen is in geste," refers to a very concrete passage in the *Fil.* (II, 84), where we are told that Griseida showed herself very discreetly from time to time to Troilo. The "folk" in the 12th, through whose writings the story of Criseyde's infidelity to Troilus has been presented to Chaucer, may be any one or all three of Benoit de Sainte-More, Guido delle Colonne, and Giovanni Boccaccio; and the asseveration of Criseyde's good intentions, as found in the 13th, may very well refer to any one of the several Troilus stories in Guido, in Benoit, or in Boccaccio. "Thise bokes," which in attribution 19th Criseyde prophesies plaintively "wol me shende," may very well refer to any version of the Troilus story produced among the writers just named, or even to Chaucer's own story of the lady's frailty, although it should be noted that the suggestion for her remark comes from Benoit" *Roman de Troie*:

        De moi n'iert ja fet bon escrit,
        Ne chantée bone chançons.   *R. de T.* (Joly) 20228-9.

But attribution 19th is hardly deserving of the name, for it contains Criseyde's, not Chaucer's, comment.

In attribution 20th, too, there is no distinct reference. It contains merely a statement that Chaucer could not discover in any of his sources how long a time, after her separation from Troilus, Criseyde remained faithful to him. Yet this statement is made, as it were, with a half regret that no author could extenuate the lady's conduct by showing how long she struggled before she succumbed to temptation and become censurable. It reveals too, curiously enough, the periodic unwillingness of the poet to depart from the authority of his sources.

Investigation of Chaucer's other references in *Troil.* proves more profitable.

The first one of our list occurs in Book I, not in the early lines, where a reference to a source might well be expected, but somewhat after the inciting moment of the great Chaucerian romance.

1st.   *And of his song nought only the sentence*
       As writ myn auctor called Lollius,
       But pleynly, save our tonges difference
       I dar wel sayn, in al that Troilus
       Seyde in his song; lo! *every word right thus*
       As I shal seyn; and who-so list it here,
       Lo! next this vers, he may it finden here. (I, 393-9).

We are here informed of a certain author "called Lollius," whose
"sentence" and possibly "every word"—much depending upon the
reader's construing and punctuating of the passage—Chaucer is about
to deliver in the poem, upon which he is working "pleynly" and
"wel."   At this point of the narrative Troilus has departed from the
temple where first the beautiful apparition enthralled him, and sits
disconsolately in his chamber, mirroring in his mind the goodly
figure of Criseyde and pondering how "good aventure" it might be
for him "to love swich oon" and "serven hir" (I, 365-70).   Finally
his lips are moved to sing.

The song that follows is Chaucer's adaptation of one of Petrarch's
sonnets, usually known as the 88th. in collections of the latter's *Rime.*
Its immediate juxtaposition to the preceding stanza of *Troil.,* referring
to "Lollius," led Miss Eleanor P. Hammond in her *Chaucer, A Bibliographical Manual* (New York, 1908) to declare "an explanation of
'Lollius' should cover a Trojan historiographer, Boccaccio, and Petrarch (p. 95)."   It has since been maintained by Dr. B. A. Wise in his
dissertation on *The Influence of Statius upon Chaucer* (Johns Hopkins,
Baltimore, 1911. (p. 5)—and the position seems tenable—that
"Lollius" here refers only to Boccaccio.   For Chaucer's "Cantus
Troili" (I, 400-20), in which the sonnet of Petrarch is used, no more
embraces the "sentence," or thought, of Troilus's song (I, 393) than
her sentiment of the two stanzas following it (I, 421-34), which are
translated bodily from *Fil.* I, 38-39, embraces them.   The translation of Petrarch's sonnet may well have been an after-thought with
Chaucer. The interpolation of it can in no way discountenance the
belief that line 421 of stanza 61 could follow quite gracefully and
naturally line 399, that is the last line of stanza 57.

       . . . lo! every word right thus
       As I shal seyn; and who-so list it here,
       Lo! next this vers, he may it finden here.   (I, 397-99)

       And to the god of love thus seyde he
       With pitous voys, "O lord, now youres is

My spirit, which that oughte youres be.
Yow thank I, lord, that han me brought to this;
But whether goddesse or womman, y-wis,
She be, I noot, which that ye do me serve;
But as hir man I wole ay live and sterve."   (I, 421-27)

But even if we are not inclined to regard the Petrarchan elements as a later interpolation, we have little reason to insist that "Lollius" refers to more than Boccaccio, i. e., to more than the author of *Fil.* After all is said and done, Chaucer in stanza 57 indicates with clearness merely that he is going to repeat not only the "sentence," or thought, of Troilus's song, as his author "Lollius" wrote it, but "every word" that the languishing youth employed in his chant to Cupid. The poet does not see the necessity of naming positively the source in which he finds the "every word" "in all that Troilus Seyde in his song" (I, 396-7), whether it be a Petrarch- or a Boccaccio- "Lollius." The preponderance of the evidence, as to the identity of the author of the "sentence" of Troilus's song, does however point to the author of *Fil.* as being here the mysterious "Lollius." To attempt to identify the latter with both Petrarch and his disciple, Boccaccio, is unnecessary.

If it be admitted, then, that "myn auctor Lollius" of attribution 1st is and can only be Boccaccio, it is next to be determined by us, how frequently the "author" referred to in the succeeding attributions of our list is to be identified with "Lollius," that is to say, with Boccaccio. Later less important suggestions may be hazarded as to how Chaucer happened upon such a substitute for the real name of his "auctor."

Now it is most interesting and most pertinent to observe that in Chaucer's 24th attribution Boccaccio— and Boccaccio only— can be identified with "Lollius."

24th. Stood on a day in his malencolye
       This Troilus, and in suspecioun
       Of hir for whom he wende for to dye.
       And so bifel, that through-out Troye toun,
       As was the gyse, y-bore was up and doun
       A maner cote-armure, *as seyth the storie,*
       Biforn Deiphebe, in signe of his victorie,

       The which cote, *as telleth Lollius,*
       Deiphebe it hadde y-rent from Diomede

> The same day; and whan this Troilus
> It saugh, he gan to taken of it hede,
> Avysing of the lengthe and of the brede,
> And al the werk; but as he gan biholde,
> Ful sodeinly his herte gan to colde.
>
> (V, 1646-59)

This attribution, we perceive, instances both the "storie" (1651) and "Lollius" (1653) as authorities. It is the only attribution in the whole of *Troil.* which employs the term "storie" in referring to *Fil.* That term, it should be observed, is used by Chaucer always in the sense of "history" or "account," i. e., in the sense of its French original *histoire*, never in the sense of a piece of literature, such as our modern short story, involving a definite and unified plot-structure. The English poet Gower in his unique use of the word "storie" in the *Confessio Amantis* (V, 6002) employs it, like Chaucer, only in this general sense. But the important thing to note in the 24th attribution is that both references, cited in it, look to "Lollius," the author of *Fil.*, for it is only in this work that Chaucer can find the picture of the "cote-armure" wrested from Diomede by Deiphebus, and borne before the latter in sign of victory throughout the town of Troy. Benoit makes no mention of a particular combat between Diomede and Deiphebus.

The "maner cote-armure" (V, 1651) is the "ornato vestimento," possessed of which Troilo in *Fil.* VIII, st. 8, heard Deifebo

> . . . tornar . . . pomposo
> Di cotal preda, e seco assai gioioso.

The "broche" that Troilus "on the coler fond with-inne" (V, 1660) is the "fermaglio" or the "fibbiaglio," which Troilo, when he took the "vestimento" into his hands "per vederlo meglio," perceived

> . . . . . . .gli occhi erranti
> Or qua or là d' intorno a tutto,
> . . . . .nel petto.
>
> (*Fil.* VIII, 9)

We have then, in Chaucer's own text, excellent testimony that the name "Lollius" is used by him only in reference to the author of *Fil.* It is never applied to the author of any one of the other sources of *Troil.* It is Chaucer's name for Boccaccio.

No further reference to a source is made in the First Book of *Troil.*, although it will be remembered by readers of Rossetti's parallel edition of *Chaucer's Troylus and Cryseyde compared with Boccaccio's*

Filostrato that in that particular section of his work the English poet follows Boccaccio's text most diligently. Chaucer shows no disposition here, where he is borrowing mainly from one source, to over-crowd his poem with acknowledgments. The significant thing to note, however, is that the poet attributes with justice his debt for the material of *Troil.* to one authority.

Our second attribution, which occurs early in Book II complicates our problem but little.

> 2nd. O lady myn, that called art Cleo,
> Thou be my speed fro this forth, and my muse,
> To ryme wel this book, til I have do;
> Me needeth here noon other art to use.
> For-why to every lovere I me excuse,
> *That of no sentement I this endyte,*
> *But out of Latin in my tonge it wryte.*
>
> Wherfore I nil have neither thank ne blame
> Of al this werk, but pray you mekely,
> *Disblameth me, if any word be lame,*
> *For as myn auctor seyde, so seye I.*
> Eek though I speke of love unfelingly,
> No wonder is, for it no-thing of newe is;
> A blind man can not juggen wel in hewis.
>
> *Ye knowe eek, that in forme of speche is chaunge*
> *With-inne a thousand yeer, and wordes tho*
> *That hadden prys, now wonder nyce and straunge*
> Us thinketh hem; and yet they spake hem so,
> And spedde as wel in love as men now do;
> Eek for to winne love in sondry ages,
> In sondry londes sondry ben usages.
>
> (II, 8-28)

We find in it (l. 18) Chaucer apparently saying as "myn auctor seyde," where it seems his "auctor" said nothing at all, for in the first 574 lines of this book he borrows little, comparatively speaking from Boccaccio. The stanza, too, which contains the reference, follows a stanza which would induce the reader to believe that Chaucer either was translating or pretending to translate *Troil.* "out of Latin," i. e., the ancient classical language of Cicero and Virgil. But the trained reader is not warranted, from this stanza, in looking upon Chaucer as a false claimant to an authority of which he is not making

use at this time.   For we have every reason to believe that the "Latin"
of which the poet speaks is nothing more or less than the language
known as the *lingua volgare* by Boccaccio and Dante, a language
which later acquired the name of Italian, the language which Boccaccio repudiated in his later years of serious work in Latin treatises,
and the language in which Dante feared at first to write *The Divine
Comedy.*   The earliest use of the word *Italian,* as the English designa-
tion of the modern language spoken in Italy, i. e., the vernacular or
the *lingua volgare* of the fourteenth century in Italy, recorded by the
New English Dictionary, dates from the year 1485, a full century
after the writing of *Troil.*   It appears in Caxton's Preface to Malory's
Morte d'Arthure.   "Moo bookes," he says, "[are] made of his noble
actes . . . as wel in duche *ytalyen* spaynysshe and grekysshe as in
frensshe."   The second use of the English word *Italian* as the name
of the language, recorded by the same dictionary, is from the year
1547.   Boorde in his Introduction to Knowledge has the words,
"Who that wyl learne some *Italicn.*"   Apparently then the word was
not early in coming into general use, for otherwise we should expect
more frequent early appearances of it in English.   There is certainly
no evidence obtainable that Chaucer knew the language of Boccaccio,
or of his "Lollius," as *Italian.*   To him it must have seemed only
vernacular Latin; and from that he was translating into English.
There is no reasonable ground, then, for any charge that Chaucer was
misrepresenting his *Troil.* to be the translation of an old classical Latin
work, in order to secure to it greater prestige by virtue of an ancient
origin.   Lydgate speaks of the language of *Fil.* as *Lumbard tong.*[1]

Lines 15-21 of this second attribution beg merely that Chaucer be
"disblamed" for writing as an "auctor" wrote before him, and so in
no way affect the results of our study.   Neither does the comment of
the following stanza, lines 22-28, affect them.   Although one might
at first be tempted to suppose it describes a change in the form of
speech from Latin to the English language within a thousand years,
it signifies merely, upon closer investigation, that the speech of love
varies with time and clime, that

> . . . to winne love in sondry ages,
>   In sondry londes, sondry ben usages,

that a pre-Homeric Troilus would not use the same amorous vocabulary as a fourteenth century esquire.

There is, in brief, nothing in the 2nd attribution to impugn the sincerity of Chaucer when he makes a reference to a source or authority.

[1] See Hammond, p. 58.

The 3rd attribution is of only negligible importance.

> . . . som men grave in tree, som in stoon wal,
> As it bitit; but sin I have begonne,
> *Myn auctor shal I folwen*, if I conne.   (II, 47-49)

Chaucer's resolve, "Myn auctor shal I folwen, if I conne," although not at once carried out in the immediate context of Book II, is later resumed and fully performed in the general development of *Troil.*

The 4th attribution, a reference to "bokes olde," containing likewise unimportant material, we shall pass over for the present in order to observe a very interesting series of attributions, in which Chaucer always refers his sources to an "auctor," an "auctor," who, we find invariably, represents Boccaccio. He is never Statius, nor Benoit, nor Guido.   These attributions are the 6th, 7th, 8th, 9th, and 11th.

> 6th.   But now, paraunter, som man wayten wolde
> That every worde, or sonde, or look, or chere
> Of Troilus that I rehersen sholde,
> In al this whyle, un-to his lady dere;
> I trowe it were a long thing for to here;
> Or of what wight that stant in swich disioynte,
> His wordes alle, or every look, to poynte.
>
> For sothe, I have not herde it doon er this,
> In *storye* noon, ne no man here, I wene;
> And though I wolde I coude not, y-wis;
> For there was som epistel hem bi-twene.
> That wolde, *as seyth my auctor*, wel contene
> Neigh half this book, of which him list not wryte;
> How sholde I thanne a lyne of it endyte?
>   (III, 491-504)

> 7th   *Nought list myn auctor fully to declare*
> *What that she thoughte whan he seyde so,*
> *That Troilus was out of town y-fare,*
> *As if he seyde ther-of sooth or no.*   (III, 575-8)

> 8th.   What mighte or may the sely larke seye,
> Whan that the sparhauk hath it in his foot?
> I can no more, *but of thise ilke tweye,*
> To whom this tale sucre be or soot,

> Though that I tarie a yeer, *som-tyme I moot,*
> *After myn auctor, tellen hir gladnesse,*
> As wel as I have told hir hevinesse.
>
> (III, 1191-7)

9th. But sooth is, *though I can not tellen al,*
> *As can myn auctor, of his excellence,*
> Yet have I seyd, and, god to-forn, I shal
> *In every thing al hoolly his sentence.*
>
> (III, 1324-7)

11th. Thourgh yow (i. e., the divinities invoked by Chaucer
to inspire him in his song.)
> have I seyd fully in my song
> Theffect and joye of Troilus servyse,
> Al be that ther was som disese among,
> *As to myn auctor listeth to devyse.*
>
> (III, 1814-7)

Boccaccio, to be sure, never makes such a statement as the "auctor" who in the 6th attribution "seyth" that some of the letters exchanged by Troilus and Criseyde, would contain

> Neigh half this book, of which him list not wryte;

yet Boccaccio is the first writer of the Troilus and Criseyde story
who mentions the letters of the lovers and who gives us anything of
their contents (*Fil.* II, 95-106), letters which Chaucer must have
found very long in the reading.

In attribution 7th Chaucer seems to be enjoying his joke in silence,

> Nought list myn auctor fully to declare
> What that she thoughte.

For it is Chaucer's Criseyde who has the opportunity to decide upon
the value of her uncle's veracity, not Boccaccio's Griseida, a woman
never deceived by the pretext of her relative that her lover is "out of
town y-fare" and never either willingly or unwillingly entrapped by
the contrivances of her kinsman and of her lover. (Cf. *Fil.* III, 21
with *Troil.* III, 575-78.) Chaucer, it is just possible, is himself filled
with a sort of satirical wonder as to what "Lollius" would think of
his innovation into the Troilus story.

The "auctor," after whom Chaucer must sometime

> . . . tellen hir gladnesse,
> As wel as I have told hir hevinesse,

(Attribution 8th, Bk. III, 1196-7), can only be Boccaccio, who is the first writer before Chaucer to introduce into the story the long scenes of the lovers' happiness.

The same is true of the "auctor" whose "sentence"—and "god to-forn"!—Chaucer declares to have "hoolly" said (Attribution 9th). This latter reference is very interesting. It is an admission of the poet's purpose to reproduce in his work the thought of Boccaccio, *without binding himself to follow it slavishly in a literal translation.* Chaucer is, in this passage, taking his "auctor" seriously.

The last excerpt from Book III, of *Troil.*, cited as an attribution to authority, i. e., the 11th, points to Boccaccio, who alone among Chaucer's predecessors in the Troilus story told of "the effect and joy of Troilus's service." This attribution looks backward to Book III, but it precedes directly Book IV of *Troil.*, a book in which, one observes by the way, Chaucer follows Boccaccio throughout with the utmost of pains. But the significant fact for us to notice is, that every one of the five times, when Chaucer refers to an "auctor" in Book III, the "auctor" referred to is always the author of *Fil.*; that is to say, every mention of an "auctor" in that book looks consistently to Boccaccio.

Now there are in the Fourth Book of *Troil.* only two attributions to authority, the 12th and the 13th. These two, we have already seen in our examination, are very inclusive. The 13th,

And treweliche, *as writen wel I finde*

That al this thing was seyd of good entente (IV, 1415-16).

so far as it is an attribution, covers all the sources wherein Chaucer finds assurance that Criseyde, or her source-prototype, intended to be faithful to Troilus, i. e., in Benoit, Guido, and Boccaccio. The 12th,

For how Criseyde Troilus forsook,

Or at the leste, how that she was unkinde,

Mot hennes-forth ben matere of my book,

As wryten folk thorugh which it is in minde. (IV, 15-18)

becomes very interesting when studied in relation to the references to authority contained in the first three books of *Troil.* Through the whole of these three books Chaucer must needs depend upon Boccaccio for whatever authority he wishes to draw upon in the weaving of his tale of Troilus, because only in Boccaccio's version is to be found that part of the story, which narrates the various episodes of the *innamoramento* of the lovers and their experiences before the exchange of prisoners compels their separation. But when Chaucer wishes to write of Criseyde's desertion of Troilus for Diomede, he finds he can employ several additional sources:—the *Roman de Troie* of Benoit, and the *Historia Trojana* of Guido. Accordingly it is most natural that the poet, released now from entire responsibility to one author, should add naively,

> As wryten *folk* thorough which it is in minde.

It is to be observed, then, that this early attribution in Book IV bears very significant witness to the accuracy of our conclusion, that in Book III of *Troil.* the "auctor" is always Boccaccio.

It is worthy of note that all eleven of our remaining as yet undiscussed attributions, occurring all but two of them in Book V, employ the terms, "bokes," "storie," or "stories." The exceptions, or the ones which do not occur in Book V, are the 4th and the 10th, both in Book III. Let us look at the 4th.

> His resons, as I may my rymes holde,
> I yow wol telle, *as techen bokes olde.* (III, 90-91)

This passage occurs in the scene at the house of Deiphebus, which we know to have been invented by Chaucer. There is, then, at this point no immediate necessity for a reference to a source. The "resons" of Troilus, i. e., of course, not his "reasons" but his conversation,— here in the way of love-pleading,—appear in all the Troilus stories. Accordingly Chaucer may, without any shadow of dishonesty or pretense, speak of the old books which have taught him. In a word the casual attribution is permissible, and there is no necessity here for a reference to the author of *Fil.* In connection with this 4th attribution, it is rather interesting to note that other manuscripts read

> His *wordes* as I may my rymes holde   (III, 90),

a fact which very clearly reveals the real meaning of "resons."

The 10th attribution,

> He was, and ay the firste in armes dight;
> And certeynly, *but-if that bokes erre,*
> Save Ector, most y-drad of any wight (III, 1772-74)

cannot really be considered a Chaucerian attribution. It is rather a Boccaccian ascription to authority, for it contains the words "*but-if that bokes erre,*" which are themselves the actual translation of a brief passage in *Fil.*,

> Egli era sempre nell' armi il primiero;
> . . . .
> . . . .*se non erra*
> La storia.   (III, 90)

Accordingly it has no bearing upon our discussion.

Let us turn to the nine remaining attributions, all involving the terms, "bokes," "storie" or "stories," and all appearing in the Fifth Book. These are the 14th, 15th, 16th, 17th, 18th, 21st, 22nd, 23rd, and 25th, or in other words all the attributions from the 14th to the 25th except the 19th, the 20th, and the 24th. The latter three attributions we have already studied. The 19th, containing Criseyde's apprehensions that books might injure her name, was unimportant. The 20th, which is the only attribution in the Fifth Book involving the term "auctor," we have already seen[1] contains no distinct reference whatever. The 24th employs, as we have noted in our earlier examination of it in connection with the first of all our attributions, both the term "storie" and the name "Lollius;" the former term being an incontestable allusion to *Fil.*, and the name "Lollius" an equally indisputable reference to the author of the Italian poem.

Continuing our observation of the series, we find that the 14th attribution,

This Diomede, *as bokes us declare,*

Was in his nedes prest and corageous (V, 799-800),

serves as an introduction to the descriptions of Diomede, Criseyde, and Troilus, found in lines 799-840. These descriptions, we know now, Chaucer derived chiefly from Joseph of Exeter's *De Bello Trojano* (Lib. IV, 61-4, 124-27, 156-62).[2] In brief, the English poet here makes use of a new source and makes an acknowledgment of it. The allusion is obviously to Joseph's book.

The 15th attribution,

And certainly *in storie it is y-founde,*

That Troilus was never un-to no wight,

As in his tyme, in no degree secounde

In durring don that longeth to a knight.

(V, 834-7),

contains a description of Troilus borrowed directly from Joseph, and so likewise refers to his *De Bello Trojano.*

The 16th, 17th, 18th, and 21st, attributions look consistently to Benoit de Sainte-More.

16th. *And after this the story telleth us,*

That she him yaf the faire baye stede,

The which he ones wan of Troilus;

---

[1] See page 157.

[2] On the origin of these descriptions the article of Professor R. K. Root, *Chaucer's Dares,* will soon be available in *Modern Philology.*

And eek a broche (and that was litel nede)
That Troilus was, she yaf this Diomede,
And eek, the bet from sorwe him to releve,
She made him were a pencel of hir sleve.
(V, 1037-43)

17th.   *I finde eek in the stories elles-where,*
Whan thrugh the body hurt was Diomede
Of Troilus, tho weep she many a tere.   (V, 1044-46)

18th.   But trewely, *the story telleth us,*
There made never womman more wo
Than she, whan that she falsed Troilus.
(V, 1051-53)

21st.   Ne me ne list this sely womman chyde
Further than the story wol devyse.   (V, 1093-94)

It is only in the *R. de T.* that we find, outside of Chaucer, reference to this present of Criseyde to Diomede of the horse, which had once belonged to Troilus.   In the French poem we find a long passage which describes the capture of this steed from his rival Troilus by Diomede, who then sends it by his squire as a gift to Briseis in the Greek camp (see *R. de T.* 14238-76).   Benoit's record of the gift is as follows:

"Sire," fet ele, "lo cheval
Vos presterai" . . . (*R. de T.* Joly. 15046-47)

The "story" then that provides us with Book V, 1037-9 is the *R. de T.*   But the story that provides us with the next two verses is Boccaccio's *Fil.!* The "broche" (1040) is the "fermaglio" or "fibbiaglio," in the Italian poem given by Troilo to Griseida, and afterward disloyally presented by her to Diomede (see *Fil.* VIII, sts. 9-10). Now there is one particularly interesting thing to note. *Chaucer's exacting sense, which permits him casually to attribute the gift of the horse to the "story" we know to be Benoit's, does not permit him to attribute incorrectly the gift of the "broche," an item borrowed from Boccaccio, to the same authority, i. e., to Benoit.*

Any one who will look at ll. 1040-1 will perceive at once that they do not contain a subordinate clause dependent upon "the story telleth us" of 1037. The poet's sense of accuracy is at this moment keen. He justly attributes the "stede" to Benoit's *Roman*, but carefully avoids attributing to it the "broche" which comes from the "fermaglio" of Boccaccio. Attribution 16th is an exceptional instance of the really serious and fair-dealing attitude which Chaucer maintains toward his sources.

The "pencel of hir sleve" (V, 1043), made for Diomede by Criseyde, it should be observed, comes also from Benoit.

> La destre manche de son braz
> Nueve et fresche d'un ciglaton
> Li baille en lieu de confanon.
>   (*R. de T.* Joly. 15103-5)

In his next stanza the English poet, once more making use of the material of the *R. de T.*, carefully adds his

> "I finde eek in the stories elles-where,"

following the words with the episode of Criseyde's grief over Diomede's wound, another feature of the story which is borrowed from Benoit (*R. de T.* 20194-274).

After exercising this care, justly to attribute his material to its several sources, Chaucer mentions twice a "story" (Attributions 18th and 21st) and once "thise bokes" (Attribution 19th), which point again directly to the *R. de T.*, all within the space of forty-four lines (V, 1051-94). Many of these lines Professor Karl Young, in his book on *The Origin and Development of the Story of Troilus and Criseyde* (Chaucer Society, 1908 p. 135), shows us by interesting parallels are further adaptations from Benoit's work.

Of all the twenty-two attributions—some of them only so called attributions we have seen—thus far examined no one has been discovered to contain any reference which can be charged with being insincere. There remain but three more, similarly accurate in spirit, the 22nd, the 23rd, and the 25th, to be considered in our study In the 22nd,

> And Meleagre, lord of that contree,
> He lovede so this fresshe mayden free
> That with his manhod, er he wolde stente,
> This boor he slow, and hir the heed he sente;
>
> Of which, *as olde bokes tellen us*,
> There roos a contek and a great envye;
> And of this lord descended Tydeus
> By ligne, *or elles olde bokes lye.*   (V, 1474-81),

reference is made by Chaucer to the old books from which he derives his material for the descriptions of the Calydonian Hunt which the prophetess Cassandra draws for her brother Troilus:—the *Thebaid* of Statius, the *Metamorphoses* of Ovid, or possibly even the *De Genealogiis Deorum Gentilium* of Boccaccio.   In the 23rd attribution,

> And thus this worthy knight was brought of lyve,
> For whom, *as olde bokes tellen us,*
> Was mad swich wo, that tonge it may not telle.
> (V, 1562-64),

the reference to old books is quite general.   The death of the worthy knight Hector and the woe occasioned by it in Troy are so common a property of histories and romances of Troy that Chaucer might have read of it in anything from the *Iliad* to the *De Bello Trojano* of Joseph of Exeter.   The 25th and last attribution,

> Of Troilus, this ilke noble knight,
> *As men may in thise olde bokes rede,*
> Was sene his knighthod and his grete might
> (V, 1752-54),

is also very inclusive.   Coming, as it does, very near the end of Chaucer's poem, it may very well be retrospective.   The poet is himself completely conscious by this time of his indebtedness to a number of sources.   He has used Ovid, Statius, Guido, Joseph of Exeter, Benoit, and "Lollius."   In many of his sources he has found encomiums on the nobility and knightliness of Troilus, and instinctively he remarks,

> . . . men may in thise olde bokes rede
> . . . his knighthod and his grete might.

The investigation of Chaucer's attributions to authority, which we are now ready to conclude, has shown us several things of significance. Chaucer, we discovered, inclined to a particular accuracy in assigning the several parts of his works to their sources.   Again and again he admitted that this or that feature was not of his own creation. His every mention of a story or of old books was a reverent one. Reticent though the poet may have been in naming his sources, he was always fair-minded enough to acknowledge his indebtedness to them.   And he never broached the name of any one of them in the spirit of any but the mildest, blithest sort of satire, as in the 7th attribution.

In order to summarize more concretely the results of our examination of the twenty-one attributions to authorities in *Troil.*, it is my desire to present now five leading facts:

I. There is no deliberately spurious claim to the use of a source, not actually employed in *Troil.*, in order that Chaucer may gain greater reverence for the poem in the minds of his readers by reason of its apparent antiquity or authority. Nor is there any reference which may be shown to be unduly facetious or insincere.

II. There is never any claim on the part of Chaucer to have created the features of the poem which he derives from the creation of some other writer.

III. The poet's attitude to his sources is consistently serious. If ever levity can be detected in this attitude, it is due to the fact that Chaucer professes very early in *Troil.* he dare serve only the servants of the god of Love and dare not appeal to Love himself for inspiration (I, 15-17). This is Chaucer's unique pose or pretense in the poem. It seems to anticipate the defense, which he is to offer later in the *Pro. L. G. W.*, against the charges advanced by Cupid.

IV. Chaucer's attitude toward "Lollius" is ever respectful. Although at all times briefly expressed and never intimately expressed, it is more definite than his attitude toward his other sources. "Lollius," i. e., Boccaccio, is the only writer, to whom Chaucer refers with the appellation of "auctor," the only one to whom he attributes "excellence" (III, 1325), and the only one whose "sentence" he insists he has "al hoolly" presented (I, 393; III, 1327).

V. Chaucer never refers to an "auctor" without meaning "Lollius," the author of *Fil.*—or as we know him, Boccaccio.

Of the five facts educed from our investigation, the first three may be omitted from further discussion. To the fourth and fifth, however, in view of the position of so eminent a scholar as Professor Pio Rajna, who, writing as late as 1903, inclines to the belief that Chaucer, for ulterior motives, refrained from proper acknowledgments to Boccaccio, one more remark may be devoted (see *Romania*, 1903, pp. 204-267, *Sulle Origini del Chaucer's Franklin's Tale*). Scanty as is the information of our fourth fact, it yet becomes significant, when supported by the evidence of the earlier three, that the poet is always prone to admit his obligations to other writers. Chaucer could have no motive, then, for the concealment of Boccaccio's name, frankly owning, as he everywhere does, that he himself was not the creator of the Troilus story.

We are brought therefore to the conclusion of our fifth fact, that Chaucer actually believed that an "auctor called Lollius" had written the *Filostrato*.   And as a corollary to that conclusion it would appear that Chaucer must have found the name "Lollius" somewhere upon the manuscript of the *Filostrato* which he used.

In connection with my conclusions in regard to Chaucer's genuine attributions to "Lollius," it is interesting to note that, within recent years, satisfactory explanations have been made of the only other enigmatic references to authors found in the whole Chaucer canon. These ascriptions were two in number: "Corinne" (*Anelida and Arcite*, l. 21) and "Trophee" (*Monk's Tale*, B. 3307).

Professor G. L. Kittredge has discovered for us the correct explanation of "Trophee."   The comment on Hercules made in the *Monk's Tale* (3307-8),

> "At bothe the worldes endes, seith Trophe,
> In stede of boundes, he a piler sette,"

he fully explains as being an erroneous interpretation of a sentence in the *Epistola Alexandri Macedonis ad Aristotelem de itinere suo et de situ Indiae*: "Ast et ad Herculis Liberique *trophaea* me deduxit in orientis ultimis oris."[1]

To Mr. E. F. Shannon we owe the correct explanation of "Corinne." Writing in the *Publications of the Modern Language Association* (27, 461-85), he shows us that, by a peculiar mistake, the writings of Ovid were, during the middle ages, sometimes ascribed to "Corinna." This "Corinna" was originally the mistress of the Latin poet, a lady whom he addressed in the *Amores*.   The latter work was circulated about in mediaeval times in manuscripts, which either were marked *sine titulo* or designated the author as "Corinna."   Chaucer, who used Ovid's *Heroides* as a secondary source in *Anelida and Arcite*, according to Mr. Shannon, attributed it to "Corinne," a name which he regarded as synonymous with that of Ovid.

With all of Chaucer's ascriptions to authority now satisfactorily explained, it would seem that we might be somewhat warranted in slightly modifying the view we too frequently assume in regard to writers of the middle ages.   We may continue to charge them with over-plagiarizing, but Chaucer, at least, we must except from the

---

[1] I have been unable to secure the original of Professor Kittredge's article, *The Pillars of Hercules and Chaucer's "Trophee"*: *The Putnam Anniversary Volume*, The Torch Press, Cedar Rapids, 1909.   It is, however, carefully reviewed in the *Archiv für das Studium der neueren Sprachen* 124, p. 428.

accusation of falsely claiming authorities for his literary works. Further investigation might relieve other mediaeval writers of the same onus. We might even discover that the instinct for accuracy existed in the minds of great clerks and men of letters in the middle ages, in hardly less palpable form than it exists in the minds of modern scholars.

It is only proper to append at this point of the present study a few brief summaries of theories hitherto advanced to explain the identity of "Lollius."

Mr. R. G. Latham in the *Athenaeum* for 1868 (II, 433) suggested that the name may have been discovered by Chaucer in a passage from one of the *Epistles* of Horace, and have been mistaken by him for the name of a writer on the Trojan War. Horace writes in allusion to Homer, "Troiani belli scriptorem, maxime Lolli, Dum tu declamas Romae, Praeneste relegi" (*Horatii Epistularum;* Lib. I, 2, 1-2).

Mr. W. M. Rossetti once believed, and afterwards changed his mind, owing to Latham's suggestion, that "Lollius" was "Laelius" and that the latter name was an appellation of Petrarch (see Hammond, p. 96).

Professor James W. Bright in the *Publications of the Modern Language Association* (19, p. xxii) proposes, "Boccaccio with its pejorative suffix means 'ugly mouth'; and to one seeking to use a synonym would suggest that its possessor was a thick-tongued babbler careless about his articulation. The English words for characterizing such a person were '*loll, lollard, loller.*' By the addition of the classical suffix -*ius* to the radical syllable, Boccaccio would be rendered by an euphonious equivalent having the semblance of an author's name." This explanation was accepted by Dr. Wise (p. 6). My chief objections to it are that, in the first place it implies charlatanry, a willingness deliberately to obscure, on the part of Chaucer, and in the second it does not at all account for the position of honour assigned to "Lollius" on the pillars of the *House of Fame* (see l. 1468).

Miss Hammond in her *Bibliographical Manual* (p. 98) hazards a suggestion that "Lollius" might have been the author of the "trophium," from which Chaucer may have drawn the name "Trophee" of the *Monks Tale* (B. 3307), and that the name "Trophee" may have "applied both to the unmarked *Filostrato* of the same volume and to the preceding Latin . . . cited by Chaucer" in the tale just mentioned. The explanation of "Trophee" by Professor Kittredge, of course, fully obviates this suggestion.

Mr. C. M. Hathaway, Jr., in *Englische Studien* (44, 159-64) conjectures that "Lollius" may have been Raymond Lully, "a famous alchemist, philosopher, and missionary, the 'illuminated doctor' of the thirteenth century," and that the Latinized form of his name "Raymundus Lullius" might in some way have been connected with the manuscript of *Fil.* used by Chaucer. The known manuscripts of *Troil.* all, however, present consistently the reading "Lollius." We cannot, therefore, by a scribal error account for it as a corruption of "Lullius."

A fifteenth century translation of the *Filostrato* into French made by Louis de Beauvau attributes the work to Petrarch. See Henri Haurette: *Les plus anciennes traductions françaises de Boccace*; Bordeaux et Paris, 1909.

The present writer was for a time of the belief that "Lollius" was Lello Stefani, one of the best loved of the friends of Petrarch, with whom he corresponded for many years, always addressing him under the name of "Laelius," the cognomen of the model friend whom we find in Cicero's *De Amicitia*. Petrarch fondly imagined that the delight Scipio found in his associations with Laelius was such as he found in his association with Lello. My conjecture was that Chaucer, knowing that the Humanist called one of his friends "Laelius" and further that Boccaccio was an intimate friend of Petrarch, confused Boccaccio with "Laelius," and, in fancied compliment to the author of *Fil.*, gave him the appellation of "Laelius" in *Troil.* The spelling "Lollius," I conjectured, was an early scribal error for "Laelius." But all the known manuscripts of *Troil.*, we know from the recent examination of them by Professor R. K. Root, read consistently "Lollius."

A further conjecture which I entertained for a time was that Petrarch, after the death of Lello Stefani, transferred the name "Laelius" to his newer friend Boccaccio. That some familiar name for Boccaccio had been employed by Petrarch, I inferred from the fact that in two of the letters of Boccaccio, we find Francesca, the natural daughter of Petrarch referred to as "Tullia." Petrarch, I conjectured then, was, to Boccaccio, "Cicero," and his daughter was to the great Humanist's disciple "Tullia," the daughter of Marcus Tullius Cicero; and to the other two, Boccaccio was their intimate friend "Laelius." Both these conjectures I have since abandoned as being extremely tenuous. I include them here only because they appear to me to contain a presumptive possibility of truth, equal to that of the conjectures previously offered by other investigators of the "Lollius" problem.

The letters referred to in my second conjecture are to be found in the *Lettere Edite ed Inedite*:

Ad Franciscum Petrarcham Laureatum, pp. 123-9.

Ad Francisum generum Domini Francisci Petrarchae, pp. 377-84.

It should, of course, be remembered that both Petrarch and Boccaccio publicly, whether or not they did it as an affectation, repudiated their early poems in the vulgar tongue. By some men in Italy their repudiation of the *Rime* must have been accepted in good faith as a sincere expression of their attitude. Filippo Villani, writing a biography of Boccaccio in the last decade of the fourteenth or the first decade of the fifteenth century, after he has presented a full list of Boccaccio's Latin works, declares: "Exstant et quamplura eius *Opuscula vulgari edita sermone*, pleraque rythmis modulata, pleraque continua oratione prosaica, in quibus lascivientis iuventutis ingenio paulo liberius evagavit, quae, cum senuisset, ipse putavit silentio transigenda. Sed non potuit revocare, neque ignem quem flabello excitaverat sua voluntate restinguere" (see page 18).

Boccaccio's works drifted about in the fourteenth century in unsigned manuscripts. Several manuscripts of the *Filostrato* have come down to us without the name of an author attached. One fifteenth century translation of *Fil.* into French, as was seen in a previous note, ascribes the authorship of the poem to Petrarch. Chaucer, it is more than possible, used a manuscript of *Fil.* which ascribed it to "Lollius."

CHAPTER IX

CHAUCER AND THE *Decamerone*

We have seen the very great improbability of Chaucer's acquaintance with any of the works of Boccaccio thus far discussed except the *Filostrato* and the *Teseide*. And in the last chapter we considered matter that argued a rather great unlikelihood that Chaucer was even acquainted with the name of Boccaccio at all, certainly not with it as that of the author of the *Filostrato*. The old question rises. "Was Chaucer acquainted with the *Decamerone?*"

I shall not attempt to answer it assuredly in either the affirmative or the negative. Yet I shall at once admit that nothing in the evidence so far presented for his acquaintance with it inclines me to frame an answer in the affirmative.

Summed up briefly, the internal evidence for Chaucer's knowledge of the *Decam.* is as follows: 1) There are some general similarities in the frame-work of the *C. T.* and that of the *Decam.* 2) There is something of likeness in certain "apologies" contained in the links or the frame-work of the two works. 3) There are two tales in the two works which are nearly equivalent.

External evidence is quite shadowy. There are no references, dating from anything near the time of Chaucer or Boccaccio, in regard to the English poet's possible familiarity with the *Decam.* There is nothing except the probability that Chaucer, acquainted with other works of Boccaccio, should have known the *Decam.*

Let us weigh, in review, first the internal evidence. The best study of the similarities in the frame-work of the *C. T.* and the *Decam.* is that of Professor Lorenz Morsbach, already examined in the section of this work on Chaucer and the *Ameto*. Professor Morsbach, it will be recalled, in his article (*Chaucers Plan der Canterbury Tales und Boccaccios Decamerone; Eng. Stud. 42, 43-52*) proposed four interesting parallels between the two works, which at the same time differentiate the two from other mediaeval collections of stories. These parallels, he concludes, establish a relationship between Boccaccio's and Chaucer's works. Condensed they read as follows: 1) The stories of both works are told by the members of a company of persons. 2) The company in each work has come together, not by chance, but with a common purpose of its members. 3) The links connecting the stories in both works describe the actions of the company. 4) One member of the company in each work acts as a director and judge of the story-telling.[1]

But these parallels are not really significant. Professor J. S. P. Tatlock, we recall, demonstrates in his article (*Boccaccio and the Plan of Chaucer's Canterbury Tales*; *Anglia*, 1913, pp. 69-117) that they are equally applicable to the *C. T.* and the *Filocolo*, or to the *C. T.* and the *Ameto*. And the *Filocolo* and the *Ameto* neither Professor Young nor Professor Tatlock, we have seen, has produced adequate evidence that Chaucer knew. Indeed it is altogether doubtful if Chaucer was acquainted with either of these two other frame-work compositions of Boccaccio. Accordingly, the complete applicability of Professor Morsbach's parallels to them much weakens the value of their own case in regard to the *C. T.* and the *Decam.* Fitting, as they do, three sets of works, their significance in any case is much to be discounted. Especially must this be the case when one realizes how exceedingly unlikely it is that Chaucer knew either the *Ameto* or the *Filocolo*, and remembers at the same time the applicability of the parallels to them. If the parallels, in a word, are fortuitous in the case of those two works, they are more than likely to be fortuitous in the case of the *Decam.* Certainly they are not convincing evidence for a relationship between that work and the *C. T.*

The next evidence for relationship to be considered is the likeness in the "apologies." Professor R. K. Root, in a brief article (*Chaucer and the Decameron*: *Eng. Stud.* 44, 1-7) points out an interesting resemblance between the *Decam.* and the *C. T.*, but without asserting that it is any positive evidence of a relationship. He finds that "both Boccaccio and Chaucer make formal apology for the freedom and coarseness of some of their tales, and defend the inclusion of these tales on precisely the same grounds, and in the same playful spirit of mock seriousness." This "formal apology" Chaucer makes in two passages—in the general *Prologue* (A. 725-742), and in the *Prologue* to the *Miller's Tale* (A. 3171-3186)—while Boccaccio makes it but once—in the *Conclusione dell' Autore*, which is appended to the *Decam.* The first instance of it in Chaucer's work, Professor Root acknowledges, "confines itself to the question of plain speech, and does not discuss the propriety of excluding objectionable stories altogether." Little indeed can be made of its very general nature. The second instance of apology, occurring in the *Prologue* to the *Miller's*

---

[1] For the complete wording and the original German of Professor Morsbach's parallels see footnote on pp. 33-35 of this text.

Tale, is more significant.   Boccaccio's apology in the *Conclusione dell'
Autore* and it resemble each other in three ways: 1) the author is
merely a reporter, "bound to relate the stories which were told" and
"not responsible for the character of them"; 2) "the squeamish
reader is bidden skip the stories which give offense" . . . "it
is not the author's fault if he choose amiss"; 3) "the author has
given his readers ample warning" by introductory matter as to the
nature of each story before they read it.   To support the testimony
of these three resemblances in regard to a relationship of the two
works no verbal parallels can be offered.   To me, however, they seem
more significant than the parallels of Professor Morsbach, in that the
expression of each one of them is restricted to one narrow passage
rather than thinly spread over many pages of narrative.   The discovery of more such really striking details of similarity might lead
to an established fact of relationship between the *C. T.* and the *Decam.*
But the discovery of them is likely to be very remote.[1]   The likeness
of the "apologies," then, too much resembles coincidence to be sufficient as evidence without further proof.

The third part of the internal evidence for relationship lies in the
fact that in the *Decam.* and in the *C. T.* are two tales which are nearly
or quite equivalent.   These are the story of Patient Griselda and
another of a knight and his faithful wife.   The former appears in
Chaucer's *Clerk's Tale* and in the tenth *novella* of the tenth Day of the
Decam.; the latter, in Chaucer's *Franklin's Tale* and in the fifth *novella*

---

[1] Professor Root does, however, in a footnote point out one very interesting
parallel between the Reeve's Prologue and the Induction to the Fourth Day of
the *Decam.* 'The Reeve,' he observes, 'though a white-haired old man, is none
the less minded to "speke of ribaudye," and explains that "in oure wil ther stiketh
ever a nayl, To have an hoor heed and a grene tayl, As hath a leek" (A 3877-3879).
In the Induction to the Fourth Day, Boccaccio is defending himself against those
who criticize him for writing frivolous tales. Among other charges, it has been
asserted that such writing was not becoming for one of his years. He replies thus:
"E quegli che contro alla mia età parlando vanno, mostra mal che conoscano che,
perchè il porro abbia il capo bianco, che la coda sia verde" (*Opere Volgari*, ed.
Moutier, 2, 146). Despite the closely similar conditions under which the example
of the leek is invoked, the obviously proverbial character of the remark makes it
unsafe to assume any direct indebtedness to Boccaccio on the part of Chaucer.
Compare Dekker's *Honest Whore*, Part II, Act I, Sc. 2, (ed. 1873, Vol. 2, p. 103):
"Tho my head be like a Leeke, white: may not my heart be like the blade, greene?"
It is, of course, possible that Dekker is indebted to Chaucer.' Professor Root is
himself skeptical about the force of the parallel he has discovered to us.   It would
indeed be rather hazardous to assume a relationship between the *C. T.* and the
Decam. on the strength of it.

of the Tenth Day of the *Decam.* But the testimony of neither of these stories is compelling.

For the story of Griselda, as it appears in the *Clerk's Tale*, Chaucer, we know, only indirectly owed a debt to Boccaccio. For it was from Petrarch's translation into Latin of Boccaccio's beautiful story that the English poet drew his materials, there being not the slightest verbal or literary evidence that he levied, by way of supplement, contributions from Boccaccio's Italian version for the *Clerk's Tale.* And this fact is itself evidence that Chaucer did not have the *Decam.* at hand when he was composing the *C. T.* It was quite foreign to the manner of Chaucer not to draw upon every source with which he was familiar, in producing a new work. In *Troil.* we saw he made use of every possible source for both descriptions and episodes. It can hardly be questioned that, if the Italian version of the story of Griselda had been available, Chaucer would have used it. Striking similarities between the English and Latin versions are, on the other hand, at once detected when one compares the work of Chaucer and that of Petrarch. And Chaucer's dependence upon that writer, which we remember the Clerk acknowledges, seems wholly to obviate any dependence in the *Clerk's Tale* upon the *Decam.* (See *Chaucer Society, Originals and Analogues,* pp. 149-172.)

As for Boccaccio's story of the knight and his faithful wife, it has so many analogues (see *Orig. and Anal.* pp. 291-340) as would make it an exceedingly difficult thesis to maintain that Chaucer drew from it the plot of the *Franklin's Tale.* Only the most meagre plot-skeletons of the two versions resemble each other. Professor Rajna is the only scholar of prominence who has argued the possibility of relationship between the *C. T.* and the *Decam.* version of this story, his argument being however little more than conjecture. He believes primarily (See *Le Origini della Novella Narrata dal "Frankeleyn" nei Canterbury Tales del Chaucer; Romania,* 1903, pp. 204-267.) that Chaucer found the material for the *F. T.* in a *questione d' amore* of the *Filocolo,* afterwards reworked by Boccaccio into the *Decam.* story (*Rom.* 1903, 234-44). But later he hazards the surmise that the Chaucerian version is also influenced by the latter account (*Rom.* 1903 244-56). But Professor Rajna's arguments and surmises, when observed carefully, also prove tenuous evidence. An examination of them, as yet to be presented in my study of the *Source of the F. T. and Boccaccio,*[1] points quite negatively. They prove neither a rela-

[1] See Chapter X, pp. 186-196 of this text.

tionship between the *F. T.* and the *Filocolo* nor between the English poem and the *Decam.*

The third item, then, in our internal evidence is not conclusive. The story of Griselda points only to Petrarch's Latin version; and the story of the knight and his faithful wife shows no clear influence from Boccaccio. Neither the *Clerk's Tale* nor the *F. T.* demonstrates assuringly a relationship between the *C. T.* and the *Decam.*

Certainly the question of Chaucer's acquaintance with the latter work cannot definitely be answered in the affirmative. Similarities in frame-work, similarities in "apologies," and approximate similarities in story-versions, alike prove insufficient to make safe such an answer.

That is to say, evidence for relationship between the *C. T.* and the *Decam.*, so far procurable, sums itself up, after all, in only the fact that the two great collections of tales are written in frame-works hardly less excellent than the tales themselves.

Over against this evidence still persists the great *argumentum ex silentio*, that, if Chaucer had known the *Decam.* and had it at his disposal, he would surely have availed himself of its splendid store of *novelle* to enrich the collection of his *C. T.*

Other arguments it is not my intention either to offer or to reiterate. But in conclusion it should be observed that no argument can safely be based on mere general probabilities that Chaucer had the *Decam.* in his library because he had there numerous other manuscripts of Boccaccio. For it has been shown in the present work that we have no adequate evidence that Chaucer used any other Italian works of Boccaccio than the *Filostrato* and the *Teseide.* With those two works only can we say categorically that he was acquainted. And very many are the chances that he did not know the *Decamerone.*[1]

[1] In Miss Hammond's *Bibliographical Manual*, pp. 150-53, may be found the most satisfactory brief summary of previous opinion in regard to Chaucer's possible acquaintance with the *Decam.*

CHAPTER X

THE SOURCE OF THE *Franklin's Tale* AND BOCCACCIO

In connection with the source of the *Franklin's Tale* a very interesting problem has risen. The tale contains a story, of which there
are but two other known mediaeval European versions, both of them
by Boccaccio; and therefore the question has become pertinent whether
Chaucer derived his version from one or possibly from both of Boccaccio's. Immediate answer to the question is difficult by reason of a
statement made by the Franklin in his link-prologue that he is going
to narrate a Breton lay.

> Thise olde gentil Britons in hir dayes
> Of diverse aventures maden layes,
> Rymeyed in hir firste Briton tonge;
> Which layes with hir instruments they songe,
> Or elles redden hem for hir plesaunce;
> And oon of hem have I in remembraunce,
> Which I shal seyn with good wil as I can.
>
> (F. 709-15)

And further objection to answering the question in the affirmative
appears in the setting of Chaucer's poem, maintained, as it is on the
whole, in the atmosphere of Brittany, whether the scenes in that
country are entirely realistic or romantic. The tale is, in a word,
told as a Breton lay, of Breton folk, and of Breton scenes. No old
French source for it is discoverable to-day, however; and that fact
makes possible the suggestion that the story's guise of Breton lay
may be only a literary fabrication of Chaucer to effect diversity in
the manner of the stories told in the *C. T.* And corollary to that suggestion follows one that the poet may have derived his narrative
material from Boccaccio. If that was Chaucer's actual procedure, it
has to be generally admitted by Chaucerians, that he disguised particularly well his Italian material in its Breton garb.

The paucity of occidental versions of the tale—itself a rather
remarkable phenomenon since oriental versions[1] are common—
makes possible a number of theories in regard to the source of its one
Chaucerian and its two Boccaccian versions. Chaucer may have

---

[1] A collection of these oriental analogues to the *F. T.* is to be found in *Originals
and Analogues of Some of Chaucer's Canterbury Tales*, edited for the *Chaucer Society*
by Furnivall, Brock and Clouston, pp. 291-340.

acquired his material from a Breton lay now lost; he may have derived it from some tale not a Breton lay and now lost, and represented it as a Breton lay; or he may have derived it from Boccaccio and represented it as a Breton lay. On the other hand Boccaccio may have drawn his material from a Breton lay and may have removed from it the Breton aspects of the tale; or he, too, may have drawn his material from some version not a Breton lay and removed from it some of its distinctive source features. If Chaucer did not borrow his material from Boccaccio, it is possible that the two poets derived their material from a common source, perhaps a Breton lay, perhaps not. In the case of a common source occasional verbal parallels in the English and the Italian versions would readily be accounted for; that is to say, the presence of any such parallels can argue nothing more than a high probability of a common source; or, in other words, the presence of the most peculiar or unexpected of such parallels would be necessary to prove that Chaucer's version was derived from Boccaccio's, unless, of course, there were external evidence pointing to that conclusion.

Several problems are accordingly left to Chaucerians. They must prove first of all whether or not the *F. T.* is a Breton lay. If it is not a Breton lay, they must yet furnish very excellent evidence before we can accept it as a story derived from Boccaccio, and at the same time satisfactorily account for Chaucer's subterfuge in having his Franklin term it a lay. To do all these things is no slight task.

Of the four leading scholars who have so far devoted themselves to a study of the problem, Professor W. H. Schofield (*Chaucer's Franklin's Tale, Publ. Mod. Lang. Assoc.*, 1901), Professor Pio Rajna (*Le Origini della Novella Narrata dal "Frankeleyn" nei Canterbury Tales del Chaucer, Romania*, 1903, 204-67), Professor Lucien Foulet (*Le Prologue du Franklin's Tale et les Lais Bretons, Zeitschrift für Romanische Philologie*, 1906, 698-711), and Professor J. S. P. Tatlock (*The Scene of the Franklin's Tale Visited, Chaucer Society*, 1914, 55-57), the first is satisfied that the material of the *F. T.* is that of a Breton lay, and the other three are inclined, with varying degrees of conviction, to believe that its material is not that of a Breton lay, but derived from Boccaccio. Before an appraisal of the various grounds for the opinions of these scholars can be made, a skeleton summary of the *F. T.* must be presented. It may be offered first altogether without the use of names for the characters.

A woman whose affections and loyalty have been pledged to one man either by marriage or merely plighted troth, in order to rid herself of the amorous attentions proffered during her husband's or lover's absence by a second man, promises to grant the latter full enjoyment of her love, provided he can accomplish a certain hitherto impossible feat. The second lover accepts the hazard, and presently, by the assistance of certain magic powers, performs the feat, much to the surprise and fear of the woman, who feels constrained to keep her promise and goes in deep distress to her husband or lover to confess the fatal promise she had made during his absence to her persistent wooer. The husband or lover, realizing that the lady never wills for a moment to be disloyal to him but is yet in honour bound to grant the second man his desire, generously instructs her to go in secret to the latter and fulfill her vow. The woman goes to the second lover, informs him that she has come at her husband's bidding to keep her promise and so preserve both her own and her husband's honour; and the astonished lover, marvelling at the generosity of her husband, refuses to take advantage of it in any way, and sends the lady home untouched. Subsequently the disappointed suitor finds himself about to become impoverished by the payments he must make to the magician who has aided him, and, telling his story with its unhappy issue to the enchanter, is greatly surprised at being freed from all monetary obligations to him by the latter, who desires to emulate the generosity of the honourable husband.

Of this simple story a number of versions have been found. Both Asiatic and European texts are common; even in Gaelic the tale has found literary expression; but in English and Italian the only mediaeval versions now known are those in Chaucer's *F. T.* and Boccaccio's *Filocolo* and *Decamerone*, while no old French manuscript containing the story has as yet been found. The latter fact, however, can argue nothing in regard to the story's not being known in mediaeval France or Brittany before Chaucer's time. We may, therefore, now weigh the evidence for its once having been embodied in a Breton lay.

Chaucer's own statements in the matter, or those of the Franklin, should first be observed. These, it can easily be shown, all are expressions of Chaucer's authority rather than of his spokesman's. Forgetting that the *F. T.* is supposed to be told from memory, as the Franklin declared in his prologue, and *viva voce*, Chaucer nods and writes presently, speaking in his own person,

> . . . . Arveragus,
> Shoop him to goon, and dwelle a yeer or tweyne,
> In Engelond, that cleped was eek Briteyne,
> To seke in armes worship and honour;
> For all his lust he set in swich labour;
> And dwelled there two yeer, *the book seith thus*
> (F. 808-813),

and later towards the end of his poem,

> . . . . .he was so weel apayd,
> *That it were inpossible me to wryte;*
> *What sholde I lenger of this case endyte.*   (F. 1548-50).

We have, then, the poet's own testimony that the *F. T.* is a Breton lay; and that testimony, in the light of our discovery that Chaucer was invariably sincere in his claims to sources in *Troil.*, becomes significant, if not certain evidence that the narrative was in origin what the poet declared it to be.

Other bits of evidence that the poem was derived from a Breton lay have been assembled chiefly by Professor Schofield, who employs them in that particular, and argument by Professor Tatlock, who is not sure that his evidence is more than a proof that Chaucer knew rather well the geography and atmosphere of the real Brittany, declaring that the *F. T.* is "too Breton for a Breton lay" (*The Scene of the F. T. Visited*, 75). Summed up briefly, these bits of evidence consist in the names of the characters of the *F. T.*, all of them demonstrably Celtic or Breton in origin; in the geographical names of the poem; in certain phenomena of Celtic legends, the precursors of Breton lays; and in similarities in nature between the *F. T.* as a Breton lay and other specimens of that literary *genre*.

The names of the three chief characters of the *F. T.*, the only three honoured with names by Chaucer, are Dorigen, Arveragus and Aurelius. The name of the lady Dorigen Professor Schofield identifies interestingly with that of the lady *Genu*issa, the wife of an Arveragus, a Celtic chieftain who appears in Geoffrey of Monmouth's *Historia Regum Brittanniae;* while Professor Tatlock, after a most scrutinizing study of it as a Breton name, concludes that "the form *Dorigen* is so striking and unusual that all the parallels mentioned above justify us in calling it Breton" (*The Scene of the F. T. Visited*, 37-41). The name of the husband, Arveragus, it has already been stated, is that of a Celtic chieftain, prominently mentioned by Geoffrey of Monmouth; and the name of the lover Aurelius, Professor Schofield further shows us, appears in a Celtic legend as that of a British King, at the behest of whom Merlin transports 'the great rocks from Mt. Killaraus in Ireland to build the celebrated Giant's Dance at Stonehenge, an undertaking so seemingly impossible of execution that the British king "burst into laughter" at the mere suggestion of attempting it' (*Publ. Mod. Lang. Assoc.*, 1901, 417). It can be seen at once then how very appropriate is the use of these three appellations of manifest Celtic and Breton origin, in Chaucer's purported Breton lay.

The three geographical names used in the *F. T.* are Penmark, Kayrrud, and Orleans. Penmark has been for some time identified with the modern Breton Penmarc'h, the name both of a headland and a commune in the department of Finisterre near Quimper in Brittany, and a little to the south of Brest. The rocks that play so prominent a part in the magic performance of the *F. T.* more than belong to this section of the coast of Brittany. The second place name, Kayrrud, Professor Tatlock studies very carefully, and, at the end of his research, he concludes, "*Kayrrud* is not only a Breton name; places so named now exist in Brittany, though not in the region which is the scene of the *Franklin's Tale*" (*Sc. of the F. T. Visited*, 16). The name of the French city Orleans need not be debated. It is not mentioned in the *F. T.* as a Breton town, but merely as the city to which the Breton Aurelius resorts in order to secure a magician's aid. All the other names, then, used in the *F. T.* are quite appropriate to a Breton lay.

Further evidence that the *F. T.* was originally a Breton lay Professor Schofield offers us in citations of narrative elements belonging to Celtic legend, to the *F. T.*, and to a few known genuine Breton lays. Already Merlin's magical removal of the rocks from Mr. Killaraus to Stonehenge, a miracle paralleling Aurelius's removal, in the *F. T.*, of the rocks from the coast of Brittany, has been cited. But the real test of the genuineness of the *F. T.* as a lay of Brittany lies in its similarities to other specimens of that type. Professor Schofield parallels a number of such correspondences. In the lay *Equitan*, by Marie de France, he points out three features resembling elements of the *F. T.*,—the introductory lines, the discussion of love and the condition of its happy continuance, and the infatuation of Equitan, a character in many ways like Aurelius, for a married woman. In Marie's lay of *Lanval* he discovers an excellent parallel to the scene in the garden of the *F. T.* where the avowal of love takes place— with the difference, however, that the rôles are reversed: it is the lady who seeks the love of the knight. The comforts administered by the sympathetic friends of Dorigen, Aurelius, and Lanval seem, too, to participate in the same spirit. In a third lay by Marie, *Guildeluec and Guilliadun*, appears a distinguished knight of Brittany happily married to a lady of rank, who after a while goes to England to take service there and carry on warfare. The wife from whom he separates to carry on conquest, like Dorigen, grieves much at her husband's departing, but is assured by him that he will remain true to her.

It would seem then, if we are to accept Professor Schofield's discussion as significant, that various elements in the composition of the *F. T.* are coincident elements in the lays of Marie de France, known to-day as lays of Brittany. There is, to conclude then, a great deal in the *F. T.* which makes for the belief that Chaucer was reshaping in it a Breton lay.

It is interesting in this connection to know that there are genuine instances of Breton lays which were translated into English during the middle ages. As early as 1886 Professor George L. Kittredge made a study of the matter in his article *Sir Orfeo* (*American Journal of Philology*, VII, 176-202). In it he discusses six Middle English poems that profess to be Breton lays. They are known as *Sir Orfeo, Lay le Fresne, Sir Launfal, Sir Gowther, Emare*, and the *Erl of Tolous*. Two of these, the *Lay le Fresne* and *Sir Launfal*, are free translations from Marie de France, who, it will be remembered, is said to have made of the Breton lay a literary convention. In his discussion Professor Kittredge demonstrated that *Sir Orfeo*, despite the fact that its theme is the classical myth of Orpheus and Eurydice, is an English translation either directly or through a French version of an original Breton lay, which presented the tale of the classical musician in combination with elements of Celtic folk-lore. *Gowther* and the *Erl of Tolous* represent similar accretions, but upon a different foundation, the one having its original source in French stories of *Robert the Devil* and the other in an Acquitanian tale. In a word, there are three other mediaeval English poems, besides the translations from Marie and the *F. T.*, purporting to be translations of Breton lays, of which it is known the ultimate origins were actually Breton lays, even though the direct source of no one of the three has been found. These poems do much to corroborate the Breton origin of the *F. T.*

Despite this mass of evidence to corroborate Chaucer's own statement that the *F. T.* is a Breton lay, Professor Rajna believes that the materials for it were drawn from Boccaccio's *Filocolo* chiefly, and probably also from the *Decamerone* (*Orig. della F. T., Romania*, 1903,

204-267). To support his belief he draws parallels and summaries from the two Italian prose renderings of the skeleton-story of the *F. T.* The first summary he draws from an untitled *questione d' amore* of the *Filocolo,* a brief version that plays a thoroughly insignificant part in the whole scheme of the *Filocolo* (*Opere Volgari,* VIII, 48-60). In this brief narrative the lady and her husband are unnamed, and we are not told of any prolonged absence of the latter from their home in Spain. To her persistent suitor, Tarolfo, the troubled wife, not doubting his officious attentions would come to the ears of her husband, promised the enjoyment of his will, if he should make "del mese di gennaio in quella terra un bello giardino e grande, d' erbe, di fiori e d' alberi et di frutti copioso, come se del mese di maggio fosse" (p. 50). In dejection the lover wanders off on a journey about the world till he discovers in Thessaly (the mediaeval land of magic) an old herb-gatherer by the name of Tebano, who learning of Tarolfo's perplexity, makes a compact to help him, and returns with him to his home. When January comes, Tebano makes by night a preliminary circuit of Europe, Asia, and Africa in a chariot drawn by dragons, and returns the third day supplied with a magic liquid, which scattered over the earth, makes of it a garden and converts the soil into a flowering meadow. Once this miracle has been performed in Spain, Tarolfo demands of the lady that she keep her pledge. The subsequent distress and course of events thereafter closely parallel the story of the *F. T.* At the end is appended the question, which among the three, husband, lover, enchanter, performed the most generous act.

The version of the story in the *Decamerone* (Gior. X, nov. 5) is not very different. Here the knight and his lady are named Gilberto and Dianora, the lover is called Ansaldo, and the enchanter, now become a *nigromante,* or necromancer, remains nameless. The importunate suitor makes his advances to the lady no longer in person, but through an emissary, and receiving the lady's promise and conditions as before resorts to the necromancer, but this time without having to travel to Thessaly in search of him. The particular method of enchantment employed to transform the January fields is not mentioned in the *Decam.* And one further slight difference occurs in this version: the lady, when sent by her husband to redeem her pledge, is accompanied at his command by two gentlewomen. At the end of the story, Ansaldo's generosity is discussed in the frame-work by the several narrators, but not here in comparison with the generosity of the other characters. To account for the differences in the two versions of

Boccaccio, Professor Rajna remarks, "Tutto sommato, per stretti che siano i rapporti, il Boccaccio non ha seguito sè stesso più di quello che altri novellieri abbiano in molti casi seguito lui senza incorrere in reato di plagio" (*Rom.* 217).   In other words he would have us infer that, if Boccaccio himself could so easily make changes in the story as he took it from the *Filocolo* and adapted it to the *Decam.*, Chaucer might very well, likewise, have made changes in it as he took it from the *Filocolo*. That Chaucer has actually done so is his belief.   Turning to the *F. T.* he declares we have in it "un racconto che a prima vista pare diverso assai, ma che, considerato da vicino, ci vien rivelando convenienze sempre maggiori.   Rivestito d' altre carni, abbiano il medesimo scheletro.   E in molta parte non si tratta nemmeno di carni" (*Rom.* 217).   It is easy, of course, to show similarities in the two skeleton-plots of practically the same story, in order to prove a relationship between them, and about as easy to show differences in the same two skeleton-plots to disprove the relationship which, some other scholar contends, exists.   But if bits of the flesh that covers the two plot-skeletons resemble each other, one finds in them a rather convincing argument for a relationship.   To disprove it is a harder task.   Yet Professor Rajna's *carni* may very well be examined. Let us, however, postpone that examination a moment in order to glance briefly at his summaries.

The one great difference between the *F. T.* and the *Filocolo* version of the story lies, as we are shown by Professor Rajna, in the two different miracles of enchantment found therein.   The Thessalian enchanter of the *Filocolo* transforms the wintry fields of January into the flowering meadows of May, while the necromancer from Orleans in the *F. T.* removes by magic from the coast of Brittany "from Geronde to the mouth of Seyne" all the dangerous rocks upon which the home-returning husband of Dorigen might at any time be dashed to ruin.   This difference looms up as an obstacle in Professor Rajna's path.   He makes efforts, not altogether impotent, to remove it, but efforts not absolutely successful.   He argues that nothing would be more natural for a grieving wife in Brittany than to wish to have the rocks upon which so many vessels and men had met disaster removed forever from the coast, while for a lady in Spain or Italy nothing could be more desirable than to have the fields abloom in January.   Chaucer, he believes, has the heroine of his poem set a task for her wooer which would be quite appropriate for a loyal Breton wife; Boccaccio on the other hand, could have no possible use for rocks or the removal of

rocks.   The argument seems thin.   If it proves that Chaucer added
the rocks, it does not yet prove that he borrowed his story from Boccaccio; and if it fails to prove that he added them, it might even be
used to prove that Boccaccio had once read a Breton lay, and resolv-
ing later to use it in a story of his own, found it advisable to substitute
some other form of magic for the miracle of the rocks, which he found
in his source.   It is furthermore worth observing that a garden abloom
in January would, as a miraculous phenomenon, suit any country in
Europe, whereas the removal of the rocks would suit only particular
regions.   Hence, an original rock story would have to be changed
for a new setting, while an original garden story could be used unchanged in any setting.

The best part of Professor Rajna's article is undoubtedly that which
contains his presentation of the *carni*, i. e., a number of parallel passages in the versions of Chaucer and Boccaccio.   The *Filocolo* story
he takes up first.   Beside the introductory words of this story of
Tarolfo and Tebano he sets the opening lines of the *F. T.*:

In Armorik, that called is Britayne,	. . . nella terra là dove nacquì, mi ri-
Ther was a knight that loved and dide	cordo essene uno ricchissimo e nobile
his payne	cavaliere, il quale di perfettissimo
To serve a lady in his beste wyse;	amore amando una donna nobile
And many a labour, many a greet em-	della terra, per isposa la prese: della
pryse	quella donna, essendo bellissima . . .
He for his lady wroghte, er she were	(Vol. VIII, 49)
wonne.	
For she was oon, the faireste under	
sonne,	
And eek therto come of so heigh kin-	
rede,	
That. . . . (F. 728-36)	

Of these two passages Professor Rajna insists that the English is
only an amplification of the Italian.

His second step is to compare the wooing of the two lovers, Aurelius
and Tarolfo.   The latter loved the unnamed lady of the *Filocolo*
with such great love that "oltre a lei non vedeva niuna cosa, nè più
disiava, e in moltre maniere, forse con sovente passar davanti alle sue
case, o giostrando or armeggiando o con altri atti s' ingegnava d' avere
l' amor di lei; e spesso mandandole messaggieri forse promettendole
grandissimi doni, e per sapere il suo intendimento" (VIII, 49).

"Aurelius," in the *F. T.*, he points out, "loves Dorigen passionately
for two years, is a neighbor and well known to her, knows of the

temporary absence of her husband, yet does not dare to reveal his passion, limits himself to poetic sighs and to demanding pity with glances neither advised nor intent." Of course, it is perfectly safe for Professor Rajna to conclude that Aurelius is as ardent a lover as Tarolfo; but further than that point it appears hardly reasonable that he should identify the two so far as their love-making is concerned. The ardor of Tarolfo is manifested in the tournament and extravagant promises of gifts, that of Aurelius in sighs and unadvised glances. It is impossible to identify the two manifestations. Momentarily Professor Rajna's case seems to be weak. And at a fatal moment he makes a desperate shift. It will be remembered that in the *F. T.* the final confession of Aurelius of his love to Dorigen takes place in a garden, whither her friends have enticed her to divert her attention from her grief and longing. To strengthen his case Professor Rajna feels that he must have a garden, and forthwith he applies a telescope to the text of the *Filocolo*, where he finds two passages which mention gardens, the first about thirty pages earlier and the second about fifty pages later than the passage in which the story we are studying occurs, and neither of them in any way connected with it. The purpose of those who seek refreshment in these two gardens and their conduct in them are, he feels, similar to the purpose and conduct of Dorigen and her companions in the *F. T.* But that similarity does not obviate the fact that the gardens which he cites do not appear within the limits of the *Filocolo* version of the story. Moreover, there is a significant plot-detail in the *F. T.* which escapes the Italian scholar. Aurelius obtains his promise from Dorigen in a garden (F. 901 seq.), while Tarolfo secures his promise through an emissary from the unnamed lady, who, her husband being at home, could not presumably meet him in such a retreat. "Ella mandò così dicendo a Tarolfo, che se egli tanto l' amava quanto mostrava . . . ella farebbe ogni suo piacere" (VIII, 50). It is, too, very interesting to note that two actual analogues to the lady Dorigen's rash promise to Aurelius in the garden appear in the gardens of the Indian and Persian versions, where similar promises are made (*Originals and Analogues, Chaucer Society*, pp. 291-97; 306-9).

Professor Rajna next seeks to identify the "young clerk roaming by himself" (F. 1173 seq.), whom Aurelius and his brother meet on their travels to the French city of Orelans, with the old herb-gatherer Tarolfo encountered in Thessaly. It is true that the two magicians, the young clerk of Orleans and the Thessalian herb-gatherer, have one similar experience, viz.—one chance encounter with a questing lover; but that one experience is hardly real ground for identifying the two men. The subsequent careers of the two, their reception of the errant knight or knights, the miracles they perform, etc., are entirely different. The clerk astounds his two guests, first by telling them exactly what is the purpose of their journey, before they say a word of it to him, and then entertains them at his house with illusions of

> Forestes, parkes ful of wilde deer

. . . .

> . . . fauconers upon a fair river
> That with hir haukes han the heron slayn
> . . . knightes justing in a playn

and even Aurelius's

> . . . lady on a daunce
> On which himself he daunced, as him thoughte
>   (F. 1190-1201);

while the Thessalian enchanter, it will be recalled, starts off on a preliminary tour of Europe, Asia and Africa. The difference in the miracles which the two perform need not again be mentioned here.

One last weak point of comparison is cited by the Italian scholar, before he adduces his most valuable evidence. He observes that the Thessalian Tebano and Tarolfo appear in the vicinity of the lady's home "assai vicini del mese" (VIII, 53), i. e., rather close to the month January, while Aurelius and the magician return to Brittany in the "colde frosty seson of Decembre" (F. 1244).

At this point Professor Rajna begins the citation of his most valuable parallels. These are expressive of the experiences, inward and outward, of Arveragus, Dorigen, and Aurelius and of their Italian analogues in both the *Filocolo* and the *Decam.*, after the performance of the miracle. They reveal only an occasional verbal similarity. Only one at all significant passage can be quoted from the *Decam.* version. Yet, until their testimony has been studied in connection with analogous passages in the Asiatic versions of the story of the rash promise, the parallels do seem cogent. It is my purpose to show how weak they become in such a connection.

Professor Rajna first parallels as follows:

And to the temple his wey forth hath he holde, Wher-as he knew he sholde his lady see. . . .	e dovendo essere il seguente giorno nella città una grandissima solennita, egli se n' andò davanti alla sua donna, . . . e così le disse: madonna, dopo

Madame. . . . . I have do so as ye comanded me; Doth as yow list. . . . He taketh his leve, and she astonied stood. (F. 1306-7, 1331, 1333-5, 1339)	lunga fatica io ho fornito quello che voi comandaste: quando vi piacerà di vederlo e prenderlo egli è al vostro piacere. La donna. . . . si mara- viglið. (VIII, 57)

To these two passages no analogue appears in any one of the oriental versions published in the Chaucer Society's *Originals and Analogues*, but that this should be the fact is only natural, since in none of them is a miracle performed, and accordingly there can be no attendant surprise. One observes, however, in the two passages quoted considerable differences. Aurelius found his lady in a temple; his Italian analogue found his lady, though the text of the *Filocolo* does not actually say so, obviously present at a *solennità*. Aurelius makes no mention of the labour he had undergone to achieve his miracle. The resemblance, in brief, simmers down to the similarity between the words *comanded* and *comandaste*, *astonied* and *maravigliò*.

The second set of parallels is a briefer one:

And hoom she gooth a sorweful crea- ture (F. 1346).	Ma la gentil donna . . . tornando nella sua camera piena di noiosa malin- conia. (VIII, 58)

Of this set it may be observed that the melancholy and humiliation felt by Dorigen are paralleled in almost all of the Oriental versions. Tears and a downcast face as well as her desire to be loyal to her husband are a commonplace in descriptions of the lady. And one sees moreover in this set no verbal parallel.

The third pair too is brief:

For out of toune was goon Arveragus (F. 1351).	che 'l signore mio vada a caccia o in altra parte fuori della citta. (VIII, 58)

Of this it may be said that the delay of Dorigen in the fulfillment of her promise, necessitated by the absence of Arveragus, is virtually paralleled in every instance in the other analogues by the lady's refusal to keep her vow before she has informed her husband or her lover of it. The postponement, not the absence, is the real parallel; and that postponement is the common attitude.

Let us observe the fourth parallel:

. . . ye sholde your trouthe kepe and save. (F. 1478)	va', e copertamente serva il tuo giuramento, e a Tarolfo ciò che tu promettesti liberamente attieni (VIII, 58).

In connection with this it is important to notice that Arveragus's injunction to Dorigen to keep and save her "trouthe" has analogues in many of the Asiatic versions. In some of them the husband even accompanies his bride to the house of the other suitor. Says one: "Alas she is in love with another man; she must certainly go, why should I make her break her word?" (*Orig. and Anal.* 294). A second, realizing that "the power of a promise is extremely great . . . , granted her leave to go" (300). A third "gave her leave to keep her promise" (311). A fourth husband answered: "Go and keep the marriage-night" (321). Furthermore, the injunction to secrecy occurs in several versions. To conclude, then, there is nothing significant in Professor Rajna's fourth parallel.

We turn to the fifth:

Aurelius gan wondren on this cas.	Allora disse Tarolfo: senza fine mi
(F. 1514)	fate maravigliare. (viii, 59)

Of this one need only comment briefly that the wonder of Aurelius, when Dorigen comes to him with her husband's message, is repeated a number of times. "Wonderful!" cried one king, "you are true to your word indeed!" (301).

The sixth set of parallels is also disposed of easily:

fro his lust yet were him lever abyde,	e fra se cominciò a dire, che degno
Than doon so heigh a cherlish wrec-	di grandissima riprensione sarebbe chi
chednesse	a cosi liberale uomo pensasse villania.
Agayns franchyse and alle gentillesse.	(viii, 59)
(F. 1522-24).	

This unwillingness of the second lover to take advantage of the generosity of the husband is paralleled in four instances. (*Orig. and Anal.* 295, 312, 313, 321).

With the seventh parallel the case is similar:

She thonketh him upon hir knees al bare,	Ringraziò la donna molto Tarolfo di tanta cortesia, e lieta si partì tor-
And hoom unto hir husband is she fare,	nando al suo marito, a cui tutto per
And told him al as ye han herd me sayd	ordine disse quello che avvenuto l' era.
(F. 1545-47).	(viii, 60)

Expressions of gratitude and delight at being released from the rash pledge occur in two of the Oriental versions (*Orig. and Anal.* 295, 309).

Even more striking is the evidence against the eighth pair of paralleled passages:

Lordinges, this question wolde I aske
    now,
Which was the moste free, as thinketh
    yow ?
(F. 1621-22).

Dubitasi ora quale di costoro fosse
maggiore liberalità.
(VIII, 60)

This question, posed by the Franklin as well as by the interlocutor
in the *Filocolo*, as to who of the several characters was most generous,
is present in one after another of the Oriental versions. At times it is
developed in them at greater length than in either Chaucer's or
Boccaccio's work. (*Orig. and Anal.* 295, 302, 310, 317, 319, 321, 325,
328) The frequency of its appearance wholly invalidates the evidence, presented in this last parallel from the *F. T.* and the *Filocolo*,
for a relationship between those two works.

Professor Rajna uses in his ninth parallel a passage from the *Decam.*
version of the story:

. . . in his herte had greet compassioun
Of hir and of hir lamentacioun
And of Arveragus, the worthy knight.   (F. 1515-17)

Just as, says Professor Rajna, 'Ansaldo, saputo della donna "ver-
gognosa e quasi con le lagrime sopra gli occhi" la grande "liberalità
di Gilberto," "commosso, il suo fervore in *compassion* cominciò a
cambiare" ' (*Romania*, 1903, 244; *Decam.*, Gior. X, nov. 5).

This parallel, when used in an argument for relationship, is quite as
unconvincing as most of the parallels drawn by Professor Rajna
between the *F. T.* and the *Filocolo*. Its only strength rests upon the
occurrence of the word "compassion" in both texts. But the attitude
of compassion, if not the mere word of it, is discovered in a number of
the Oriental versions; and in several of them the idea of subduing
passion, as Ansaldo subdued his, appears prominently (*Orig. and Anal.*
295, 311-12, 316, 319, 324-5).

Summarizing, it becomes evident to one who reviews carefully the
passages, quoted by Professor Rajna from the *F. T.*, the *Filocolo* and
the *Decam.*, to make his theory of relationship secure, that very few
of them offer conclusive evidence. All, except the first one, which
appears, both in the text of Chaucer and in that of Boccaccio, after
the part of the story in which the performance of the miracle is described,—we have found, have analogues in one or another or in several
of the Asiatic versions; and sometimes the analogue is very striking.
Moreover, it is always an analogue which occurs in some version
unquestionably unknown to both Boccaccio and Chaucer. In a word

then, it seems safe to maintain that, in each of the kindred passages, we have in Boccaccio and in Chaucer the survival of certain thought-phenomena present originally in the primitive version of the tale. So, of course, we have in no one of them any positive proof that Chaucer used either of Boccaccio's versions of it, unless we were to base a relationship on the accidental appearance of the three words, *comandaste, maravigliò,* and *compassion,* in the Italian and the three, *comanded, astonied,* and *compassioun,* in the English.

If now we turn to the earliest bits of the *carni* cited by Professor Rajna, viz.—the introductory words of the *F. T.* and of the *Filocolo,* we cannot rate very high their force in an argument.   The rich and noble "cavaliere" is not necessarily the

>knight that loved and did his payne
>To serve a lady in his beste wyse;

the "perfettissimo amore" of one who loved a noble lady of his country is not necessarily equivalent to the devotion of another who

>many a labour, many a greet empryse
>. . . for his lady wroghte, er she were wonne;

and the "donna . . . bellissima" is not necessarily the same as Chaucer's

>faireste under sonne,
>And eek therto come of so heigh kinrede.

Ladies of such birth and beauty, and knights of such wealth, nobility, and willingness to labour in a lady's service, are but the stock figures of mediaeval romance.   To prove relationship between such knights and ladies, more unique pictures must be shown than those introduced by the Italian scholar.

To conclude then, I feel certain that neither Professor Rajna's citations of *carni,* clinging to the plot-skeletons, nor his parallels offer satisfactory evidence for any relationship which constitutes an influence of Boccaccio over Chaucer in the writing of the *F. T.*   And that conclusion, I cannot help believe, is ample warrant—especially in view of Professor Schofield's and Professor Tatlock's studies— for us to return to the belief that Chaucer did after all use the material of a Breton lay in the *F. T.*   And we are once more brought to the knowledge that we have no reasonable ground in either Professor Young's study of the *Filocolo* and *Troil.,*[1] or in Professor Rajna's study of the *Filocolo* and the *F. T.,* for believing that Chaucer knew Boccaccio's long prose romance.   Furthermore we see that no real

[1] See Chapter I.

evidence for Chaucer's having known the *Decam.* is offered in Professor Rajna's article.

Besides these two scholars, it will be remembered, one other inclined to the belief, that Chaucer had employed the *Filocolo* in the *F. T.* This was Professor Lucien Foulet (*Zeitsch. für Rom. Philol.*, 1906, 698-711). In his article he contends, in contravention of Professor Schofield, that Chaucer could not possibly have known the lays of Marie de France, since her works had been forgotten even in her own country (Marie probably lived in England,[1] rather than in France!) by the end of the fourteenth century; and furthermore that none of the works of the thirteenth century which Chaucer knew could have furnished him the sense which he gives to the word *lay* in the prologue of the *F. T.* That word, he asserts, Chaucer uses as a general rule in the sense which was current in contemporaneous French poetry, i. e., in the sense of a brief song. It is unnecessary for us to go into Professor Foulet's definition of the term, for whether or not Chaucer knew any manuscript, of either the thirteenth or fourteenth century, containing the word *lay* as employed by Marie de France or others, it is still true that Chaucer did use the term *layes* which the Bretons *"of diverse aventure maden."* And he could hardly have made such use of the term, if he had nowhere previously heard of its use, or if he had known nothing of the literary school or of the folk-literature to which the Breton lays belonged. Professor Foulet in no way strengthens the case for relations between the *F. T.* and the *Filocolo*.

Several tasks remain to be accomplished by the scholars who believe that Chaucer did not use a Breton lay, or that Chaucer used the *Filocolo* in the *F. T.* They must explain to us why Chaucer should attempt the feat of writing a pseudo-Breton lay in an age when Englishmen were still translating genuine lays; they must convince us that such a convention—if convention it is—would secure greater favour among the contemporary readers of Chaucer; they must explain satisfactorily to us Chaucer's motives in disguising Boccaccio's story or stories; and they must more satisfactorily account for the several great differences between the English and the Italian versions.

To a list of these differences I can do nothing better than prefix the additions to the story which Professor Schofield shows us Chaucer makes: The discussion of the cause of evil in the world, *à propos*

---

[1] According to the *Encyclopædia Britannica* Marie de France lived in Anglo-Norman England, probably at the court of Henry II and his wife, Eleanor of Provence.

of the existence of the dangerous rocks on the Breton coast, the abundant references to astrology, the complaint of Aurelius to Apollo, and Dorigen's complaint to Fortune (*Publ. Mod. Lang. Assoc.* 1901, 444-48). To these I would add as being real differences between Boccaccio's and Chaucer's versions rather than only additions to the story, the following points:

I.   The suit of Arveragus, with its unique conditions, before he finally wins the hand of Dorigen (F. 736-802).

II.   The residence of Chaucer's characters among French and Breton scenes.

III.   The departure of Arveragus to a far country and his absence for two years (F. 809-13).

IV.   The walking of Dorigen by the sea, sighing for the return of her lord (F. 847-58).

V.   The confession of Aurelius to Dorigen of his passion directly— and not through an emissary or emissaries—in a garden where her friends were seeking to divert her with dancing during the absence of Arveragus (F. 898-905, 960-78).

VI.   The presence of a brother to Aurelius, whose sympathy was enlisted in the cause of the latter, and through whom the arrangement for the miracle was finally made with the magician of Orleans (F. 1082-1086, 1105-87).

VII.   The entertainment with its several forms of illusion (none of which are mentioned by Boccaccio) which the clerk of Orleans furnishes to Aurelius and his brother at the time of the negotiations, and before the performance of the miracle on the coast of Brittany is suggested to him (F. 1189-1208).

VIII.   The very different nature of the miracle performed in the *F. T.*, i. e., the removal of the rocks, instead of the making of a garden to bloom in January.

CHAPTER XI

CONCLUSION; CHAUCER AND BOCCACCIO

The results of the foregoing investigation of the relations of Chaucer's and Boccaccio's works have been almost unvaryingly negative. We have seen that we do not possess adequate material for establishing Chaucer's acquaintance with any of that writer's Italian works other than *Filostrato* and the *Teseide*. We have seen, too, that we have no good evidence that the English poet knew those two poems as works of Boccaccio. We are accordingly brought to a difficult position. We cannot on the one hand look upon Chaucer as a literary disciple of Boccaccio, and on the other we cannot deny his very great indebtedness to the Florentine poet. We can do little more than sound the note of caution, and that note seldom has a really pleasing quality within.

Unless there should some day be discovered some further, actually contemporaneous documentary evidence in regard to Chaucer's journeys and experiences in Italy, we must continue to believe that Chaucer and Boccaccio were personally unacquainted, and we must continue to doubt the English poet's knowledge even of the existing person of the Italian writer. With such doubts besetting us, we cannot safely postulate any theory that the *Decamerone* was of any help whatsoever to Chaucer in the inception, or in the composition of either the frame-work of the *Canterbury Tales* or of the *Tales* themselves.

Furthermore we are left with the position that, except in *Troilus and Criseyde* and the *Knight's Tale*, Chaucer's narrative art remains unaffected by the art of Boccaccio. There is no ground for any inference that under Boccaccio's influence Chaucer learned to tell a story better. In the case of the two poems which he, in a sense, translated from Boccaccio we have seen that he employed methods differing not only from those of his sources but differing radically from each other. In *Troilus and Criseyde* he followed a principle of increase, and in the *Knight's Tale* a principle of reduction. Moreover, examination of Chaucer's other tales and legends reveals no significant similarity in the ways in which the two poets elaborate setting, plot or character in their works. There is no particular resemblance in their methods of maintaining suspense or preparing surprise. As different as are the Florentine ladies and gentlemen who tell the stories of Boccaccio's

Decamerone from the pilgrims of Chaucer's *Canterbury Tales*, so different are the two poets in their management of narrative art. Boccaccio is primarily a teller of fascinating, diverting stories; Chaucer is primarily and always an interpreter of life. And that fact is true despite the fidelity to life and to the laws of psychology that one seldom loses sight of in the characters of Troilo and Griseida and Pandaro as one reads the *Filostrato*.

That Chaucer looked upon the author of the *Filostrato* and the *Teseide*—if indeed he supposed the man to be one and the same—as a source rather than as a model is apparent, too, when one considers Chaucer's versification. In narrative poetry he never adopts either the *terza rima* or the *ottava rima* of Boccaccio. His few rare uses of the former rhyme scheme may readily be traced to Dante's influence. The second scheme he never employs. It is, however, highly probable that he was influenced to narrate *Troilus and Criseyde* and the *Parliament of Fowls* and several of the *Canterbury Tales* in stanzaic form, i. e., in rhyme royal, by his knowledge of how well the author of them had used the stanzaic form of *ottava rima* in the long narratives of the *Filostrato* and the *Teseide*. Further than that we cannot say that the prosody of Boccaccio influenced that of Chaucer.

In the main, Chaucer's debt to Boccaccio is that of a borrower. The English poet served no apprenticeship to the Italian. He never became a literary disciple to him. He did not weakly imitate him as a master. What of Boccaccio he drew upon he drew as from a storehouse; and, like the materials he drew from numerous other literary storehouses, he fitted it deftly into the great mosaic of his own work. The two Italian poems only furnished a few more strands of fiction and truth, of reality and phantasy, of comedy and tragedy for him to weave into the great pictorial tapestry of mediaeval life which Chaucer's complete works will ever represent.

The English poet's indebtedness to Boccaccio, not wholly an unacknowledged one and not wholly a conscious one, is yet a very great one. The fairest of the gardens and the temples in his tapestry, the most beautiful of his ladies, the most chivalrous of his knights, the most pathetic of his youthful characters, and the most human of his middle-aged ones, come many of them from Boccaccio. And from Boccaccio they bring the breath of old romance. But Boccaccio owes a great debt also to Chaucer. It was Chaucer who made him in *Troilus and Criseyde* and in the *Knight's Tale* part and parcel of English Literature. And admission to a share in such a realm, and through such a hand, is no slight privilege.

BIBLIOGRAPHY

Ovid: *Metamorphoses; Heroides.*

Boccaccio: *Genealogiae cum demonstrationibus arborum designatis et cet.* Venice, 1511.

Thomas Tyrwhitt: *The Canterbury Tales of Chaucer,* 2nd edition, Oxford, 1798.

Josephi Iscani: *De Bello Trojano,* in *Dictys Cretensis et Dares Phrygius* (Accedunt Josephi Iscani Libri Sex, v, 364-576) Londini, 1825.

Boccaccio: *Opere Volgari,* Florence, 1827-34. 17 vols.

Philippi Villani: *Liber de Civitatis Florentiae Famosis Civibus,* Florentiae, 1847.

R. G. Latham: Chaucer Note, *Athenaeum,* II, 433, 1868.

F. J. Furnivall. (See *Lansdowne MS* in the Chaucer Society's *Six-Text Edition of The Canterbury Tales.* 1868-79.)

Bernhard ten Brink: *Chaucer Studien,* Münster, 1870.

W. M. Rossetti: *Chaucer's Troylus and Cryseyde Compared with Boccaccio's Filostrato. Chaucer Society,* 1873.

Boccaccio: *Lettere edite ed inedite.* Florence, 1877.

John Koch: *Englische Studien,* 1877, pp. 249-93.

G. L. Kittredge. *Sir Orfeo, American Journal of Philology,* VII, 176-202, 1886.

E. Koeppel: *Chauceriana, Anglia Zeitschrift für Englische Philologie,* 1891-92, 227-67.

A. W. Pollard: *Chaucer Primer,* London, 1893.

W. W. Skeat: *The Prioress' Tale,* Oxford, 1893.

Bernhard ten Brink: *History of English Literature* translated by W. C. Robinson, New York, 1893.

Henry Morley: *Chaucer, English Writers,* Vol. V, London, 1893.

H. Oskar Sommer: *The Recuyell of the Historyes of Troye, Written in French by Raoul Lefevre, Translated and Printed by Caxton, about A. D. 1474,* 2 vols., London, 1894.

W. W. Skeat: *The Complete Works of Chaucer,* 6 vols. Oxford, 1894-1900.

J. J. Jusserand: *Histoire Littéraire Anglaise.* Paris, 1896.

Marie de France. *Die Fabeln der Marie de France,* ed. Warnke, 1898. An earlier edition of the *Lais* by Warnke was published in 1885 at Halle.

F. J. Mather: *The Date of the Knight's Tale,* in the *Furnivall Miscellany,* 1901.

W. H. Schofield: *Chaucer's Franklin's Tale. Publications of the Modern Language Association,* 1901.

G. L. Hamilton: *Chaucer's Indebtedness to Guido delle Colonne.* New York, 1903.

Pio Rajna: *Le Origini della Novella Narrata dal "Frankeleyn" nei Canterbury Tales del Chaucer. Romania,* 1903, 204-67.

A. W. Pollard: *Chaucer Primer.* London, 1903.

Benoit de Sainte-More: *Le Roman de Troie.* ed. L. Constans, Paris, 1904-1906.

Lucien Foulet: *Le Prologue du Franklin's Tale et les Lais Bretons, Zeitschrift für Romanische Philologie,* 1906, 698-711.

R. K. Root: *The Poetry of Chaucer.* New York, 1906.

J. S. P. Tatlock: *Development and Chronology of Chaucer's Works. Chaucer Society,* 1907.

Dante: *La Divina Commedia,* riveduta da G. A. Scartazzini, Milano, 1907.

Giacomo Leopardi: *Rime di Francesco Petrarca.* Successori Le Monnier. Firenze, 1908.

Eleanor Prescott Hammond: *Chaucer, A Bibliographical Manual.* New York, 1908.

Karl Young: *The Origin and Development of the Story of Troilus and Criseyde.* Chaucer Society, 1908.

Henri Haurette: *Les plus anciennes traductions françaises de Boccace.* Bordeaux et Paris, 1909.

Émile Hyacinthe Legouis: *Geoffroy Chaucer.* Paris, 1910.

J. L. Lowes: *Chaucer and the 'Miroir de Marriage' of Eustache Deschamps. Modern Philology,* VIII, 305-34.

B. A. Wise: *The Influence of Statius upon Chaucer.* Hopkins Dissertation, Baltimore, 1911.

R. K. Root: *Chaucer and the Decameron. Englische Studien,* 44, 1-7.

E. F. Shannon: *The Source of Chaucer's Anelida and Arcite. Publications of the Modern Language Association,* 1912, 461-485.

Émile Hyacinthe Legouis: *Geoffrey Chaucer,* translated by L. Lailavoix, J. M. Dent & Sons, London, 1913.

W. G. Dodd: *Courtly Love in Chaucer and Gower. Harvard Studies in English.* Boston, 1913.

J. S. P. Tatlock: *Boccaccio and the Plan of the Canterbury Tales. Anglia,* 1913, 69-117.

J. S. P. Tatlock: *The Scene of the Franklin's Tale Visited. Chaucer Society,* 1914.

Koeppel: *L'Intelligenza. Englische Studien,* 20, 156-7.

Lorenz Morsbach: *Chaucers Plan der Canterbury Tales und Bocaccios Decamerone. Eng. Stud.* 42, 43-52.

C. M. Hathaway: *Chaucer's Lollius. Eng. Stud.* 44, 159-164.

E. Kölbing: *Zu Chaucers Knightes Tale. Eng. Stud.* 2, 528-32.

C. G. Child: *Chaucer's Hous of Fame and Boccaccio's Amorosa Visione. Modern Language Notes,* 10, 379-384.

Boccaccio: *Il Filostrato,* ed. Paolo Savj-Lopez. *Bibliotheca Romanica,* 146, 147, 148. Strasburg.

Eustache Deschamps: *Oeuvres Complètes. Société des anciens textes français.*

G. L. Kittredge: *The Pillars of Hercules and Chaucer's "Trophee,"* in the *Putnam Anniversary Volume.* The Torch Press, Cedar Rapids, 1909. Reviewed in *Archiv für das Studium der neueren Sprachen,* 124, 428.

F. J. Mather: *The Prologue, Knight's Tale, and Nun's Priest's Tale. Riverside Literature Series.* New York, 1899.

J. W. Bright: *Chaucer and Lollius. Publications of the Modern Language Association,* 19, p. xxii.

J. L. Lowes: *The Prologue of the Legend of Good Women Considered in its Chronological Relations. Publ. Mod. Lang. Assoc.* 20, 749-864.

J. L. Lowes: *The Date of Chaucer's Troilus and Criseyde. Publ. Mod. Lang. Assoc.* 23, no. 2, 285-306.

G. S. Robertson: *Elements of Realism in the Knight's Tale. Journal of English and Germanic Philology,* 14, 226-255.

Furnivall, Brock, and Clouston editors. *Originals and Analogues of Some of Chaucer's Canterbury Tales. Chaucer Society.*

R. K. Root: *Chaucer's "Dares."*   *Modern Philology.*

Guillaume de Lorris et Jean de Meun.   *Le Roman de la Rose*, ed. Ernest Langlois. Paris, 1914-1915.

G. L. Kittredge: *Chaucer's Discussion of Marriage.*   *Mod. Phil.* IX, 435-467.